Across Many Borders

THE DIARY OF A WANDERING EXPLORER

Shyama P. Chakroborty

PAGE PUBLISHING, INC.
New York, NY

First originally published by Page Publishing, Inc. 2018

ISBN 978-1-64298-328-9 (Paperback)
ISBN 978-1-64298-329-6 (Digital)

Printed in the United States of America

C O N T E N T S

CHAPTER 1

Introduction

I have traversed a long, winding, and arduous path since my childhood in a small town on the Indian subcontinent. I faced, head-on, numerous extraordinary events as I hopped around the incredibly acrimonious social and religious divides created by the turbulent sociopolitical history of pre-independence India. For years I moved across many national boundaries and religious divides in search of my spiritual identity and a place where I would be accepted, welcomed and could finally call home. My destiny was to eventually find that home in America, the land of opportunity.

I spent most of my early childhood in a Brahmin (the highest Hindu caste) family in the predominantly Muslim country of East Pakistan (now Bangladesh), before my family was forced to migrate to India to escape unbearable religious persecution. Originally Bangladesh, Pakistan, and India comprised one vast country ruled by a central king or emperor in addition to many other regional kings, maharajas, and nawabs until the British gained their foothold in India.

The improbable British presence in India initially resulted from the heinous treachery of Mir Jaffar, the chief general of Nawab Sirajudolla, the last independent nawab of the Bengal, Bihar, and Orissa regions of India. The British traders of the East India Company in India promised Mir Jaffar the reign of the region if he colluded with them in dethroning the nawab. Mir Jaffar conspired with the other nobles opposed to Nawab Sirajudolla and sided with the British traders. After Nawab Sirajudolla was dethroned and killed, Mir Jaffar did not, however, ascend to the position as he was promised. This inglorious act of infamy is the singular event in the annals of Indian history from which subsequent black events and turbulence flowed throughout the country. His treachery gave the East India Company its foothold in India. Subsequently, for two hundred years English monarchy subjugated India to its direct rule.

When the British finally left India in 1947 in the wake of the Indian freedom movement spearheaded by Mahatma Gandhi, the Indian subcontinent was partitioned into two countries, Pakistan for the area that had a predominantly Muslim population, and India for the area that had a predominantly Hindu population. Pakistan was created with two separate territories separated by several thousand miles: East Pakistan located on the northeastern fringe of India, and West Pakistan, located on the northwestern fringe of India. The common bond between the two territories was religion, i.e., Islam. The rest of the subcontinent became what is known today as India, a predominantly Hindu state.

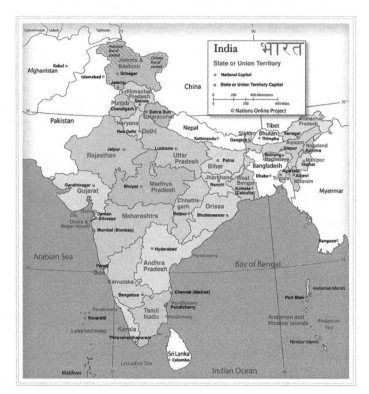

At the time of the partition of the Indian subcontinent, 15 to 30 percent of the population in various regions of East and West Pakistan were Hindu and there was a 15 to 20 percent Muslim population in India. There was a huge scramble as these minorities migrated across the border to realign their religious identities with their country of residence. As history would tell, riots broke out in communities throughout the subcontinent, and millions of people were killed when they tried to cross the border to resettle on the other side.

Almost all my elder brothers and sisters left our ancestral hometown within a few years of partition and moved to settle in India. However, my parents, one younger sister, two younger brothers, and I did not immediately move until the tumultuous political and social upheavals preceding the separation war between East Pakistan and West Pakistan in 1971 forced the remaining members of my family to move to India.

My father was a successful and highly respected lawyer in East Pakistan. He held a master's degree in economics and a law degree from the University of Calcutta, at that time one of the most prestigious universities in India. It would have been natural for him to move to the Indian side and settle there immediately after partition. Unlike his other siblings, however, he did not opt to move immediately and stayed in Pakistan as member of the Hindu minority, just as there was a Muslim minority in the predominantly Hindu India.

Preceding the time when East Pakistan seceded from West Pakistan in 1971 with the help of the Indian Army and became Bangladesh, I rushed back to my ancestral hometown to help my parents and my remaining siblings move to India since the harassment of Hindus had become unbearable and dangerous. Our ancestral home was bombed and utterly destroyed by the Pakistani Army during this war. My family entered India as destitute refugees and started to rebuild their new lives there. After moving to India, my father opened his law practice near Kolkata (formerly known as

Calcutta)[1] and went on to become one of the most successful and respected lawyers in that region. As they say, genius never dies. He was elected the president of the District Bar Association in Barasat near Kolkata and held that position until his death at the age of eighty-eight in 1992.

By 1971, I had already graduated with a bachelor's degree in mechanical engineering, and after I helped the remainder of my family move from Bangladesh to India, I applied for the MTech program at the prestigious Indian Institute of Technology (IIT), Kanpur, and was preparing myself to enroll there. Instead, I took a calculated risk and joined a utility company which had close collaboration with an American company, Parsons Corporation, one of the largest environmental and construction companies in the USA. The job took me to Dacca, the capital of newly independent Bangladesh. A large contingent of American engineers was stationed there. I forged a friendship with many of these people who appreciated my hard work and sincerity. I also acted as their communication channel since they hardly spoke the local language.

The sixty-eight-year-old Mr. Dale Long, who was originally from Columbus, Ohio, was one of these men, and he loved me like a son. He knew of my deep interest and childhood ambition to go to the USA for higher studies. He said Ohio State University (OSU) was one of the top universities in America, although as a native of Ohio he was probably biased. He promised to assist me if I needed help to attend the university. I have been blessed with many chance encounters with outstanding individuals like Mr. Dale Long who gave me hope and inspiration to dream big and achieve my goals.

I started to apply to American universities and was accepted to some of the more prestigious schools based on my TOEFL (Test of English as a Foreign Language) and GRE (Graduate Record Examination) scores, but ironically it was only OSU that prom-

---

[1] In recent years India has been reverting the names the British used for various cities back to their original names. For example, Calcutta, Madras, Bombay, and Bangalore were renamed as Kolkata, Chennai, Mumbai, and Bengaluru.

ised me a graduate assistantship. Going to OSU was a life-altering experience.

On March 16, 1974, I set out for the USA, the land of opportunity. I landed in Columbus, Ohio, on a severely cold winter night without a warm winter coat and only $9.57 in my pocket. America received me with open arms and gave me the home and spiritual identity I'd missed growing up in the volatile post-independence Indian subcontinent. I spent my entire adult life in my adopted country, and America provided me with enormous opportunities that allowed me to enrich my life personally, professionally, and spiritually.

These limitless opportunities allowed me to have an eventful and exciting professional career as a well-recognized space scientist. I served the National Academy of Science, the highest scientific body that advises the president of the United States and Congress on scientific matters of national importance. I was to also play a key role in many major defense and space programs.

In addition to my professional career, I was fortunate to undertake many extraordinary adventures that took me to Russia for cosmonaut training at the Gagarin Cosmonaut Training Center and a flight in a supersonic Mig 25 fighter plane to eighty-five thousand feet at a speed of more than Mach 2.2. I travelled to England and completed an assisted swim across the English Channel between England and France. I trekked to the North Pole and climbed up to the base camp of Mount Everest. I traveled all over the world to speak and present scientific papers at many major international conferences. I met my wife, a white American student, at OSU in 1975. My life was enriched through meeting and interacting with many extraordinary personalities. All of this was a far cry from my childhood when mere survival had been a challenge and my family bounced across sociopolitical and geographical boundaries.

My family's tortuous and painful experience has enabled me to reflect on how intolerance in humanity can cause enormous suffering simply because of a difference in how they perceive God and practice their faith. My close examination of the core beliefs of the world's major religions has revealed the universal themes inherent in all religions of goodness and righteousness based on the acceptance and tolerance for others. Unfortunately, mankind has suffered immensely when religious extremists have tried to impose their spiritual beliefs on others because they differ from them.

My life in America sometimes feels like a reincarnation after enduring and surviving the turbulent history of the post-partition Indian subcontinent. My story is probably not unique. There are possibly millions of others who have similar stories and experiences to share about America and its magnanimity. America gave me an identity and a home away from my home country of birth. This eternal truth shines brightly in my life.

CHAPTER 2

Early Childhood

My birthplace, Bagerhat, was a small subdivisional town in the southern part of Bangladesh. A small river flowed gently through this peaceful town. It had no industries of which to speak. The only commercial activities were centered around the local bazaar that housed a few small department stores in impoverished buildings and huts in addition to an open-air market where the residents went for their daily groceries, particularly fresh fish that the local fishermen caught in the river. The famous Ilsha fish from the Padma River, a favorite of most Bengalis, came from other parts of the country.

I have always wondered how the huge local population supported their families with so little business activities and opportunities. Miraculously, they all sustained themselves, and life seemed to flow in a peaceful manner.

There were several elementary and high schools for boys and a single high school for girls only. The local PC College, named after the legendary chemist Acharya Prafulla Chandra Ray, was a good educational institution open to both boys and girls dating back to the pre-partition era. *Acharya* means "sir" in Bengali, and he received the title when the king of England knighted him during colonial times. Even though he was a Hindu, the Muslim rulers of East Pakistan never changed the name of the college as they did in other similar institutions.

There were professionals such as doctors, lawyers like my father, teachers, professors, and many government officials who administered the town's affairs. There were vendors and traders who ran thriving businesses supplying the daily necessities of the townspeople. The subdivisional officer (SDO), who was normally a member of the prestigious and highly competitive civil service corps, ran the administration of the subdivision. There was a police station and a jailhouse. At that time, there was only one automobile in Bagerhat, a jeep belonging to the SDO. The SDO drove around town in the jeep like a chieftain to various official functions, commanding utmost obedience and reverence. He presided over the criminal court. The civil courts were presided over by the low-level justices, or the munsefs, as they were called in Bengali. The SDO presided over or attended the official and cultural functions in the town and almost always was the chief guest at all the athletic competitions involving the schools and the local teams when they played against each other or other visiting teams.

My father maintained a good personal and working relationship with all the SDOs who normally stayed for two to three years before moving up to district-level jobs. Many of them went on to become top officials at the central or provincial government. One of them eventually became the secretary to the governor of East Pakistan, and another became the secretary to Sheikh Mujibur Rahaman, the founder and first prime minister of Bangladesh before he was assassinated in 1975.

The river separated the subdivisional headquarters from the villages on the other side. Some of the rich people in town owned a large swath of agricultural land in the village that was cultivated mainly for rice. Many of the poor from the villages tilled this soil for them to earn a meager living, while the richer people lived a comfortable life from their sweat and labor.

One of the most interesting characters in our household staff was Modhu. We called him Modhuda, as *da* is the abbreviation of *dada*, meaning "elder brother," and in this way, we could show our respect to someone older than us. He came to our house to get his breakfast very early each morning. Then my mother would give him about 30 to 40 rupees (US $4 to 5 at the exchange rate at that time) to go to the nearest market to purchase groceries and fresh fish for the day.

Normally he came back from the market three to four hours later. One day my mother sent me to check where Modhuda was as he was so late, the lunch would not be prepared in time for the children before school or for my father before court. I went to the market and saw Modhuda sitting on the side street of the market with several items arranged neatly in front of him, e.g., vegetables, fish, stationery, etc. Intrigued, I asked the adjacent shopkeeper what was going on. He laughed and said it was Modhuda's daily routine. He normally bought an assortment of goods, including fresh vegetables and fish early in the morning, then he would sell them at slightly marked-up prices when the supplies ran low, sometimes making as much as a 100 percent profit. He took advantage of the supply and demand principles of economics. He made anywhere from 30 to 40 rupees in profit, depending how much my mother gave him in the morning. He was very clever. The first thing he bought was quality fresh fish such as the Ilsha fish from the Padma River, which was always in short supply. Shoppers who came late to the market were forced to buy it from Modhuda who would sell the excess over what was needed for our home for profit. The day I showed up to check on him, there was a surplus supply of the Ilsha fish and other commodities that Modhuda was trading, so it was taking a longer time to sell them. Even though I admonished Modhuda for his business tactics, assuming he was misappropriating our money, over the years I developed a tremendous amount of respect for the business acumen of this simple and uneducated man. His shrewd investment strategy generated a quick turnaround and a hefty profit while providing our family the goods he was asked to get and supporting his large family of five children. Most of the income he brought in to support his family was from the daily shopping for our family!

Years later I heard of the eccentric chief minister of Bihar, later the Indian Railway minister, Lalu Prosad Jadav, who was invited by the Harvard Business School to speak about how he turned Indian Railways into a profitable enterprise. It immediately made me think about Modhuda. There were some lessons to be learned from his proven ability to turn a quick and hefty profit from small seed money.

Another man with innovative business acumen was the family patriarch of another Hindu family in our neighborhood. Atul Babu had a small tea stall near the PC College campus that catered to students and their professors. In addition to tea, the stall served sandesh (a Bengali sweet delicacy) and biscuits. He bought the sweets from the main bazaar and came up with an innovative way to add other inexpensive ingredients to significantly increase the volume of the product, and even though it compromised the quality and taste, it was within the acceptable limit for the customers. He would sell these at a marked-up price, providing him with a razor-thin profit. The tea stall did not seem to be a great source of income, but he somehow managed to support his wife, four daughters, and two sons. The family had a simple and austere lifestyle and maintained a very peaceful and tranquil family life. They were happy. Atul Babu came home from his tea stall late in the evening on his bicycle, ate his dinner, and played the esraj (an Indian musical instrument similar to a sitar) for relaxation. His soothing music broke the silence of the night, and we would enjoy his music from our home. They ultimately moved to India to seek safety, security, and new opportunities for their children.

My father had two legal secretaries who handled the paperwork and coordinated the administrative matters related to a case. Gyanda was almost like a family member. He called my mother Ma, meaning "mother." My parents actually adopted and treated him like a son. All my siblings and I treated him like an elder brother, who in turn always looked after us. He was simple, humble, and very honest. He was very protective and loyal to my father. Nani Mukherjee, on the other hand, was a very complex man with a sleek personality. He was audacious and always attempted to project an image of sophistication to impress others around him. He wore fancy gold chains and bracelets and groomed himself meticulously with cropped-up hair with a lavish use of Brylcreem. He was a very fair-complexioned and handsome man and used talcum powder heavily to spruce himself up. When he came to work at my father's chamber early in the morning, he would pick up the English newspaper the *Statesman* from Kolkata that we subscribed to. He would then situate himself in his chair and start reading the newspaper loudly. Obviously, he was not very proficient in English and did not know or understand many of the words. Whenever he would encounter any of the words he did not know how to pronounce or what it meant, he would simply make a mumbled sound like "Rrrau ... Rrau ... Ah . . . Uh . . ." and jump to the next word he was familiar with. Many of my father's clients were poor and uneducated farmers who were trying to establish their legal rights to their disputed land holdings. So when they came in to secure my father's services, the two legal secretaries were jockeying using their distinctly different persuasive tactics to lure the new clients to their desk. After all, whoever succeeded in their initial registration would continue to be the legal coordinator for the case, thus ensuring a portion of the income from the case. Many of these simple and honest farmers would be impressed listening to the sleek man projecting an aura of sophistication with his loud recitation of the English newspaper and would go to his desk and sign up with him. After a while, my siblings and I had to come to Gyanda's rescue by informing our father, who in turn randomly assigned many of the cases to Gyanda.

Then there was the neighbor known around town as Falk Daktar. He was a homeopathic doctor and hence the Bengali colloquial term *daktar* was added to his name, Falk, to identify him as a doctor. But he was not known for his skills as a doctor, and so everybody called him a *faitkay dactar*, meaning a "useless doctor." He was deaf and walked with a heavy limp since one leg was noticeably shorter than the other. He did not have any significant practice, but he was one of the most good-natured persons anybody could ever meet. He called my mother *pishi*, meaning "a father's sister." When anybody in the family got sick, we would call the best doctors in town with medical degrees from the renowned Kolkata medical colleges. They were mostly our family friends and used for house calls, but we would also always call Falk Daktar as a routine whether we used his medicine or not.

He had a small metal box with different compartments that each held a small amount of white powder. It was possibly the same powder in each but gave the impression of providing a variety of medicines to address various types of medical conditions. There were also a large number of small bottles (*shishi* in Bengali) that contained some type of liquid, supposedly something with medicinal value. Intrigued, I started watching Falk Daktar when he came for the house call whenever somebody became sick. It looked like he took the powder and the liquid from the same bottle or compartment irrespective of the nature of the illness. However, the saving grace was that we hardly ever used his medicine. My mother just wanted to call the good-natured man to make him feel good. Astonishingly, he charged us just one rupee (about twelve cents at the time) for each of his visits. Even though it was almost fifty years ago, it was still a very small amount of money. He did not have an extensive list of clients, so it must have been a challenge for him to support his family.

Falk Daktar had four children living at home, while his eldest son was sent away to settle in India as many Hindu families did with their children. His youngest daughter was a close friend of my youngest sister, Mona, and would invariably come to our home in the morning and start her day with a nice breakfast. She basically spent most of her day at our home like a family member, and thus her food was taken care of.

It is a tragedy that when the Bangladesh war broke out between India and Pakistan, the Pakistani Army and their local extremist cohorts, the Razakars, rounded up many helpless and weak Hindus like Falk Daktar and shot them point blank. To this day, I still cannot fathom how any human being, even if he or she belonged to a warring army, could harm or even kill such a helpless and physically handicapped person so mercilessly. One of Falk Daktar's sons, Gora, a handsome young man in his early teens, was shot and killed by the Razakars during this war. He became just one of millions of helpless Bengalis who were killed. Hindus were killed for just being Hindus as they were perceived as being sympathizers of India and the Bengali liberation war against Pakistan.

There were numerous individuals or families in the neighborhood with meager means who seemed to always be at our home. We just treated them as part of the family and took care of them. Our family cooks were always busy making tea and snacks through the day. I do not remember our kitchen ever out of use.

We had many private tutors who came to our home. One of them, Mahendra (whom we called Mahendir Sir), was a teacher at the local elementary school with a salary of 26 rupees (about US $3.50 at the time per month) and taught me and my siblings from first grade all through our elementary school years. This diminutive man, who was around five feet tall and had only a high school diploma, was the proven hand in getting us kids started on the right path to learning the alphabet and basic math.

In later years, Mahendir Sir would remind me of the life story of Professor Abdus Salam of Pakistan who received the Nobel Prize for his groundbreaking discovery in theoretical physics. Professor Salam belonged to the nonmainstream Ahmadiyya sect, which was persecuted in the Sunni Muslim majority of Pakistan. Professor Salam was tutored by a Hindu teacher during his formative years in pre-partition India in a town that eventually became part of Pakistan. Many years later, when Professor Salam was awarded the Nobel Prize, he travelled home via India to pay grateful homage to his old Hindu teacher who had settled in India after partition. After all, this humble teacher laid the foundation that put Professor Salam on his remarkable journey to the highest pinnacle of success as a scientist. Similarly, the memory of Mahendir Sir, the humble and dedicated teacher, is etched in my heart forever.

My eldest brother, Gour, down to Deba, my youngest sibling, all started their educational journey under the tutelage of Mahendir Sir, a period that covered over three decades in our family. He was a teacher for the first and second grades at Minayr School, the local elementary school that required tuition fees of about six rupees per month, which would be about seventy cents per month at that time. Even in the 1950s that was a miniscule amount. However, the perception was that it provided a better education compared to the other local primary schools that provided free education up to the sixth grade.

Mahendir Sir came to our house faithfully every evening to tutor us. By the time I had him as my teacher, five of my elder brothers and sisters had already graduated from the local high school and moved to India to pursue their college education before subsequently settling in various successful careers. I still fondly remember how diligently he helped us build our foundations in math by starting with the multiplication tables and urging us to repeat them loudly over and over again at the top of our voices—"dui dugonay char" (two times two is four), "tin dugonay chhoy" (three times two is six), and so on. I must admit I was bored most of the time as I was well ahead of his simple teaching methods that were based on rote learning. However, the discipline of studying every day was instilled in us from the very early days of our childhood.

Mahendir Sir also doubled as the local Brahmin priest for local Hindu communities and performed the religious ceremonies during various pujas (worshiping of gods and goddesses) in Hindu homes. In his role as the town's Hindu priest, he also performed hatay khori, a Hindu ritual that involves offering prayers and soliciting blessings from the goddess of learning, Swarashati, as the formal beginning of the learning process for small children.

Mahendir Sir performed the Laxmi (goddess of wealth) and Swarashati (goddess of learning) pujas at the homes of many Hindu families in our neighborhood. Starting from his home on the outskirts of town, he would perform the puja ceremony at the first Hindu home nearest his and then progress house by house after completing, with each ceremony lasting an hour or more. Our home was at the edge of the neighborhood. So by the time Mahendir Sir came to us, many hours had elapsed. The puja had to be performed within a certain time of the day in accordance with the panjika (a religious calendar) that defined the logno (auspicious time period) in which the puja needed to be completed. So one year, Mahendir Sir, in his desperate attempt to complete the Swarashati puja at our home before the ideal time period expired, started to skip many of the mantras (religious phrases from the Hindu holy scriptures) and rituals. My father, who was a devout and orthodox Brahmin and very familiar with the rituals, blew his fuse and admonished Mahendir Sir in his heavy Bangladeshi accent, "Haramzada, tumi Ma-er shathay faislami martaso?" (You stupid man, how dare you insult the goddess?) and forced him to start at the beginning.

I have many fond memories of the annual Durga Puja, the worshipping of goddess Durga, the biggest event of the year in the Bengal region of India, and equal to Christmas in Western countries. Durga Puja is mostly celebrated as a community affair. Each suburb or town celebrates with elaborate festivities, impressive platforms that house the idols of the goddess, food stalls, cultural functions, and dazzling lighting decorations that are funded by the contributions of families living in the neighborhood. The fund-raising for some of these pujas involved a good amount of persuasion and sometimes even coercion by the organizers. In recent years, the Durga Puja in major cities in the Bengal region on both sides of the India-Bangladesh border, particularly in Kolkata, has created a carnival-type atmosphere with many elaborate and exotic pandals or mandaps (stalls that house the idols) that cost millions of rupees. Neighborhoods compete to try to outdo each other.

Sayem Kazi, the richest man in town, was an interesting and colorful character. He was a very successful businessman. He held my father in high esteem. When he bought the first car in town, a German Volkswagen Beetle, he made sure my father was the first to get a ride in the car. He owned the only movie house in town that showed Bengali movies from Kolkata as well as Hollywood movies. Interestingly, he would often come to pick up my father in his car to go to the movie house whenever a good Bengali or Hollywood movie was being screened. If they were late, he would direct the operator to start the movie from the beginning. He would say, "Babu eshechen. Prothom thekey chalao," meaning, "Honorable Sir has come. Restart the movie!" The regular customers mostly put up with it or, in some cases, assumed it to be due to a mechanical malfunction.

The Hindus and Muslims in our town mostly lived in peace without any open sign of hostility toward each other. Children crossed the religious lines and sometimes became the best of friends.

They played at each other's homes without any inhibitions either by their families or societal norms. However, the Hindus in general were always self-conscious about their minority status and watched their steps in projecting their loyalty to Pakistan. The Hindus were generally considered to be sympathizers of India, which in fact was somewhat true. The deep-rooted distrust between the communities would only come to the fore during political turmoil or tension between India and Pakistan. When this happened, it put the local Hindus in harm's way more often than not.

I have often wondered whether my sentimental attachment and inherent devotion to India had anything to do with my resentment or animosity toward Pakistan. In reality, I never harbored any ill-feelings toward Pakistan or Muslims in general despite the painful experiences my family endured in Pakistan. As a Hindu, my sentiment was naturally attached with India, which was slated to be an independent state for the Hindus, even though it was designated as a secular state after the partition with equal protection for other minority segments of the population. Similarly, I do not believe all Israelis are inherently anti-Palestinian. It is their Jewish sentimentality that is inherently attached to the Jewish cause and protective against any real or perceived threat from other external entities, particularly the Palestinians.

During any sporting event such as cricket or hockey matches involving archrivals India and Pakistan, it is not uncommon even to this date to see the Indian Muslims audaciously cheering with firecrackers when Pakistan scored a goal or won a match against India. In Pakistan, cheering for Pakistan's opponent, particularly India during a sporting event, would be expected to bring a very harsh response from the local population or even the government. Recently, a young Pakistani fan of Virat Kohli, the Indian cricket team captain, was dealt with very harshly by the Pakistani authorities when the young fan openly expressed his love and admiration for the Indian cricket team captain!

Even though my family suffered immensely at the hands of the Muslims during the few years after partition when we stayed there as a minority before moving to India, I never held any animosity toward the Muslims in general. I always took the persecution or discrimination as a natural consequence of the harsh geopolitical reality caused by the partition of India along religious lines. I am certain many Muslim families from India who immigrated to Pakistan before or after the partition would have similar experiences.

CHAPTER 3

Turbulent Years

Even though the partition of the Indian subcontinent was based on the religious majority of each region, there were certain regions or pockets of population where the division was not so clear. I have been told there were great uncertainties whether Khulna district, which included my hometown of Bagerhat, would be part of East Pakistan or West Bengal state in India. Many years later, my father confided to me that it was one of his saddest days when the Pakistani flag was hoisted at the district headquarters in Khulna on August 14, 1947. Most of the Khulna district, and its three subdivisions including Bagerhat, had a large Hindu population. There were two choices for these Hindus. Either they could migrate or move to India or simply assume the risk of living as minorities in Pakistan and being subjected to potential persecution or discrimination by the Muslim rulers as well as by the orthodox, extreme right-wing sections of the Muslim population.

I have always wondered why my father opted to stay in East Pakistan instead of moving to India immediately after partition rather than doing so many years later in the 1960s. His three elder brothers had already established their residences in Kolkata long before partition, so their families did not have to suffer the trauma of making a desperate dash to the other side of the country like millions of other Hindus and Muslims. My uncles were all professionals: one was a doctor, one was an engineer who worked for the Geological Survey of India, and the eldest one, whom we fondly called Jethamoshai ("elder brother of the father"), was a teacher at a school in Kalighat, a suburb of Kolkata.

However, like most Hindus in Pakistan, my father had a deep affinity for India just like Jewish persons around the world feel for Israel. So he started to send his children to India one by one. My four eldest brothers and one elder sister moved to India after they finished high school in Bagerhat. Three of my elder brothers, Gour, Arun, and Amiya, were all first boys (top students) at Bagerhat High School and passed their school finals with high honors. They headed to India in the 1950s for their university education before embarking on successful professional careers. Hashi, my eldest sister, left in 1960. My immediate elder brother, Anil, continued another two years after high school at the local PC College and passed the intermediate arts degree (twelfth grade) with high distinction before he left for India in 1962 to continue his studies in Kolkata.

In most cases, my siblings who were sent across the border to India by my father while still in their teens would find my eldest paternal uncle's home as the base to establish themselves, starting with little or no resources. My uncle was a schoolteacher with a modest home on the banks of the Ganges River in Kalighat, a suburb of Kolkata where the holi Kali temple was located. While my father was a highly respected and successful lawyer with a lucrative practice in Bagerhat, he had great difficulty in remitting any money legally to India to support my siblings. Consequently, they had to face many challenging circumstances while pursuing their education.

My uncle's home was a very busy hub and was perpetually crowded with other family members who came to Kolkata from other far-flung areas of Bengal from both sides of the border for their various pursuits in Kolkata. My elder brothers got their start in India here and, once they got their footing, moved out on their own. Gour[2] joined the Indian Air Force at a very young age. While on his meager starting salary in the Indian Air Force, he supported Amiya through college. After a moderately rewarding stint working in the radar area, Gour left the Air Force to become an engineer

---

[2] We called Gour borda, a Bengali term to address the eldest brother.

and went to the USA, Canada, and Europe for advanced education and training before becoming a successful senior executive at an alloy steel plant in Durgapur, just a few hundred miles away from Kolkata. Amiya went on to get his engineering degree in electrical engineering from Jadavpur University in Kolkata and subsequently had a very successful career as a top-level executive in the industries owned by the illustrious Birla family. Amiya married Sikha, a beautiful art graduate of the famed Kolkata Art College. By the time Amiya[3] was about to get settled after getting his first job as an engineer, my other elder brother, Anil, and eldest sister, Hashi, appeared on his doorstep. My father sent them to India for their continued education and new life in India.

Amiya was duty bound to support and help them through their college education. It was all about managing and getting by with Amiya's starting engineer's salary.

It was very difficult for my father to remit money to India without getting into serious trouble with the Pakistani government and local Muslims who were perpetually hostile toward India. He was able to circumvent the system from time to time to transfer some money. The process was locally known as hoondi. My father would give the money in Pakistani currency to a local Hindu businessman who was a family friend. This man had many of his own children and relatives settled in India like our family and countless other Hindu families in East Pakistan. He also had a number of businesses in West Bengal in India run by his family members, so he would take the money from my father and invest it in his business locally while his family would give the equivalent money in Indian currency to my brothers in India. Obviously, there was a fee on top of the exact amount based on the going exchange rate. Needless to say, it was done very carefully and discreetly since there was the potential for catastrophic consequences if the Pakistani authorities caught on.

Anil did well in his studies first at Ashutosh College and then at the Calcutta University, earning a master's degree in political science and a law degree. He subsequently passed and qualified for the

---

[3]   We called Amiya sejda, literally meaning "third eldest brother."

highly prestigious administrative service before starting his professional career in Jalpaiguri in West Bengal. Hashi, who was not a top performer academically, managed to get her BA degree and married a railway divisional engineer posted in Kharagpur in the Bardwan district.

During the early sixties, my father found a match for my younger sister, Anju. The boy, Shankar, was settled in India, but just like our divided family, some of his relatives were still living in Pakistan. Shankar came from Kolkata, got married to Anju, and went back to India. With great difficulty, we were able to send Anju to join her husband in India a couple of years later.

Unfortunately, a sad disaster befell our family. Anil, while still in his late twenties, died in an accident in Kolkata at the prime of his life. This was the second disaster as my second eldest brother, Arun, had also passed away in India prematurely a few years earlier. My parents and I got the news from the other side of the border. There was nothing we could do to change the harsh reality faced by countless divided families like ours. With strict rules guiding the travel across the border, we could not go to India in time to be part of the cremation ceremonies. Sejda and our cousin Shambhuda arranged and performed his last rites in accordance with Hindu religious customs.

Many years later when I shared our family situation with a Jewish colleague of mine in the USA, he said that the stories of my family would strike a chord with many Jewish families living in different parts of the world. He mentioned how his Jewish parents living in pre–World War II Germany and later in New York started sending his siblings to Israel over the years. He was born and brought up in the Bronx, New York, but spent almost thirty years in Israel before moving back to New York. Unfortunately, his father, who always aspired to move to Israel and settle there, never made it as he died of a heart attack after a setback in his business in New York. Most Jews living in other countries feel duty bound to settle in Israel or serve and support in various other ways such as in the army as the country is on a perpetual war footing with its hostile Muslim neighbors. This is another region that has experienced, and continues to experience, immeasurable miseries stemming from its sad geopolitical realities with no immediate end to the turmoil in sight for either the Jewish or the Muslim population, particularly the Palestinians.

We had an austere home in Bagerhat, but my maternal uncle had a huge mansion down the road. My father never invested any significant resources in building a big home in Pakistan. It was obvious his sentimental attachment was with India, and it's also possible he knew that someday he would permanently move to India and integrate the family.

On the other hand, my maternal uncle Charu Roy, who was a lawyer with a scant practice, had a huge mansion befitting a zaminder (owner of large land properties) in Bagerhat just a block from our home. Actually, a number of homes on that street belonged to my maternal uncle, whom we called Mama. He inherited his fortune from my maternal grandfather who owned hundreds of acres of land and made his fortune from the agricultural products from this land holding using cheap labor. In fact, the street of our home was named after my maternal grandfather at that time.

The difference between my father and my maternal uncle was the extent of tact they used to live and survive as a minority in Pakistan. Mama was very audacious and never shied away from expressing his deep sentiment and affinity for India in the public forum. Undoubtedly, it was the most politically incorrect way to live and survive there. However, most local people considered him an eccentric person and put up with him. In 1965 when war broke out between India and Pakistan and the Indian Army was inching into Pakistani territory, Mama went into the local bazaar and announced that the Indian Army had conquered a number of major cities in West Pakistan including Lahore, the capital of West Punjab province, and the Pakistani Army had suffered a shameful and humiliating defeat. This is the equivalent of a Palestinian man going into the heart of Tel Aviv and declaring Hamas has just destroyed or taken over Israeli settlements in East Jerusalem, or a Jew going to the Gaza Strip and declaring Israel has crushed Hamas in Gaza or Hezbollah in Lebanon. The reaction of local Muslims was swift and hostile. They reported him to the authorities, and he was arrested and locked up by the police. He was in Khulna district jail without trial for a few months until the war was over.

Mama was constantly feuding with local Muslims and on many occasions took them to court, contending they were trying to illegally confiscate his properties. During the height of martial law, the Pakistani Army searched his mansion to check if he was hoarding any substantial amounts of rice, which was in shortage at the time. They confiscated a large amount of rice, although it was quite natural for a zaminder-commanding farmland to have huge inventories of rice to sell on the open market. But his Hindu status was not acceptable to the Pakistani military. To our horror, Mama filed a lawsuit against none other than Field Marshall Ayub Khan, the military strongman and dreaded martial law ruler of Pakistan at the time. The poor low-level Bengali magistrate in Bagerhat, who was handling the lawsuit in his court, was put on the spot and probably did not know what to do. We were all very concerned that he was about to be locked up again. My father kept on saying, "The man just simply does not get it!" Mama was angry with my father for not taking his case and representing him legally. My father, on the other hand, thought he was too stupid for his own good to dare local Muslims and the authorities. It seemed that he was always courting trouble, mostly unnecessarily.

Then, one day the jubilant Mama came to the front of our home and announced that the judge had ruled in his favor and released his rice. The judge made him pay a small fine for hoarding large quantities of rice without the knowledge of the authorities. We were astonished. One of the influential Muslim local leaders confided to my father that the military officer in charge of Pakistani Army headquarters in Khulna had instructed the judge to make the decision in order to show the world as part of their propaganda that minority Hindus were not persecuted and got justice in accordance with the law.

My father, on the other hand, walked a fine line through the complex web of dynamics involving the minority Hindus that played out in every phase of the society. Even though there were no open hostilities between the Hindus and the Muslims in our town on a day-to-day basis, the Hindus were meek and timid and led a pacifist lifestyle, constantly mindful of their position in the society and doing everything to showcase their loyalty to Pakistan even though most of them had a close affinity toward India. They knew that they were always looked upon with suspicion by the Muslims due to their inherent loyalty and sentimental attachment to India. The Hindus always felt that they were just one step or misstep away from potential trouble. I am sure it is the same for many Muslim families living as minorities in India or other minorities that live in countries affected by sectarian conflict.

Hindus would often proclaim, "Pakistan Zindabad," i.e., "Long live Pakistan," at any official functions as a way of displaying loyalty in a very audacious way. One of my lifelong memories from my childhood in Bagerhat was of Kali Prosad Chatterjee, popularly known as KPC, a highly respected teacher who sometimes doubled as the physical education teacher and guided students through a routine of drills before classes started. He would always end his routine by shouting, "Pakistan Zindabad" at the top of his voice. And if he ever saw any Muslim government official or police officer passing on the road, he would blurt out "Pakistan Zindabad" to make sure his loyalty was clear and loud. Many years later he said to me, "Tagore [using the nickname that had attached to me in honor of the great Nobel laureate poet of India, Rabindra Nath Tagore], what a pity that I had to tell all those lies during our drills!"

My father was considered the leader of the Hindu community in Bagerhat. He worked with government officials, including the top government civil servant, the subdivisional officer (SDO) who administered the affairs of the town. He was on the board of all the schools and was an elected member of the town council.

Many civil servants who came to Bagerhat as the SDO went on to become high officials in the central or provincial Pakistani government in Dacca. They fondly remembered my father as a very competent and respected Hindu leader. With their recommendations, he was selected as a member of Pakistan's Minority Board. This was probably created by the Pakistani government as part of their propaganda to demonstrate to the outside world that Pakistan took care of its minorities and their welfare. My father traveled to Dacca a number of times to attend the Minority Board meeting, which was chaired by the central interior minister of Pakistan.

During the 1960s, my father was informed that he was being considered as a minister in the East Pakistan government. There was always a portfolio, normally a noncritical one that was given to a Hindu. However, during this time the whole country became engulfed with political unrest and demonstrations that forced General Ayub Khan out of power and Army chief General Yahya Khan into power, so my father never became a minister.

In spite of his sincere efforts to show his loyalty, it simply was never enough to secure the confidence of the authorities. When war broke out between Pakistan and India in 1965, he was interned for a few months in Khulna under the defense of Pakistan law. Then again, he was the same man who was once considered for a cabinet position. There are probably many parallels in the histories of other nations. Hundreds of thousands of Japanese-Americans were interned in the USA and forced to live in encampments after the attack on Pearl Harbor by the Japanese during the Second World War.

My father inspired and exhorted all his children to excel in school and extracurricular activities as a way of overcoming the disadvantages we experienced as a minority in Pakistan. All my brothers were first boys (top students in the class) in elementary school (grades one through six) and then at the local Bagerhat High School. My parents encouraged us without putting unnecessary pressure to excel in our academic endeavors.

I was the top student in the class every year from the first grade to the sixth, and later I enrolled in the seventh grade at Bagerhat High School and was the first boy from the seventh to the tenth grade. At the school final, my teachers expected me to be the top performer among all the high schools under the Rajshahi Board, which covered eight districts of East Pakistan. When the results came out, I was ninth out of many thousands of students. Even though it was an impressive performance, I was deeply disappointed. This was the first time I had not been the topper even though the board test had involved hundreds of schools in the eight districts. All my teachers were in disbelief when they saw my scores in various subjects. I let-tered in all the science subjects except geography where my score was only 50 out of 100. My geography teacher Keshav Sir knew my notebook contained extremely detailed answers to all the questions in the board test. When he looked at my notebook with the answers to the questions in the board test, containing proofs such as the earth was not flat but curved, he opined that even an MSc student in geography at Dacca University or Calcutta University could not have given any better or more detailed answers than what I provided. It was obvious that somebody at the board office had arbitrarily changed my score in geography, possibly to prevent a Hindu from being the topper in the board examination! Neither I nor any of my teachers could think of any other justification for the inexplicable score. I was actually expecting a score of close to 100. If I had received even the letter mark of 80 I would probably have topped the board examination as only a few points separated my score from the student who stood first.

Unlike my elder brothers who moved to India immediately after high school, I stayed for my two-year pre-engineering (intermediate science degree) at the local Bagerhat PC College. Strangely, the final results following the completion of my two-year studies at the college brought me great dismay similar to what happened with the high school board results. This time I stood third in the board exam with letters in every science subject, i.e., mathematics, chemistry, and physics, but the score in one of the English courses was only 38 out of 100, just barely above the minimum passing mark. Many of my classmates whom I tutored scored significantly higher in English. If I had received just a few points more, I would have topped the board test. It was a consensus among all my friends and the professors of PC College that my score was arbitrarily changed by an official at the board office in order to stop me from topping the board test covering all the colleges that came under the board's jurisdiction. The principal of the college, even though he was a Muslim, was so furious he wanted to appeal with a demand to investigate the scoring by a neutral examiner. My father and I were resigned to the fact that this was the harsh reality of living as a minority in a country where discrimination of various forms raised its ugly head time and time again, even though there was rarely open hostility and Hindu and Muslim neighbors were amicable on the surface. Most of my close friends were Muslims, and when my sister's friends came to our home, they would socialize and mingle like sisters.

I took the college board results in my stride. It was, after all, still a very high achievement to come in third among the thousands of students, and I had only missed first place by a few points. Still to this day, when I reflect, I am convinced I was ruthlessly denied my rightful place as the topper while I was still a teen in East Pakistan.

By that time, I decided to go to India to pursue my engineering studies. So in 1965, I left for India. However, the deadline for admission in any of the engineering universities in Kolkata or in any of the IITs (Indian Institute of Technologies) had passed. My brother Amiya was an electrical engineering alumni of Jadavpur University and went directly to the then vice chancellor Dr. Triguna Sen (who later became the education minister of India) to seek his help in getting around the admission deadline. However, during this same time when I was about to embark on my undergraduate engineering studies in India, the political situation in the Indian subcontinent was very tense just before the war between India and Pakistan broke out in 1965. My father was in a vulnerable position in East Pakistan being a prominent Hindu leader there. He was actually detained under the defense of Pakistan rule by the Pakistani military government just before the war broke out. So the pursuit of my undergraduate engineering studies in India ended prematurely. I rushed back to my hometown in East Pakistan to be supportive of my remaining family. I was heartbroken as my long-cherished goal of pursuing my engineering studies in India had to be put on hold since I was duty bound to respond to a higher calling. I was still in my teens at the time, and the welfare of the family rested on my shoulders! Subsequently, I spent a few years in East Pakistan before moving back to India. It is an irony that my second attempt at pursuing my engineering studies in India a few years later also did not come to fruition. I went through the rigorous written and oral test and was about to get admitted in the MTech program in one of the most prestigious IITs in Kanpur, India. It was exciting to see my name in the list of the selected students considering that most of the candidates who took the test for the highly competitive M.Tech program were the top engineering graduates from all the major engineering universities in India. But it was not my fate to pursue the M.Tech program at IIT, Kanpur. While working for a utility company at the time, my admission and assistantship in the Mechanical Engineering Department at the Ohio State University came through.

I departed for the United States in March of 1974 to pursue my doctorate in mechanical engineering. I started a new chapter in my life that stood in stark contrast to my chaotic and turbulent experiences in the Indian subcontinent.

CHAPTER 4

Social upheavals in East Pakistan and Perilous Journey to India

Political turmoil was sweeping East Pakistan in the late 1960s prior to the Bangladesh liberation war that ultimately led to the creation of Bangladesh in 1971. At the time, I had just started working as a lecturer in mechanical engineering at a regional engineering college.

I spent most of my time reading at my lecturer's flat or socializing with a small group of faculty members and their families on the campus. A girlfriend who was attending the local medical college at the time visited me from time to time. While the visit by a twenty-something medical student to her university lecturer boyfriend would not raise an eyebrow in any Western society, it was major gossip in conservative Eastern culture. Any open display of friendship or intimacy between a boy and a girl before marriage is a social taboo in conservative South Asian countries. In Eastern cultures, open relationships between boys and girls before marriage are frowned upon, and as a result there can be some negative repercussions. In extreme cases, particularly in conservative Muslim societies in Asia, there have been documented cases of boys and girls facing severe punishment including public lashing or death by stoning. This would be unthinkable in most Western societies. So my challenge was to walk a very fine line and manage my girlfriend's visits as discreetly as possible. Interestingly, some of my colleagues' socially progressive wives, particularly those who spent time in Europe or America during their husbands' graduate studies, were very sympathetic to my situation and made sure that the wave of gossip and rumors about my moral compass or the lack thereof did not go overboard and hurt my reputation.

Within a year, I left my lecturer's position and accepted a job that took me to Dacca, the capital of East Pakistan, to join a utility company that had a number of collaborative projects with the Parsons Corporation, one of the largest environmental companies in the United States. My parents and three younger siblings were still living in Bagerhat. The country was in political turmoil. The Awami League under the leadership of its charismatic leader, Sheikh Mujibur Rahaman, had just swept the parliamentary elections and captured all but a handful of seats in East Pakistan. Bengali nationalism was sweeping Bengali-speaking East Pakistan.

The election outcome in West Pakistan was just the opposite. The majority of the parliamentary seats were won by the Pakistan People's Party (PPP) headed by Zulfiqur Ali Bhutto. The PPP did not get a single seat in East Pakistan, and the Awami League was similarly unsuccessful in the west. However, due to the slight difference in population, there were a few more parliamentary seats in East Pakistan. According to parliamentary rules, Sheikh Mujib should have been poised to head the central government as the prime minister of Pakistan, but it was not meant to be!

The economy and politics of Pakistan were dominated by the West Pakistani elite. The military dictatorship was mostly comprised of West Pakistanis. The Bengalis of East Pakistan were discriminated against and treated as second-class citizens. So thanks to the population gap, the West Pakistani political elite like Zulfiqur Ali Bhutto and the then military strongman General Yahiya Khan realized that parliamentary democracy would inevitably give East Pakistan the majority in the parliament, and if a single party swept the election, a Bengali from East Pakistan would become prime minister. That prospect did not sit well with them, so Bhutto and General Yahiya Khan colluded to nullify the election results. This brought an unprecedented level of protest and outbursts from the Bengalis, and the whole of East Pakistan was engulfed in violent protests. On March 25, 1971, the Pakistani Army unleashed a brutal attack in the middle of the night on various residential dormitories of Dacca University, a hotbed of political activism, and other civilian centers across East Pakistan. Sheikh Mujib was arrested and incarcerated in West Pakistan. He was never heard from until after the secession of East Pakistan and the creation of independent Bangladesh following the Bangladesh liberation war.

The rampage unleashed on March 25, 1971, by the military continued for a few days before they withdrew to their barracks. The Hindu neighborhood of Dacca, Shakhari Bazaar, was savagely attacked, and there was a heavy human toll. After all, Hindus were always perceived as sympathizers of India, which openly supported the cause of the Bengalis in East Pakistan. By that time, India was openly supporting Sheikh Mujib and his quest for the emancipation of the Bengalis from the yolk of Pakistan's domination and suppression. News of mass murder and brutality committed by the Pakistani Army and its local collaborators, the Razakars, started to come in from all corners of the country.

When I went back to work at Parsons Corporation a few days later, there was a very solemn atmosphere. The few who showed up were all frightened. Most of my colleagues urged me to leave Dacca immediately as Hindus were being specifically targeted. They pointed out that the Shakhari Bazaar neighborhood was savagely attacked and thousands of Hindus in that suburb had been murdered by the Pakistani Army.

I called my close Muslim friend Farooque, who was then a lecturer in chemical engineering at East Pakistan University of Engineering and Technology (EPUET) in Dacca. He hailed from my hometown. Obviously he was also anxious to leave Dacca as no young and able-bodied Bengali was safe. He came from a very liberal and progressive Muslim family. The Army was targeting the Bengali progressive intelligentsia and younger population. I also needed to go to Bagerhat to check on my family. So Farooque and his family arranged an escape plan from Dacca. First, a bus would take us to the outskirts of Dacca, and then we would travel by an unpowered rowboat to Bagerhat with a stopover in Faridpur, a district town on the way. Nuru, another friend, was from Faridpur. He and his family also joined us on this trip. This trip actually saved my life. Later, after the liberation war when I came back to Dacca, I was told that the local cohorts of the Pakistani Army, the Razakars, came to my workplace and my apartment looking for me. Obviously, if they had found me at that time, they would have killed me and I would have become one of the statistics in the massacre that claimed several million Bengali lives.

First, we took a bus from Dacca that drove us about four hours to the ferry station from where we would take the boat. It was a slow ten-hour boat ride in cramped conditions as there were close to ten people onboard including Farooque's and Nuru's families. The most dangerous part was rowing across the big Padma River in the dark of night. We stayed in Faridpur for a couple of days. Faridpur was yet to be attacked and ravaged by the Pakistani Army. The local population there had not yet realized the devastation caused by the Army.

After a couple of days, Farooque arranged another boat to go to Bagerhat. It was another long boat ride in a small manually powered boat. Once we reached Bagerhat, I stayed with Farooque's family in their village home for a day before I went to see my family in the suburb where my parents and two of my younger brothers and a younger sister lived.

When I went to my childhood neighborhood, the entire area looked deserted, particularly the Hindu homes. Hindus there had been threatened and harassed by the Razakars, and no one was at my home. One of the neighbors told me that my parents and my siblings were living with some family acquaintances in some of the villages on the other side of the river. For the next three to four months I moved the family from village to village to hide from the Razakars who were seeking out pro-independence Muslims and all Hindus in general.

One day, one of the Muslim family friends came to our hideout and told us that our family home in Bagerhat had been bombed and burnt to ashes by the Pakistani Army. A few of our Hindu neighbors who had been brave or stupid enough to stay back were killed during this assault. Our family doctor, Dr. Falk, an old and feeble man in his seventies, was dragged from his home and shot at point-blank range. Joshoda, a tailor who lived just around the corner, suffered the same fate. Another, an octogenarian, Kiron Das, who was a very rich landlord (zaminder), was also shot at his palatial mansion.

When we received this information from Bagerhat, we were alarmed. We would move from one house to another, and at night, the younger males slept in the jungle in case our homes were invaded by the Razakars. Only the women and the elder men like our fathers were left in the house. When the local Razakars informed Hindus that the only way to escape severe punishment and survive was to convert to Islam, my goal became finding a way to take my family to India. Millions of people started to stream into India from East Pakistan to avoid the atrocities committed by the Pakistani Army against the Hindu population. Young civilians and Bengali soldiers who had deserted the Pakistani Army assembled in various camps in neighboring West Bengal and Assam states in India with the full support of the Indian government headed by Prime Minister Mrs. Indira Gandhi. India provided all the necessary training, material, and logistical support for the Mukti Bahini, the freedom fighters who started to launch attacks on Pakistani interests and their local cohorts by crossing the border and launching carefully crafted assaults using guerrilla tactics.

My first attempt was to arrange a couple of boats that would take us to India through a series of rivers by evading the local Razakars and the Pakistani Army. Very early in the morning, long before sunrise in May 1971, my family including my parents, two younger brothers, and a sister, and seven members of Rabinda's family started on the perilous journey to India. Rabinda was a professor of philosophy at Pirozpur College near Bagerhat. My family had been living with his in the village for about a month before we attempted this escape. Rabinda's family consisted of his wife whom I called Boudi ("wife of an elder brother"), his three-year-old daughter, his parents, uncle, aunt, and a nephew.

Our two majhis (boatmen) dutifully and laboriously rowed for close to four hours, weaving through a series of small rivers heading toward the Indian border. Many boats crossed our path and gave us a curious and suspicious look. We had a curtain hanging on the cabins of the two boats to hide the female members of the entourage. We were particularly worried about my younger sister who was nineteen and very pretty. Rabinda's wife was a very pretty young lady as well. We were aware that the Razakars had an eye for pretty Hindu women. We knew that the beautiful daughter of one of our neighbors in Bagerhat was forcibly taken from their home and brought to a village on the other side of the river. This unfortunate girl was a classmate of my elder sister Hashi and had a master's degree from Rajshahi University. She was tall, slim, very fair complexioned, and extraordinarily beautiful. After her abduction, she was forced to convert to Islam and marry an illiterate Muslim.

Finally, we started to realize that a number of boats were following us and closing in on our two boats. After playing cat and mouse for a while, they finally surrounded us. With shouts of "Allah hu akbar" ("God is great"), they jumped into our boats. I desperately tried to talk them into letting us go. They finally realized that I was the spokesperson for our group and wanted me to talk to their leader, a middle-aged guy with a long, bushy black beard who had the look of a Muslim religious zealot.

The man asked me repeatedly why we were leaving the country when there was no reason to do so! I desperately tried to explain that we felt threatened and we just wanted to go to India temporarily and someday we would come back when things returned to normal. Obviously, he had no interest in our fear and sense of despair. He asked us how much money and jewelry we were carrying. He wanted to know how many family members were inside the boat cabin. He specifically asked about any girls or women on board and their age. By that time the other invaders had torn open the covers of the two cabins and saw everybody there. They were shamelessly showing interest in my younger sister and Rabinda's wife.

As part of the negotiation with the leader, I gave them a large sum of cash that I gathered from all the family members and practically all the gold jewelry they had accumulated over their lifetimes. I kept some cash that was tied around my upper thigh under the lungi (a traditional Bengali skirt). I made a deal with the leader that they could have all the cash and the jewelry, but they could not take any of the girls or the women away from us. After a relentless discussion back and forth and after I showed my loyalty to Islam with a recitation of the Quran, which I had memorized by heart as part of my survival acumen, the leader finally let us go, not toward India but back to our village. He ordered his men to let us go. The men followed us for an hour or so to make sure that we were indeed heading back to our starting point in the village, and not on a path to India. So we returned to Rabinda's family home sometime late in the evening, after almost twelve hours of our abortive and disastrous attempt to flee to India.

From that point on, my whole energy was focused on devising another daring plan to escape the atrocities of the Razakars and the Pakistani Army. By that time, I had grown a long beard in an attempt to blend in as a Muslim. I made two trips into Bagerhat and contacted a couple of Muslim leaders who were close family friends and who had great respect for my father. They were very afraid to provide any help in case they were implicated. So I decided to go one bold step further to meet another Muslim family friend, a banker in the district town of Khulna about twenty-five miles from Bagerhat, closer to the Indian border. I was counting on his help in our attempt to flee to India. He and his family had been our next-door neighbors before subsequently moving to Khulna to take up a new job. The challenge for me was to travel those twenty-five miles, either by a narrow gauge train or by a three-wheel auto-rickshaw on a bad roadway that ran parallel to the rail track. Then it would require crossing the Rupsha River in a small rowboat. In all, it would be a challenge to get to the house of this Muslim family friend and take over four to five hours.

Before this troublesome situation developed in the country, I was a very well-known, recognizable boy who excelled in academics and athletics and was the son of the most renowned Hindu leader in Bagerhat. So I was tremendously worried that I would be recognized by the Razakars or their cohorts, and there was a high chance my superficial camouflage with a long beard and the look of a poor

Muslim laborer would not succeed. Once I was caught they would definitely torture or kill me.

While I was considering this trip to Khulna to finalize our escape to India, the situation in the villages where we were hiding became precarious. The younger members of our families, including my younger brothers, dared not sleep in the hut at night, fearing the Razakars would round them up and slaughter them. We would hide and sleep in the jungle hoping, praying that the women and young girls would be safe. During this time, the local Razakar leader actually arranged a conversion ceremony presided over by a mullah or imam and converted many of the Hindus hiding in the village. At first all the young people were forcibly gathered in the compound of the local Razakar leader and were told to go through the rituals and recite the Quran—"La ilaha illallah Muhammadur Rasulullah" or "There is no God, only Allah, and Mohammed is the prophet of Allah"—for the conversion to Islam. The shout of "Allah hu akbar" ("God is great") pierced the stillness of the night. Obviously, nobody went through the rituals voluntarily. It was coerced.

I was very grateful that my family escaped this inglorious experience somehow as it would have destroyed my father if he lost his religious identity as a devout Brahmin Hindu.

One morning, I finally gathered enough courage to set out for Khulna. My parents tearfully wished me luck and warned me to be careful. Baba, as I called my father, kept on hitting his head with both hands in a prayerful and customary Hindu gesture to seek God's blessings.

The first hurdle was to cross the river that separated the villages where my family was in hiding from the town center in Bagerhat. Then I travelled twenty miles by road to the Rupsha River that I needed to cross to get to Khulna. As I was trying to hire a boat to take me across, I noticed a bearded and menacing-looking individual was closely watching me. I immediately recognized him as one of the notorious local miscreant who was known as a Hindu hater in Bagerhat even during peaceful days. Obviously, he knew me but was probably struggling to correlate my new shaggy and bearded look with the old clean-cut Tagore, the highly popular and adored scholar athlete from the most respected Hindu family in town!

Fortunately, I was able to get onto the boat and pushed the boatman to start rowing right away. The miscreant kept on looking at me as our boat started to draw away from shore. It was a missed opportunity for the miscreant for a good catch. After I reached the other side, it was a matter of finding a rickshaw driver who was familiar with the neighborhood as I only knew the name of the bank where our old family acquaintance was employed and did not have his office or home address. It was also very important that the rickshaw driver did not become too suspicious as he could be a local cohort of the Razakars and by extension the Pakistani Army. A young man in his early twenties could easily be mistaken as a member of the Mukti Bahini, the Bengali freedom fighters who were waging guerrilla war from their camps across the Indian border.

After an hour of futile efforts to locate the bank, I told the rickshaw puller to go to any bank branch in the neighborhood. I inquired inside one, and the bank officer told me our old family friend was assigned in another branch and gave me the name and directions. The officer could tell something was suspicious, but I could see the sympathy in his face, and when I was leaving he whispered in my ear, "Shubdhanay thakben, joy Bangla," meaning "Be careful! Victory to Bangladesh." After all, most Bengalis were supporters of the ongoing liberation war and would express their sentiment discreetly in selected safe situations. When I went to the other branch, I immediately recognized my old neighbor from Bagerhat. He was shocked to see me and probably in disbelief that I had undertaken such a brazen venture in broad daylight with the risk of being seen and caught.

He immediately took me to his office and closed the door. He told me it was too risky to stay there long since my shaggy look would raise suspicion. We immediately bolted out of the door and took a rickshaw to his home about a mile away. There I pleaded with him to help me secure a van to transport my family to the Indian border. He was initially very nervous and hesitant but in the end relented and agreed to help. The plan was to have the van available at the ferry site on the Khulna side of Rupsha River two days later, very early in the morning so that as soon as we crossed, we could get into the van and head toward India. The driver had to be trustworthy with the lives of so many people at stake. The driver had to also be familiar with all the back roads to the Indian border to avoid the strongholds of our tormentors.

After finalizing the escape plan with him, I returned to my family. This time I decided to go back after dark to avoid being recognized. Once I had returned, I held a family meeting and informed everybody about the plan. Needless to say, everybody was frightened. Baba (Father) kept asking, "Tui nishchinto acchish toe, shob nirapaday hobay?" ("Are you sure everything can be done safely?") How could I give him that assurance?

Two days later, on a day that would become one of the most remarkable days in the life story of our family, we got up early, long before sunrise. Rabinda's family gave us some hastily prepared breakfast. My father and mother, who were in their late sixties at the time, and my two younger brothers, Shiba and Deba, and my youngest sister, Mona, who were all in their teens, would make this daring trip with their lives and security riding on my shoulders. Everybody was told to pack a small handbag with just a few clothes and basic necessities. Baba was in pants and shirt with a Muslim cap without his customary Hindu dress of a dhoti and Punjabi. The women were in burka, the black robe that fully covered the women head to toe and was normally worn by conservative Muslim women. I was in a lungi and a Muslim cap, commonly worn by the poor and ordinary religious Muslims.

I had arranged four rickshaws the day before with the help of a trustworthy Muslim family friend to take us from our hideout in the village to the river. There a boat would take us to Bagerhat on the other side. How trustworthy were the rickshaw pullers? How did we know they would not inform the Razakars about our trip? Obviously, the payment of a few hundred rupees for a fare that would normally cost just a few rupees probably made the difference. Also, there were many good-hearted and well-meaning Muslims who sympathized with Hindus who were being ruthlessly tortured and killed. By the time we reached the riverfront, dawn had not yet broken and part of the plan was to avoid the local miscreants who would still be in bed. The prearranged boatman was waiting to take us to the other side of Bagerhat River. The boatman was again very heavily compensated in our attempt to keep our trip under the radar as much as possible.

After we crossed the river, we hurriedly got into a couple of auto-rickshaws arranged by a local Muslim friend and sped away. The road ran parallel to the narrow-gage rail line between Bagerhat and Khulna. I had taken the slow train many times growing up in Bagerhat, but I'd decided to avoid this train since I did not want my family to be confined in a train where we could be recognized. After all, our family had been very well-known during the period preceding the turmoil. The actual distance between Bagerhat and Khulna was only about twenty miles. But with seven or eight stops, the train took close to two hours to traverse this distance. Taking an auto-rickshaw provided us with a more covert and faster means of travel.

It took us about an hour to reach the ferry stop on the Bagerhat side of the Rupsha River. This was also the end point of the Bagerhat-Khulna train line, so it was a very busy place. There were a large number of people there, including those who commuted from Bagerhat to the district town of Khulna for work or business. They would normally take the manually rowed boat to cross the Rupsha River to go to Khulna. With all the women covered in full burkas and the men in shaggy clothes and Muslim caps, we looked like a lower middle-class orthodox Muslim family. My beard ran to my chest. To my horror, I noticed a notorious Razakar leader at the ferry station. Fortunately, he took a boat just ahead of us. It was a close call. Even with our disguises, he could have easily recognized us. If we had arrived at the ferry stop even a few minutes earlier, we would have been on his boat and possibly identified and killed; it was miraculous timing that saved us all.

We negotiated with a boatman to take us all to Khulna on the other side of the Rupsha River. The heavyset boatman had a long, bushy black beard and wore a Muslim cap. He looked menacing and intimidating. I chose him intentionally as nobody would expect a Hindu family to travel with such an orthodox-looking Muslim. I tried to make the boat ride seem as authentic as possible and give the impression of a poor Muslim family on a trip to Khulna. My greatest challenge was to keep my father's hands from hitting his forehead repeatedly in a Hindu gesture of prayer. I sat next to him on the boat and kept a tight squeeze on his hands to immobilize them.

After our boat reached the other side of the Rupsha River, we disembarked hastily. After I paid the menacing-looking boatman and was about to push the family into our prearranged waiting van, the boatman softly whispered in my ear, "Babu [a traditional way to address an honorable Hindu], khoob shabdhanay thakben. Haramzada Pakistan Army ar shala razakar-ra shob juygatay achay!" ("Sir, be very careful. The evil Pakistan Army and their lackey Razakars are everywhere!"). I was startled. The man had known all along what we were up to. We had not fooled him. But contrary to my earlier apprehension about him, he was one of those many good-hearted secular Muslims who made up the majority of Bangladeshi society and supported the liberation movement wholeheartedly. I replied, "Thik achhey, khoda hafez," a common Muslim way of saying, "All right, goodbye."

Our old family friend kept his commitment. He had a big van waiting right at the ferry station. To this day I wonder what would have happened if there had been no van waiting when we arrived. The Indian border was still a good thirty-five to forty miles away with the two district towns of Khulna and Jessore in between! I'd taken a big gamble based on the simple commitment of our old Muslim neighbor.

After we got into the van, we put all the women with the burkas in the window seats. The men with beards and Muslim caps were in the middle seats. Our old neighbor was brilliant in hiring a driver with a long beard and a Muslim cap who was in reality a sympathizer of the Bengali liberation war at heart. Everything was done to make it look like an innocent Muslim family taking a simple family trip. As I learned several years later after the liberation war was over, the driver's two sons, one a student of Dacca University and another of Rajshahi University, joined the Mukti Bahini and were in India with the liberation forces fighting the Pakistani Army and frequently crossed the porous border to engage the Army and ambush the Razakars. So he was yet another good-hearted Muslim who had taken a big risk himself to help a Hindu family trying to dash to India and save their lives.

As our car started driving through the busy streets of Khulna, we passed, followed, and were tailed by many military vehicles. At one point, we were just behind an armored military vehicle with two Pakistani military officers sitting in the front and a number of military personnel with automatic weapons ready to shoot positioned in the back seats. My heart was racing uncontrollably. I simply could not control my father's hands. He would start doing his prayer gestures with both hands, reaching to touch his forehead. I kept bringing them down and desperately tried to keep them immobile. Finally, after almost fifteen minutes of following the military vehicle, the harrowing episode ended. The military vehicle took a turn, and we continued our drive toward Jessore and our dash for the Indian border.

During the hours we spent driving across the district towns of Khulna and Jessore, our ploy mostly worked. We were stopped only once at a checkpoint where a group of policemen asked us where we were heading. The driver responded that the family was going to attend a family emergency in a village just five miles away. They looked at us closely. Still, to this date I do not know what they really thought of our true intentions. Possibly they were sympathizers of the liberation war and had figured out what we were up to, but we were allowed to continue. After another hour of driving through a maze of rural unpaved roads, we finally reached a village on the outskirts of Jessore.

The driver told us that he would not be able to continue due to the condition of the road and because he was running out of fuel. In other words, we were on our own and on our feet from that point on. The Indian border was still a good five to ten miles away so we started our trek on foot. My father was sixty-eight, and my mother was close to that age. My two younger brothers and sister were in their teens and more frightened than tired. We could hear the roaring sounds of machine-gun fire being continuously exchanged between the Pakistani Army which was manning the border and the Mukti Bahini who were waging guerilla warfare from the Indian side.

At least a couple of times, we had to cross roads that were being used by military vehicles. We would wait until there were no vehicles in sight on either side, then dash to the other side of the road and blend into the wooded jungle and continue our trek. As we moved closer and closer to the Indian border, we started to encounter more and more Hindu families who were converging from different directions in their own flight toward the border. I was almost carrying my mother by this stage, as she continuously kept on saying, "Oh, Tagore, are hut-tay parchhi na" ("Tagore, I cannot walk any further!")

We then faced the biggest and last challenge of the trip: a one-hundred-foot-wide river crossing via a narrow, wobbly bridge made of bamboo perched just ten feet above the water. The water below was flowing quite fast, and the current looked daunting. Assuming my younger siblings would be able to handle the task on their own, I told them to start crossing the bridge. It required careful position of the feet while holding on to the side rail.

I positioned myself behind my father and helped my mother to position herself on the bridge next to me. My mother literally leaned on my shoulder, grabbing me with one hand and holding the bamboo side rail with the other hand. I was wedged between my father and mother as we inched step by step toward the other side. This was probably one of the most frightening moments of my entire life. We were halfway across the bridge when my mother froze and started to cry. We could see the fast-moving water below us, and any misstep would have been catastrophic. I told my father to be very careful and start moving on his own so that I could totally concentrate on carrying my mother. I told my mother to hold on to me as firmly as possible with both hands while urging her to focus on her feet on the narrow bridge. From that point on, I literally carried her inch by inch across the bridge. Finally, the nightmare ended and we were on the other side. This was the first time we felt that most of the danger was over, and we were told by the local villagers that the Indian border was only a mile or so away.

We decided to rest for a while as we were totally exhausted and drained. We had hardly eaten or drunk anything for close to twelve hours! We did not have any food or water, but a local volunteered to give us some fruits (mangos and bananas) for a few rupees. Fortunately, I had strapped a few thousand rupees under my lungi to my upper thigh when we set out for the trip. I had used this money to pay for the ferry and the van and only had a small amount of cash left.

After a rest of about an hour, we resumed our trek. It was getting closer to evening, and our plan was to cross the border before nightfall and then take a bus or other available transportation to go to my brother's place in Kolkata.

The last mile seemed like an eternity. I was literally carrying my mother. My father was faring rather well under the circumstances. Possibly he was invigorated with the knowledge that the Indian border was almost within sight. I suppose knowing that we were mostly out of danger also helped lift his morale exponentially. Finally, we came across a milestone that declared we were about to cross into Indian territory. I will never forget the satisfied smile on my father's face. He could just manage to blurt out, "I-ssha gachi!" in his heavy Bangladeshi accent, which meant, "We have arrived!"

We then came across a forward military post manned by the Indian Regular Army. I exchanged some pleasantries with them in my broken Hindi. Obviously, the soldiers were now very accustomed to seeing an endless stream of desperate and destitute Hindus crossing into India to seek safety and security. It is now a historical fact that millions of Hindu refugees and Muslim Bengalis who joined the liberation forces crossed into India during the Bangladesh war of 1971. I started to talk to the locals about the most inexpensive and the quickest way to go to Kolkata, which was at least seventy miles away from this border town.

We were able to secure our seats on a long-distance bus to take us to the outskirts of Kolkata. Once we got near Kolkata, our plan was to find another means of transportation to get to Amiya's apartment in Tollygunj, a suburb of Kolkata.

My brother was an electrical engineer in his early thirties and recently married. I had never visited his flat before this time. After we reached the bus stop near Kolkata at around 9:00 p.m., I tried to get a taxi that would be willing to take all of us and our small bags. I did not want to separate the family in case we lost one another, and as we were close to running out of money I wanted to avoid incurring the fare for two cars.

While I was trying to convince reluctant taxi drivers to take a group of refugees for a ride, we were noticed by an elderly Sardarji (a Punjabi Sikh) driver who obviously felt sorry to see us in such a sad state. He offered to take us to our brother's flat. I gave him the address, but it was not easy to locate and we got lost several times. When we finally got there, we found my brother had already moved away. We had not been in touch with him during the months we had spent in hiding, and one of his neighbors told us that he had moved a month ago to Asansole, a city several hours' train ride from Kolkata to his new job at the Pilkinton Glass Manufacturing Plant.

It was a very helpless situation. It was getting close to midnight. We were all very tired, exhausted, thirsty, and hungry. We had to quickly come up with another option. One of my paternal uncles (Jetha Moshai) and his family lived in Kalighat, a suburb of Kolkata.

We were very fortunate that the Sardarji driver was very kind and patient. By that time he had been with us for almost two hours. I assumed he had seen the same human misery day after day as countless numbers of helpless and destitute Hindus streamed into India. A large portion of these refugees came to Kolkata or the adjacent areas along the Bongaon-Shealdah railway line.

By the time the taxi stopped in front of Jetha Moshai's home on a very narrow lane, it was close to midnight. Jetha Moshai's home was on the banks of the Ganges River near the Chetla Bridge. Obviously, everybody was asleep, and the second floor of the home where they lived was dark. True to the local norm, the taxi driver started to honk his horns. Finally, it woke them up, and my cousin Shambhuda came out to inquire what was going on. Once they saw us, it was a combination of extreme surprise and joy at seeing us all alive. After all, they had been following the events in East Pakistan through the newspaper and other media. They were all aware of the atrocities committed against the Hindus by the Pakistani Army and their cohorts. Shambhuda asked Dulalda, another cousin, to come down and help us unload our meager belongings and help us upstairs. Shambhuda's and Dulalda's wives had woken up by that time and started the earthen oven to cook some food for us. Jetha Moshai, who was in his late seventies, also woke up. Shambhuda cleared one of the bedrooms so we could lie down on a few simple satarnchis (simple mats) on the floor. Each was given a small pillow to sleep.

This was the start of a new chapter for our family. It was never the same again. However, needless to say, the image of that Sardarji taxi driver who showed us compassion and kindness beyond any measure has remained forever etched in my heart.

CHAPTER 5

Family's New Life in India

Jetha Moshai's home in the Kalighat suburb of Kolkata was built over a hundred years back. During our childhood, my father took the family to India every year, mostly during the Durga Puja. During these trips we stayed at or visited Jetha Moshai's place. This humble home provided shelter for much of our extended family who came from far-flung areas including East Pakistan. Jetha Moshai's family never turned any of them away.

Shambhuda, the second eldest son of Jetha Moshai, worked for the Kolkata Municipal Corporation and ran a tight ship to make sure the limited resources spread across everybody who lived there at any given time. Even to this date, I am simply amazed how so many people found refuge in that home in times of desperate need before they eventually made a soft landing elsewhere and found a footing on their own.

Four of my eldest brothers, Gour, Arun, Amiya, and Anil left East Pakistan in the 1950s immediately after high school and started their new lives in India at Jetha Moshai's home. Gour went on to join the Indian Air Force and eventually held important positions in radar operations. He always boasted about the fact that Air Marshall PC Lal, who ended his career as the chief of the Indian Air Force, interviewed him personally for a critical position in the radar operation when they were posted at the same Air Force base during the early stages of Air Marshall PC Lal's illustrious career. After leaving the military, Gour had a remarkable career in the steel industry and retired as a senior executive. He traveled to the USA, Canada, and Europe for training.

While living at Jetha Moshai's home in Kalighat, Amiya attended Ashutosh College and then Jadavpur University in Kolkata where he graduated with a degree in electrical engineering and went on to become a senior executive vice president of the famed Birla industrial empire. Arun died tragically while still in college, while Anil went on to earn a master's degree in political science, a law degree from Kolkata University and then qualified in the prestigious and highly competitive Administrative Service Cadre. Unfortunately, a tragic accident took his life just as he started his career with a posting as a administrative service officer in Jalpaiguri in West Bengal.

After a couple of days at Jetha Moshai's home, my parents and my younger siblings went to live with Gour in Durgapur and Amiya in Assansole so as to lessen the burden on any one of them. Subsequently, my father went to the home in Barasat, which he had built over the years by sending money from Pakistan.

While my elder brothers and sisters were already educated and settled in India, my younger siblings who had just arrived would launch their new lives in India from this point. Even though he was a very successful lawyer in East Pakistan, my father had to start his law practice in India from scratch. He had actually done all his education including his master's degree in economics and law degree at the prestigious University of Calcutta in India during the 1920s. Still, he had to reacquaint himself with the current Indian laws and other legal protocols.

As they say, genius never dies. My father went on to become a top lawyer in that part of the country within a few years. He argued in front of judges in his heavy Bangladeshi accent. Even though it was frowned on by the local Bengalis (colloquially known as Ghotis) who had lived in West Bengal all their lives, my father was so highly respected by his peers, it was of no major consequence. He was elected the president of the District Bar Association in Barasat and held that position until his death at the age of eighty-eight. Some years after his death, I went to the district court in Barasat to visit my father's old office in the building that housed the offices of all the senior lawyers. The main room of the building was decorated with the pictures of the national leaders such as Mahatma Gandhi, Jaharlal Nehru, and so on. I was proud to see my father's picture prominently displayed on the wall. At that time, it was the only picture on the wall other than those of the national leaders.

At first my younger siblings struggled to gain their footing until my father reestablished his law practice and was able to support the family. My elder brothers, particularly Gour and Amiya who were both engineers with decent jobs, tried their best to support the family even though they had their own families. After I went to the USA in 1974 to do my PhD in mechanical engineering, I sent $60 from my $280-per-month assistantship to help the family. I shared the pain. However, it took my father just a year or so to establish his law practice and make his mark. Both my younger brothers went on to have successful careers in the banking industry after obtaining their master's degrees from the University of Calcutta. In addition, my youngest brother went on to become one of the most successful lyricists in India even though it was a side hobby for him. He wrote the lyrics for many famous and legendary singers such as Manna Dey, Lata Mungeshkar, Asha Bhosle, Kabita Krishnamurthy, Anuradha Parwal, Alka Yagnik, Kumar Sanu, Shreya Ghosal, Babul Supryo, Jojo, Shan, and many others.

My youngest sister, Mona, had married Nimai, my father's legal secretary back in East Pakistan. Nimai was a self-made boy. Coming from a humble background, he went on to get a master's degree in commerce and later did management training from a prestigious management school in Hyderabad, India, before embarking on a successful career in a number of major business enterprises in Mumbai. He also became general manager of a major multinational company.

Both my younger brothers subsequently lived at the home in Barasat that my father built. They continued to share the sprawling home after my father's death in 1992. Over the years, this turned into an imposing two-story house with over fifteen rooms.

CHAPTER 6

Minority Experiences

I spent most of my childhood in a predominantly Muslim country witnessing and experiencing life as a minority there before my family eventually moved to India. Very few countries in history have witnessed such gargantuan religious turmoil and human suffering as the minority communities of the Indian subcontinent who lived on the wrong side of the border at the time of partition in 1947. Religion has been the dominant force that has shaped the social and political dynamics on the Indian subcontinent for hundreds of years. It became more pronounced at the time of the partition when millions of people perished during their desperate dash to align their religious identities with their adopted country.

I have always struggled to make sense of the immeasurable negative impact religion imparts on the social and political dynamics of the subcontinent. The traumatic experience of religious persecution has had a lifelong impact on my family. I have always wondered why there is so much intolerance and hatred across the religious and sectarian divides around the world. Long before the Arab traders who started to come to India around the sixth century immediately before the time of Prophet Muhammad and the Muslim invaders who came subsequently from outside and ruled India for hundreds of years, most Indians identified with the same historical and cultural heritage and lineage dating back to thousands of years BC.

The ensuing spread of Islam, Buddhism, Christianity, and other faiths created a complex society built around a web of religious, ethnic, and cultural diversities, which in turn resulted in devastating sufferings due to intolerance of one segment of the society for another. Even to this day, almost every part of the world is engulfed in social upheaval emanating from religious persecution of one form or another and atrocities committed in the name of religion.

The Middle East has been in a perpetual state of instability ever since the Zionist state of Israel was created in 1948. As a result, millions of Palestinians were displaced from their ancestral home, forcing generations of Palestinians to live in refugee camps in subhuman conditions. While the Israelis and the Jews from all over the world considered that the land had belonged to them for thousands of years, the Palestinians held the same claim or rights to this land. The Palestinians have involuntarily become refugees in their own land. Wars and constant fighting between the Israelis and the Palestinians have not resolved any of the core issues, and these senseless human miseries of such enormous proportions seem to have no end in sight. While there are many moderates on both sides who would be willing to live in harmony in a two-state solution, the extremists on both sides such as the conservative, ultranationalist, and orthodox Jews in Israel and the Hamas on the Gaza Strip or the Hezbollah in Lebanon do not seem to find any common ground. Each side seems to be determined to simply annihilate or drown the other side in the ocean.

On the surface, it would seem that Israel has taken a very heavy-handed approach based on total distrust and contempt in dealing with the Palestinians. The conflagration in Gaza in 2014 resulted in the deaths of thousands of innocent civilians on the Palestinian side. The Israeli Army also suffered an uncharacteristic heavy level of casualties. It is a cycle of vicious retaliations from both sides, each blaming the other for the flare-up of any violence. Israel claimed the recent fighting in 2014 would not have started if Hamas had not abducted three young Israeli teenagers and killed them. The retaliatory abduction of a sixteen-year-old innocent Palestinian boy by the Israeli mob before burning him to death was also a senseless crime. However, these scattered incidents were only the superficial manifestation of the much deeper issue built around the centuries-old distrust and intolerance that exist between Jews and Palestinian Muslims. A similar situation involving Hindus and Muslims exists in India as I have painfully witnessed and experienced.

Many argue that human beings anywhere in the world would act in the same desperate mode if they had been subjected to the same level of inhuman treatment handed down to the Palestinians. None other than Jimmy Carter, the former president of the United States, underscored this point more precisely. Obviously, his stand did not bring any adulation from the Israelis. But the counterargument has always been the fact that the Israelis, with the exception of the new Jewish immigrants from all over the world, have also lived in the land for centuries and could not be simply driven from their ancient land into the ocean.

I can relate to the plight of the Palestinians as our ancestral home in Pakistan was burnt to ashes by Muslims. Our land holding was confiscated as enemy property by the Muslim government, forcing us to flee to India as refugees where we had to start and rebuild our lives from scratch. One of the major stumbling blocks in the path of resolution of the Israeli-Palestinian conflict was the right of the Palestinians to return to their homes from which many of them were forced out during the creation of Israel. This is similar to the experiences of millions of Hindus who were displaced from their homes in Pakistan. Many Muslim families who voluntarily or involuntarily moved from India to Pakistan likely have similar stories and unpleasant experiences to share.

Nelson Mandela, one of the most towering personalities in the history of mankind, showed the world that two archenemies can set aside their past political, cultural, and religious differences and live in harmony in a new order. He was subjected to twenty-eight years in solitary confinement on Robben Island by the South African National Party before he led South Africa to freedom from the yolk of apartheid. Yet, when he became the first president of independent, postapartheid South Africa by way of a free election based on "one person, one vote," he assured the nation that South Africa could thrive and prosper only in an all-inclusive society and there was no place for retaliation against the white minority, particularly those who had championed apartheid and subjugated the majority black and other minorities as second-class citizens in their own homeland for hundreds of years. As a result, all South Africans found a balance based on mutual trust and tolerance to live in harmony, contrary to the apprehension that the country would descend into anarchy once the white minority lost their hold on power. It is no wonder that South Africa turned out to be one of the most politically, socially, and economically stable countries compared to most of the other countries in Africa.

The modern history of Zimbabwe (formerly Rhodesia) sadly paints a diametrically different picture compared to South Africa. After power was wrested from the colonial white rulers when Robert Mugabe became the first prime minister in 1980, the country descended into lawlessness and anarchy with the black majority unleashing unprecedented retaliation against the white minority population. With direct encouragement from Robert Mugabe, they forcibly took lands from white farmers, claiming it to be their rightful land that was taken away from them many years ago. Many white farmers were slaughtered, and those who survived fled the country. Zimbabwe, which had been the food basket of Africa for hundreds of years, turned into a basket case while Robert Mugabe became president and ran the country as a tyrannical dictator. He held on to power even when it was widely believed that he lost the rigged election. Eventually he was forced out of power by the military in response to widespread popular unrest resulting from the failed economy. This was in sharp contrast to Nelson Mandela who left the presidency after just one term once the affairs of the state were steadied for others to continue his peaceful path. The stark contrasts of how postapartheid South Africa and Zimbabwe turned out demonstrate that a society based on tolerance for others irrespective of caste, creed, or color has far more stable foundations.

In recent years, many regions and countries in Africa have seemed to be in a perpetual state of upheaval. Many of the problems appear to be perpetrated by Muslim extremist jihadists. They have committed unprecedented atrocities in the name of religion. Two of the extreme groups, Al Shahab in Somalia and Boko Haram in Nigeria, have killed innocent civilians, abducted young girls, in many cases subjecting them to rape, sexual mutilation, or sexual slavery, and justifying such actions in the name of religion. It has become commonplace for Muslims to kill fellow Muslims and members of other tribes, sects, and religions if their religious or political agenda are at odds with each other.

Millions of Armenians were subjected to torture, expropriation, deportation, and starvation during the Armenian genocide. Millions of Armenians were slaughtered during this genocide by the Turks of the Ottoman Empire during and immediately after WWI. During the Rwandan genocide in 1994, close to a million Tutsis were slaughtered by the majority Hutu government, and hundreds of thousands of Rwandans became destitute refugees. Thousands of Bosnian Muslims were killed by the Bosnian Serb forces during the Bosnian genocide. In addition, a wider ethnic cleansing was perpetrated against the Muslim Bosniaks and Bosnian Croats by the Bosnian Serbs during the 1992–1995 Balkan war, leading to the mass killing and deportation of tens of thousands of innocent civilians. Many other similar human tragedies in history resulted when two warring factions of mankind were on the opposite ends of the differing political, religious, or cultural spectrum and the destructive forces of the stronger segment prevailed and vanquished the weaker one.

The animosities and fighting between the Shiite and the Sunni sects of Islam have resulted in atrocities committed against each other all over the world. In the aftermath of the pullout of United States and allied troops from Iraq, the Shiites and the Sunnis started to inflict unprecedented havoc on each other. Sacred religious shrines that have stood for hundreds of years were burnt and destroyed, innocent civilians including children and women were slaughtered, and in many cases, attempts were made to forcibly convert minority sects in the region to Islam.

In Sunni-dominated Pakistan, Christian, Shiite, other Muslim sects such as the Ahmadyya, Hindus, and other minorities have come under ferocious attack from orthodox Sunni zealots. Frequently their places of worships have been burnt, and worshippers have been slaughtered when they congregated for religious rites and prayers. Many minorities were falsely persecuted and harshly punished for fictitious or overly exaggerated charges brought against them using the draconian blasphemy law.

It is a documented fact that the famed physicist, Dr. Abdus Salam, the only Pakistani scientist to ever receive the Nobel Prize, did not receive the honor, dignity, and recognition in Pakistan he deserved since he belonged to the Ahmadyya sect of Islam. He came from the Punjab region in Pakistan where he'd received his early education. Actually, his family descended from the Punjabi Rajput lineage that embraced Islam in the twelfth century. Dr. Salam was a devout practicing Muslim, but his scientific endeavors were not driven by any religious convictions.

It is also a well-documented fact that the Ahmadyyas have been routinely persecuted in Pakistan. Many extremely conservative Muslims in Pakistan even openly declared that the Ahmadyyas do not deserve to live. There was even a well-publicized controversy associated with Dr. Salam's burial in Pakistan. The epitaph on his tomb originally mentioned "First Muslim Nobel Laureate," but the word "Muslim" was subsequently removed by order of a magistrate, resulting in the nonsensical "First Nobel Laureate" on his tomb. Dr. Salam, who is credited with ushering Pakistan into the modern scientific age after establishing himself as one of the foremost theoretical physicists in the world, actually left Pakistan for England out of disgust when the Pakistani parliament designated the Ahmadyyas as non-Muslims. As a devout Muslim, he deeply resented that designation. Dr. Salam was a remarkable human being who was above any shallow man-made religious divide.

Even in countries like China and Russia, social unrest and fighting are commonplace due to ethnic unrest. In the Xinjiang region of China, the Han Chinese and Uyghur Muslims have frequently clashed, and hundreds of Uyghurs lost their lives in the rioting with the Hans. The Chinese authorities controlled this unrest with heavy-handed force to prevent the situation from getting out of control. There has been universal condemnation of the Chinese government's ill treatment of Uyghur Muslims in regards to violation of their civil rights.

Muslims in Chechnya, Dagestan, and Ingushetia in the Northern Caucasus region continue to fight Russian authorities as part of their own secessionist movements. From time to time, they unleash terrorist activities in other parts of Russia, including Moscow, with bomb blasts in residential areas, schools for children, and theaters.

India has experienced and continues to experience frequent terrorist activities committed by homegrown Indian mujahideen or by other infiltrators who have crossed over from Pakistan to fight a proxy war encouraged by the Pakistani military establishments such as the Inter Services Intelligence (ISI). Many innocent lives have been lost in bomb blasts in public places such as bus stops, train stations, shopping malls, and hotels. In November 2008, terrorists from Pakistan came to Mumbai by sea and occupied a number of major businesses and cultural institutions such as the Oberoi Trident and Taj Hotels, the Chhatrapati Shivaji Railway Terminus, Leopold Café, which was a major attraction to foreign tourists, the Nariman House Jewish Community Center, and CAMA Hospital in Mumbai. Mumbai police and the Indian National Security Guards (NSG) conducted Operation Black Tornado to flush out and kill the terrorists. The only surviving terrorist, Ajmal Kasab, confessed that the operation was launched with the direct support of the Lashkar-e-Taiba organization, which had been tagged as a terrorist organization by the United States and other countries. Over two hundred innocent lives were lost before the terrorists were killed or captured by Indian security forces.

After the withdrawal of US soldiers from Iraq in 2013, the Sunni insurgency led by the brutal members of the Islamic State of Iraq and Syria (ISIS) captured a large swath of land in Iraq and Syria and unleashed a reign of terror on the members of other Islamic sects such as the Shiites, Turkmen, and Kurdish Muslims as well as the Christian community. They destroyed Shiite mosques, some of which were sacred and had been revered for hundreds of years. The Christian minority community was subjected to ruthless persecution. Their churches were burnt down. The Yazidi Christian sect was forced to flee their villages in Syria when they were given the ultimatum to be converted into Islam or be beheaded. Thousands

59

of these Yazidis fled to the mountains to escape, and many children and women died from thirst, hunger, and exhaustion. Those who were abducted were sexually violated. The United States helped these trapped Yazidis by air-dropping food and undertaking a massive air strike campaign against ISIS that provided the Yazidis with an escape route from their stranded position in the mountains. Based on the perceived threat to the social order in the Middle East and by extension to the world, many countries including Great Britain, France, Germany, Russia, Denmark, Belgium, and Turkey joined the United States in their efforts to check, stop, degrade, and eventually destroy ISIS.

In recent years, Afghanistan has turned into an epicenter of human disaster due to the infighting between different Muslim factions after US soldiers and its international allies started to pull out after a protracted war lasting over fifteen years. Originally, the US defense forces went into Afghanistan in the aftermath of the 9/11 attacks in 2001 to root out the jihadist terrorists led by Osama Bin Laden. While the jury is still out regarding the effectiveness of the US campaign in Afghanistan in rooting out the terrorists who were hell-bent to harm US and Western interests, the withdrawal of US and international forces from Afghanistan posed another threat. The Taliban insurgency was solely driven by its intent to either come to power or simply destabilize the whole country through terror. Most of the Taliban leadership, including Osama Bin Laden and Mullah Omar, fled to Pakistan and continued to wage a clandestine terror campaign from their hideouts in Pakistan and Afghanistan. Osama Bin Laden was killed by US Navy SEALs in Abbottabad, Pakistan. Mullah Omar died from natural causes in Pakistan. These fundamentalists seemed to be determined to take the world back to the medieval ages by imposing their draconian orthodoxy on those who disagree with them. Under their regimes, women are barred from even pursuing a basic education, and they are viciously intent on introducing Sharia law in all aspects of life.

The Afghanistan Taliban was created by the Pakistani military establishments during the Russian occupation of Afghanistan. Now the glass in their own windows was shattered. The Pakistani Taliban started to cause havoc in Pakistani society once the military stepped in to stop their terror campaign inside Pakistan.

On the surface at least, it seems that a majority of the troubled spots in the world involve fundamentalist Muslims in one form or another. In some cases, their fights are based on reasserting their lost rights as is the case in Palestine. But in many cases, such as the persecution of the Yazidis by ISIS in Iraq and Syria, it is dictated by the core belief and conviction that members of other religions are infidels whose spiritual salvation can come only by way of conversion to Islam by force or otherwise.

There is a strong perception in many European and Western countries that the Muslim immigrant minorities are becoming increasingly vocal in pushing and imposing their lifestyles on others. Even in England, they have been vocal in arguing to introduce Sharia law. In Australia, during one such campaign, one of the Australian ministers opined that Australia had opened its door to immigrants belonging to different religions, and if any of the newcomers did not like the local social or religious customs, they could have stayed in their own countries. While they were at liberty to practice their religion freely in their adopted country that had received them with open arms, they had no right to impose their way of life on others.

France has one of the largest Muslim communities in Europe, accounting for close to 10 percent of its population. Most of these Muslims are immigrants from its former colonies such as Algeria. Historically, France has had a difficult and convoluted experience in its relations with Muslim minorities and their assimilation into French society. The French government has remained steadfast in not yielding to the pressure of the French Muslim community to allow the hijab, the head covering for Muslim women in public in addition to other Muslim customs that are at odds with the traditional secular French culture. There are some neighborhoods in France with a heavy concentration of Muslims including many who hold extremist religious or jihadist views. From time to time, these extremists have struck in Paris and other parts of France in recent times with devastating consequences.

In January 2015, extremists attacked the offices of the satirical weekly newspaper *Charlie Hebdo* in retaliation for cartoons that depicted the Prophet Muhammad. They killed eleven people and injured scores of other innocent victims. The attack received worldwide condemnation and the phrase *Je suis Charlie* became a worldwide slogan of solidarity and support for the French people. Subsequently in November 2015, Muslim jihadists attacked a number of high-profile sites including the Stade de France where the French President was in attendance for a friendly soccer match between Germany and France, the Bataclan Theater where an American rock band was performing, and a popular restaurant, Le Petit Cambodge. The mayhem led to massive human casualties and incited a widespread negative backlash against the entire Muslim community. Millions of people updated their Facebook profile with pictures wrapped in the French flag in solidarity with the French people. Ironically, the terrorist acts were perpetrated by only a few extremist Muslim jihadists who lived on the fringe of the world's second largest mainstream religion, which has over a billion peaceful adherents. The French government declared war against the jihadists, and its warplanes started to hit terrorist hotbeds in the Middle East, particularly in the ISIS-held territories, in collaboration with other allies including the United States, Russia, the UK, and others.

A few weeks after the Paris attack, two Muslim jihadists, a man and a woman in their twenties, armed with automatic weapons, killed fourteen innocent people and injured scores of others who were mostly their coworkers who had gathered in their office in San Bernardino, California, to celebrate the holiday season. The man was born and brought up in America by his Pakistani immigrant parents, and the woman had come from Pakistan on a fiancée visa and subsequently married him. After the carnage which ended with their deaths in a shoot-out with the police, a huge cache of weapons and ammunition including bombs and bomb-making materials was uncovered at their home. The woman had declared her allegiance to the ISIS leader immediately before undertaking the terrorist carnage. Many young jihadists have bought into the draconian doctrine of the ISIS leadership that exhorts its followers all over the world to kill both civilian and military with the dictate, "If you can, kill a disbelieving American or European, kill the disbeliever whether he is a civilian or military." It is encouraging to note that this dictate of the ISIS has been universally rejected by mainstream Muslims all over the world.

The backlash against Muslims immediately after the San Bernardino carnage quickly engulfed America, including the extreme views of some of the political leaders such as Mr. Donald Trump who went on to win the presidential election and propose to ban the entry of all Muslims into the United States and institute large-scale surveillance of the Muslims and their places of worship. This policy was swiftly condemned and rebuffed by most of American society; the terrorist acts of just a few jihadists brought unwanted, unfavorable, and obviously unfair characterization of the entire Muslim religion by those who operated simply from a sense of fear and anxiety rather than any rational or objective basis.

When I am confronted with such heinous acts of violence, I always pause and reflect about the immorality and absurdity of such acts in the context of my family's suffering and that of millions of others in Pakistan at the hands of extremists who misinterpreted the teaching of a peaceful religion to justify their carnage.

I spent a major part of my early childhood in Bangladesh before my family immigrated and settled in India. Many of my childhood friends who went to school with me also went to the USA and many other parts of the world to pursue their higher education like I did. Many of them secured PhDs and went on to have very successful careers in academia and industry. Most of them were moderates with a secular mind-set. But sadly, there were some Muslims who lived on the fringe with a mind-set and philosophy that were firmly anchored in the idea that all non-Muslims are infidels (nonbelievers). Some of these Muslims firmly believe in the need to convert humanity to Islam by choice or coercion.

Some years ago, on board a flight to New York on a business trip, I sat next to a Muslim gentleman. With his long, bushy black hair and traditional Muslim attire, it was quite evident he was a pious, orthodox Muslim. We engaged in small talk, which he soon turned into a discussion of religion which I normally avoided in an open public forum, but was unable to dodge this time. He asked me if I had ever read the Holy Quran, and if I had, was I convinced it was the ultimate holy book that should be the guiding light for all humanity. Then to my great surprise, he asked me if I believed that all humanity would someday embrace Islam and if I had ever considered it personally. This was a person with an advanced degree from an American university holding a good job in an American company and returning to his home after attending an Islamic conference. I told him I was at peace with my Hindu identity and that all religions had the same core message of the supremacy of truth and righteousness and were based on the belief in one supreme god. I said the only difference was in the way that belief was demonstrated in day-to-day conduct.

He pointed out that Hindus believed in many gods and they worshipped idolatry. I argued that this simplistic interpretation of the complex issues pertaining to the Hindu faith was the result of ignorance and the lack of knowledge. He challenged me to explain and convince him. I told him about an incident involving the great Hindu saint Swami Vivekananda who electrified the audience at the World Parliament of Religions in Chicago in 1893. When Swami Vivekananda was traveling all over India during his spiritual journey, he was in the court of a king who was one of his patrons or devotees. When asked to explain the concept of worshipping idolatry, the venerable swami asked the king's staff to take down the paintings of the king from the wall and put them on the floor. Then he asked them to stomp on them with their feet as a mark of disrespect. While still being reverent to the swami, the staff was startled and extremely reluctant to do so as it would come across as an act of defiance and disrespect toward the king. Then Swami Vivekananda looked at the king and said that the reason the staff was so hesitant to comply with his request was because they all saw the king in those paintings or pictures. They were not just ordinary pieces of canvas or paper to them, but rather the king himself was manifested in those paintings. The paintings were the personification of the king. Hindus personify the various attributes of God through various idols depending on the occasion, form, and format of family traditions and culture. For example, while seeking God's blessings for learning, they would personify God through Swaraswati, the goddess of learning.

After almost three hours of friendly but intense argument and counterargument, the Muslim gentleman appeared to be frustrated in his inability to convince me that Islam was the only true religion and anybody who was still opposed to that idea was a nonbeliever. He did not say outright that nonbelievers would be dealt with harshly on the Day of Judgment, but the insinuation was quite clear. Out of desperation, I said the Muslims' core belief in "La Ilaha Illallahu Muhammadur Rasulullah" (*"There is no deity worthy of being worshipped except God* [Allah], and Muhammad is the messenger [prophet] of God") only stated a simple factual truth that was not inconsistent with any facts or tenets of any other religions. I said every religion, including Hinduism, believed in one monotheistic supreme god. The manifestation or the personification of that monotheistic god as polytheistic gods by the Hindus as explained earlier did not contradict the Muslim belief in one God. Also, other religions had their belief in their own prophets or messengers of God such as Jesus Christ, Buddha, Rama (among other Hindu avatars) for Christians, Buddhists, and Hindus respectively. There was only one fact that would always hold true: the purpose of the prophets. They had all descended to earth to right wrongs and establish moral order at different times in history in different parts of the world. So any argument to establish the sole claim for any one religion as the only religion and their prophets as the only messengers of God for all of humanity was not based on a sound rationale.

Then I asked him two simple questions: Would humans born before Islam was introduced in the sixth century who had practiced other religions receive favorable consideration on the Day of Judgment or not, and if the answer was no, what was their fault or culpability? And secondly, would newborns born today into families practicing a religion other than Islam be given less favorable consideration by the divine power through no fault of their own? Obviously, I did not get a clear answer even though he remained very steadfast in his position. By that time, I was somewhat exasperated and tired. With the pretext of going to the restroom, I went to the front of the plane looking for an empty seat. I talked to one of the stewardesses and told her I did not feel comfortable to go back to my seat and would appreciate her help in finding me a different seat. There were another two hours left in our flight before landing in New York. Interestingly, the stewardess told me that she had overheard most of our discussion and arguments with amusement and that it was so heated and loud that many other passengers had heard it as well. The stewardess went to the front of the plane and after a while motioned me forward to an empty seat in first class. I sat there the remainder of the flight. My rehabilitation in first class came with a couple of free alcoholic drinks, and I assumed my good fortune had resulted from karma with divine intervention to alleviate my mental anguish. However, I was not about to declare that my position and arguments were right and everything I heard from that pious Muslim gentleman was wrong. After all, it was all about what we believed in and practiced. As they say, "Bishashay miluy bastu, tarkay bahudur," a Bengali saying meaning, "Faith achieves much and arguments bear nothing!" I strongly believe that the majority of Muslims are peace-loving and tolerant toward others and Islam is a religion of peace, which is wonderful given that a large segment of humanity to the tune of over a billion are adherents.

I also believe the gentleman I encountered on the plane did not represent mainstream Muslims. Possibly, he held a skewed view contrary to the noble teachings of the Prophet Muhammad and the sacred Quran. Practically all the Muslims I have encountered during my childhood in Pakistan, until today, have been moderates who professed tolerance and acceptance for other religions. Only those on the fringe such as the Islamists of ISIS, Al Shahab, Boko Haram, and similar groups continue to commit atrocities driven by their intolerance toward other faiths.

My devout Roman Catholic wife, Ann, had a similarly strong conviction that Catholicism was the only "true religion"—a term she often used. During many weekends, we used to have a number of visitors to our home who would come to preach and spread the message of God. Many of them were smartly dressed young boys and girls belonging to the Mormon Church (the Church of Jesus Christ of Latter-Day Saints), Jehovah's Witness, or other religious denominations. I would always open the door and talk with them and would attempt to exchange my ideas of God and spirituality. After they would leave, I would be seriously challenged to pacify my furious wife who thought I had wasted my time by listening to others who did not practice the "true religion."

There are many views on the issues related to the commonality and/or differences that exist between different religions. I have never practiced organized religion on a daily or weekly basis; however, I celebrated all the Hindu festivals and pujas with devotion. My Hindu identity has been based on subscribing to the core beliefs of Hinduism, i.e., truth (pursuit of knowledge and truth pertaining to the essence of the universe), dharma (righteousness built around right conduct and moral values), karma (the concept of cause and effect, action and reaction where our action or deeds have corresponding effects in the future in this life or during the next incarnated life), and tolerance toward other beliefs.

The concept of reincarnation is based on death and rebirth of the soul (atman) through transmigration from one physical body to another future body based on the karma (action in previous life) until moksha (liberation of the soul) is achieved with unity with the Brahman, the Supreme One, through duty, knowledge, and devotion or surrender to God. So in a sense, the concept of the judgment day as defined in other religions is inherent in each death and rebirth cycle of Hinduism as the consequences of the current life cycle manifesting in the next life cycle with the migration of the soul to a different physical body until moksha is achieved.

The perception that Hindus worship many gods is the oversimplification and contradiction of the core belief of all Hindus in a supreme, limitless, formless, all-inclusive true god. To many in the outside world, the simplified perception is that Hindus worship many gods, goddesses, and deities. It is widely believed that Hindus believe in 33 crore (330 million) variants of gods. In reality, it is the personification of certain aspects of one and only one supreme god that manifests itself as different gods depending on the occasion,

67

family tradition, regional culture, and customs, allowing the Hindus to worship God in infinite forms, formats, and social settings.

When we got married, we agreed that our children would be brought up in the strict tradition of the Catholic faith. Even though I never practiced any organized religion on a day-to-day basis other than following the teachings of the Hindu scriptures in my day-to-day code of conduct, I went to weekly Sunday mass with the family every week without exception during my twenty-nine-year marriage to my devout Catholic wife. During the ritual when everybody knelt to pray, I would close my eyes and imagine I was sitting in front of the goddess Kali at the famous Kali temple in Kolkata and pray for peace and happiness for everybody I loved and cared for. My sense of spirituality was based on one simple core belief: God is omnipresent, and one has to find his or her own way of connection to God irrespective of their affiliation to any particular religion. I remain convinced that I was reaching up to the same supreme god that the other Catholic worshippers were praying to during the Sunday mass or indeed the same being adherents of other religions prayed to. I am sure my wife was very proud of me for my devotion to Jesus and God seeing me in a prayerful gesture in the church.

CHAPTER 7

Role of Religion in Social Dynamics

In my attempt to put my own family's negative experiences in perspective, I have often reflected on the essence of different religions and searched for an answer as to why humanity has suffered from their misuse. This endless search was driven and shaped by the unfathomable persecution my family endured.

India has had a very convoluted and complicated history of religions for thousands of years. The subcontinent gave birth to some of the oldest religions in the world such as Hinduism, Sikhism, and Buddhism and provided the platform through which other religions such as Christianity, Judaism, and Islam have established their roots and flourished.

No religion or sacred book has ever advocated any ideology that would even remotely support or encourage one segment of humanity to inflict harm and injuries on another. Yet, all through its history, India has witnessed the persecution of one segment of the population by another. Many times in its history, India has witnessed the forced conversion, mass killings, and other forms of brutal persecution by invading Muslim conquerors or rulers. The unwillingness to accept other religions and the forced imposition of one faith on others have left a long and bloody trail of suffering for millions of people.

Dr. APJ Abdul Kalam, the pioneering rocket scientist and former president of India, once opined that "for great men, religion is a way of making friends; small people make religion a fighting tool." I found this statement to hold true not only in modern times but all through history.

I have always wondered and questioned why one religion would consider adherents to other religions as nonbelievers or infidels. All Abrahamic and other major religions have a common ground in their beliefs in the existence of a supreme god, and the concept of reward in heaven and retribution in hell based on our deeds on earth. Then why there would be so much intolerance toward those born into families who simply practiced a different religion or faith?

I have tried to reflect on the similarities or differences among the various religions and understand how each faith perceived God, spirituality, and other philosophical issues pertaining to the code of conduct in life on earth in the current life cycle, death, and afterlife.

My father was a practicing orthodox Hindu who followed every minute ritual which he believed an absolute necessity for his spiritual well-being. However, he was always very tolerant and respectful toward other religions. I have not been as observant in practicing my faith in a traditional way that is built around going to the temples, reciting religious mantras (hymns), or performing routine rituals. My spiritual well-being has been always rooted in the essence of righteousness while leading a life built around honesty and dealing with all fellow beings with compassion and empathy. I have always believed that all religions held the same universal messages about goodness. Just like all the rivers and tributaries flowing through different paths which converge to a greater common ocean, the paths of all humans must inevitably lead to the same common creator regardless of our affiliations to respective organized religions. Yet humankind has suffered, and continues to suffer immensely, due to the misuse of religion by zealots and fanatics pursuing their own shallow agenda.

I have always struggled in my search for an answer as to why the almighty and merciful God would allow so much suffering and injustice? Why would s/he allow the tsunami to wreak so much havoc in Japan? Why would s/he allow a ruthless dictator like Hitler to annihilate over six million Jews during WWII? Why would s/he allow the massacre of one religious sect by another? Why would s/he allow the senseless devastation and human suffering in the Middle

East? Why would s/he not resolve all political and historical issues in the Middle East in the twinkling of an eye that would allow all Palestinians to move away from the unbearable suffering in refugee camps while all the Israelis would get their ever-elusive security and recognition as a nation in peace? Why would s/he allow millions of people in Africa to suffer malnutrition, deadly diseases, famine, and unspeakable atrocities inflicted by religious fanatics like Boko Haram and Al Shabaab? Who is God then? How does s/he interject or manifest in the affairs of the universe or humanity? The answer to any of these questions is the greatest mystery in the universe and will continue to elude us forever.

Some years ago, I heard the story of a little innocent girl who was working on a painting assignment in class. When her teacher asked her what she was painting, she replied she was painting God. When the teacher reminded her that nobody knew what God looked like, she replied that they would know it soon once she was done painting him or her. The innocent comment resonates with the attempts by many to picture, depict, or define God to suit their own beliefs and imaginations. In the same way ten blind people may define an elephant differently by simply touching it in different spots, attempts to define God have led to countless competing notions. Sadly, humanity has suffered throughout history when attempts were made to force a certain belief and notion about God on the adherents of an alternate faith.

The persecution of minorities is not unique to any region or religion. No other religion has suffered as much as the Jews for simply being Jews. Over six million Jews were exterminated during WWII by the Nazis. Yet it would seem Israel has committed a high level of atrocity against the Palestinian population. For generations, the Palestinians have been homeless and strangers in their own homeland. They have been forced to live in subhuman conditions in refugee camps for generations. So some may argue that they have every moral right to fight for their survival or even commit retaliatory atrocities. Israel has the right to security and survival, yet extremists in the Palestinian movement and their external benefactors such as Iran simply want to annihilate Israel and drive Jews into the ocean.

"Live and let live" does not seem to be part of anybody's agenda, and so the vicious cycle of violence continues.

The fight between the Catholics and Protestants in Northern Ireland, the heavy-handed subjugation of the Rohingya Muslims in Myanmar (formerly Burma), the treatment of Muslims in Sri Lanka by Buddhists spearheaded by monks, the subjugation of Tamils by Sinhalese Buddhists in Sri Lanka, the fighting between Shiite and Sunni factions in Iraq, and the persecution of minorities in Pakistan all have a common theme: an imposing will that is pushed onto others by the use of force or coercion.

The endless search for a relatable identity of God has resulted in many competing beliefs. The theist believes in a god who created the universe, but does not believe in a divine revelation or the doctrine of any trinity. It is consistent with the core belief in the classical concept of god as inherent in any of the Abrahamic religions such as Christianity, Islam, and Judaism, or in Hinduism and Sikhism. Atheists reject the belief that there is even one deity representing God. Agnostics contend that nothing is known or can be known about God beyond the material world, but unlike an atheist display neither disbelief nor faith in God in the classical sense.

In the Abrahamic religions, God lives in heaven and is distant and unreachable by mortals on earth. This is validated by the Lord's Prayer:

> *Our Father, who art in heaven,*
> *Hallowed be thy name,*
> *Thy kingdom come,*
> *Thy will be done,*
> *On earth as it is in heaven.*

While the Hindu religion believes in one god, it believes that God is omnipresent in all aspects of the universe (seen and unseen). The Hindu religion is built around the cycle of creation, preservation, destruction, and renewal. The personifications of God in the Hindu trinity include Brahma, the creator of the universe; Vishnu, who maintains order and equilibrium of the universe as the preserver; and Shiva, the destroyer who initiates the renewal of creation at the end of the cycle. Shiva is also worshipped as the destroyer of all negative vibes and energy and is thus often an integral part of any religious rituals.

The elephant-headed god, Ganapati, also known as Ganesha, is another personification of God who is the remover of obstacles. In many parts of India, such as Maharashtra, Ganesha puja or annual Ganesha festivals create a carnival-type atmosphere. In 2007, I went to Hyderabad in Andhra Pradesh (and now also the capital of Telangana) to attend and speak at the International Astronautical Federation Conference where many leading space scientists from all over the world had converged. One of the four-day proceedings was badly disrupted since most of the scientists could not make the trip from their respective hotels due to traffic jams created by the annual religious procession at the conclusion of the Ganesha puja and festival.

The core principles of Hinduism as we know and practice them today existed in India for several thousand years since its inception in the Indus Valley region. Unlike other major religions such as Buddhism and Abrahamic religions that each have a single prophet or spiritual personality such as Buddha, Jesus Christ, Mohammad, and Moses who are credited with the founding and propagating of each religion, no single prophet is credited or recorded with the founding or propagating of Hinduism. However, Hindus believe that various avatars of Vishnu, the preserver of order and equilibrium in the Hindu trinity, have descended to earth at various times to establish the moral order. Other principle entities include Rama, the beloved Hindu prince depicted in the epic *Ramayana* who fought and defeated the demon king Ravana of Lanka (modern-day Sri Lanka and erstwhile Ceylon); and Krishna, the revered teacher of Hindu scripture Bhagavad Gita who mentored Arjuna, the warrior prince who, along with his other righteous Pandav brothers, defeated their evil Kaurav cousins in the epic battle of *Kurukshetra* as depicted in *Mahabharata*.

Many variant religions or sects evolved from Hinduism. However, they did not deviate from the main messages of the

Hindu scriptures. The day-to-day practices of sects such as the Jains, Vaisnavs, and similar groups might give the impression of distinct differences at least on the superficial level, even though the core messages of Hinduism are not lost.

Jainism sprang from Hinduism several hundred years BC. Jainism provides insight into the differences and similarities between the adherents of different faiths and underscores that no single faith or religion alone was the moral standard bearer of all humanity or represented the truth about God and the creation. The acceptance of a plurality of viewpoints of different faiths is rooted in the fundamental doctrine of Jainism, Anekantatavada. The failure to accept such pluralism of different faiths led to intolerance and the intent to harm others who held a different viewpoint with respect to God and spirituality. Mahatma Gandhi championed the core principles of Jainism in the form of ahimsa, which denounced all forms of intolerance and intent to harm others who held different beliefs. Satyagraha, meaning "insistence on truth," formed the basis of his nonviolent civil disobedience movement against British rule in India.

The monastic and nonascetic Vaishnavs are rooted in the veneration of Vishnu, the preserver of the creation in the Hindu trinity, and are involved in meditative practices and ecstatic chanting. Their beliefs are rooted in the Upanishads and related to the ancient puranic scriptures such as the Vedas, Bhagavad Gita, and the Padma Purana, Vishnu Purana, and Bhagavata Purana.

Buddhism was founded in India based on the teachings of Siddhartha Gautama, a Brahmin warrior prince who was born around four hundred years BC in Lumbini, Nepal. While on a walk, he encountered a sick man, an old man, a dead man, and a monk, and began to reflect on the frailties of life, e.g., sickness, old age, and death. He renounced all forms of material indulgence and luxury and led a life of asceticism and meditation under a bodhi tree in Bodhi Goya in India for many years before attaining enlightenment and becoming Buddha, the enlightened one.

The teachings of Buddha were articulated and recorded by his followers after his death and formed the basis of Buddhism. The differences in the interpretation of Buddha's teachings by his followers subsequently led to two main variants of Buddhism: *Theravada*, which spread to Thailand, Sri Lanka, Cambodia, Laos, and Myanmar; and *Mahayana*, which spread to Japan, China, Nepal, Korea, and Vietnam.

The great emperor Asoka embraced Buddhism following the battle of Kalinga where he inflicted great material devastation and human misery. He sent emissaries far beyond the borders of India. They reached all the way to Greece to spread the teachings of Buddha. Buddhism received patronage from many Greek kings, and numerous Greek monks helped spread Buddhism to other regions including Alexandria, which was later an early center of Christianity.

Today, there are over five hundred million Buddhists worldwide. The proselytizing of Buddhism by Asoka and subsequently by his emissaries would underscore the fact that the spread of any faith or religion does not have to follow the path of bloodshed and forced conversion that the world has witnessed from time immemorial.

There are Four Noble Truths of Buddhism related to human sufferings: Dukkha (there is a lot of suffering in human life), Samudaya (all suffering is caused by excessive craving for sensual and material pleasures, fame, and fortune), Norodha (attainment of liberation and nonattachment by letting go of excessive craving for material pleasures), and Magga (embracing a life of moderation, which encourages avoidance of excessive luxuries and indulgence but does not require giving up all forms of material pleasures or embracing unnecessary hardships).

The core principles of Buddhism as enunciated in its five precepts would resonate with similar principles in other religions such as the commandments in the Christian faith: do not speak ill of others or tell lies, lead a decent life, avoid drugs and alcohol, do not harm or kill other living beings, and do not take things if they were not given to you of free will.

Buddhism was subjected to persecution at various points in history. Buddhists were persecuted, and many stupas and monasteries built by Asoka were destroyed during the Sunga dynasty (185–73 BC). During the Tang dynasty in China under Emperor Wuzong, the Buddhists, along with other religions such as Christianity and

Zoroastrianism, were subjected to heavy-handed persecution in the ninth century. During the tenth century, Buddhism experienced a sharp decline with the revival of resurgent Hinduism, Jainism, Vaisnavism, and the missionary work of the Sufis. A great center of learning, Nalanda University, built during the Gupta dynasty (fourth to sixth century BC), was destroyed by Bakhtiyar Khilji in 1197 CE during the ruthless and brutal Mamluk dynasty.

Sikhism, another major religion, originated in India about five hundred years ago. Many of its core beliefs are rooted in Hinduism and are consistent with those of other major religions. Guru Nanak's declaration following his morning bath in a local stream called Kali Bein, "There is no *Hindu*, there is no *Muslim*" (in Punjabi, "*Nā kōi hindū nā kōi musalmān*") ushered in the dawn of Sikhism. The teachings of Guru Nanak, considered as the first guru, and the subsequent nine gurus formed the basis of the Guru Granth Sahib, the holy scripture of Sikhism, regarded as the eleventh and final Sikh Guru.

When I looked closely at the core beliefs of Sikhism, I saw they reflected similar messages inherent in Hinduism and other major religions. My Hindu identity is in total harmony with the essence of Sikhism that includes beliefs in one creator, equal treatment for all of humanity irrespective of gender, race, or caste, shunning all forms of ego (homai) by avoiding pride (ahnkar, the sense of arrogance and self-importance), lust (kaam, pursuit of extramarital pleasures and promiscuity), anger (krodh, harmful conduct resulting from outbursts or rage), and greed (lobh, pursuit of excessive material things over and above what is needed for a decent and peaceful life). I also believe the code of conduct inherent in my Hindu upbringing reflects the three main guiding principles of Sikhism of *Naam Japna* (connecting with God through meditation), *Kirat Karo* (earning an honest living) and *Vand Chakko* (sharing material possessions with others and providing service to others. Guru Nanak actually introduced the idea of the communal kitchen, or langar, to share and serve others).

In general, the code of conduct as enunciated in the Sikh Reht Maryada (SRM) would reflect any other religion even though there may be superficial differences in the form and format of the day-to-day rituals.

Sikhism encourages five daily prayers called nitnem banis. Muslims are also expected to offer five daily prayers. Many Hindu families have prayer rooms in their homes that are used for daily prayers.

The universality of the messages of Sikhism did not shelter it from persecution by the ruthless and intolerant Muslim rulers in India since its inception. The fifth guru, Arjun Singh, who compiled the teachings of the first five gurus and many other Hindu and Muslim saints in Adi Granth (meaning literally the First Book), was tortured and executed by Emperor Jehangir in 1606 when he refused to make changes to the granth. Guru Tegh Bahadur, who championed the cause of religious freedom and who was approached by the Kashmiri Hindus who were being persecuted for their refusal to convert to Islam, was executed by the Mughal Emperor Aurangzeb, probably the most communal of all the Mughal emperors. Banda Singh Bahadur, the commander in chief of Khalsa (the collected body of all initiated Sikhs), was executed by Emperor Farrukh Siyar for refusing to accept his offer of pardon if he agreed to convert to Islam. These types of persecutions became the catalyst that transformed the Sikhs into a formidable and disciplined social and military force to protect their social and religious rights and independence. Subsequently, it led to the formation of a vast Sikh empire encompassing what is now part of Afghanistan, Pakistan, and Northern India, mainly Punjab. The rituals and traditions of Sikhism flourished over several centuries, leading up to the time of King Ranjit Singh and later his son, Maharaja Duleep Singh, in the nineteenth century. The Sikhs and the British fought many battles to establish authority until the Sikh empire was annexed by the British Raj.

Mardana, a Muslim by birth, was Guru Nanak's companion during his spiritual journey across India and Asia to spread the message of Sikhism, and remained close to him until his death. However, Sikhs suffered persecution throughout the Mughal reign. The Sikhs retain bitter memories of the persecution wreaked on them by Emperor Aurangzeb and other preceding Mughal emperors. They feared continued persecution if they stayed in Pakistan after the division of India along religious lines in 1947. They continued to covet a free sovereign state with the rivers Chenab and Jamuna as its borders even though they mostly settled in the Punjab state of India. During the partition of India, the Punjab region was the scene of mass upheaval as it was not only Muslims and Hindus crossing the border, but Sikhs as well.

The Sikh desire to establish their own sovereign state came to a head under the Khalistan Movement in 1984, even though it was originally dismissed by many Indians as coming more from the Sikh Diaspora. Originally, the Akal Dal started a nonviolent movement to establish Sikh and Punjabi rights. However, when Jarnail Singh Bhrindanwale became the leader of the Damdani Taksal in 1977 and took refuge in the Golden Temple in Amritsar with militant followers to push his agenda, Prime Minister Mrs. Indira Gandhi ordered the Indian Army to flush them out. Operation Blue Star was launched and resulted in the death of Bhindranwale, many of his followers, and civilian devotees who were visiting the Golden Temple at the time.

A few months after Operation Blue Star, Mrs. Indira Gandhi was assassinated by two of her Sikh bodyguards in New Delhi. Violence and rioting flared up across India between Hindus and Sikhs who until then had enjoyed a very close affinity for hundreds of years. Many Sikhs were killed during this rioting. General A. S. Vaidya, the Army chief during Operation Blue Star, was assassinated in 1989 as retaliation for designing and executing the operation to flush out the Khalistan commandos from the Golden Temple.

Islam has played a great role in shaping the political and religious histories of India. There had been Arab traders in India dating back to the pre-Muslim era. These Arab merchants came to India even before the life of Prophet Muhammad. They sailed to the west coast of India to trade spices, gold, and African goods. After the Arabs started to convert to Islam during the time of Prophet Mohammad, they carried the message of Islam to India. The first mosque, the Cheraman Juma Masjid, was built in Kerala during the life of Prophet Mohammad in 629 AD.

Islam was introduced in the Bengal region by Muslim mission-aries and sufis in the eighth century, and the subsequent Muslim invasions helped spread it. Bengal was ruled by the Sena Dynasty before the Muslim invasion in the thirteenth century. The Buddhist Pala Dynasty ruled Bengal for well over four centuries, starting in the middle of the eighth century until it was supplanted by the Sena Dynasty in the thirteenth century. The Sena Dynasty, based on the conservative and orthodox Decan culture, cultivated a Brahminical caste system, creating the high and low echelons in the society as opposed to the social liberalism of the earlier Pala Dynasty. The Buddhists were subjected to systematic persecution by the Brahmans. The lower caste did not have much opportunity for upward mobility and were dominated by the upper caste. The simplistic message of equality portrayed by Islam was attractive to the lower echelon of society who started to convert to Islam. Even though there was no widespread forced conversion initially, subsequent Muslim invaders at one time or another plundered and killed many non-Muslims, leading to mass forced conversion to Islam during their seven-hun-dred-year rule in India.

India has been invaded and ruled by Muslim intruders for hun-dreds of years ending with the Mughal Empire. The first recorded Muslim invasion was by Mohammad Bin Qasim in 715 AD. After that, there have been a series of external invaders who conquered and plundered the wealth and treasures in the land they vanquished.

Mahmud of Ghazni invaded India seventeen times between 1001 and 1027 AD to plunder its wealth. He was a fanatical Muslim determined to destroy Hindus and other local religions and spread Islam. He invaded Somnath in 1025 and looted the enormous trea-sures of its fortified temple. Feroze Tughlaq of the Tughlaq dynasty was known to be very intolerant toward other religions. He invaded Jajnagar in 1360 to destroy the Jagannath Puri Temple and later invaded Nagarkot to destroy the Jwalamukhi temples. After his demise, the dynasty started to disintegrate. The last ruler, Muhammad Nasiruddin, ruled from 1395 to 1413 AD. Mughal ruler Timur invaded in 1398 AD and killed thousands of people, destroyed many temples, and plundered Delhi for many days. Muhammad fled but later returned to rule until 1413 after Timur went back to Samarkand with his loot.

The invaders who were already in India as rulers constantly fought to expand their rule. Many independent-minded Hindu kings and Maharajas fought with Muslim rulers and invaders to maintain their religious and political independence.

The Mughal dynasty was established after Babur, the ruler of Kabul, invaded India. Babur, with an army of ten thousand, defeated and killed Ibrahim Lodhi and his army of one hundred thousand in the first battle of Panipath in 1526. This ushered in the Mughal Dynasty, which ruled India from 1526 to 1707 AD before India was colonized by the British East India Company, leading to the direct rule of India by the British monarchy.

The first Mughal emperor, Babur, faced numerous problems and resistance from the Afghans and Rajputs. After he defeated Rana Sanga of Mewar in 1527 in the battle of Kanwah, the power of the Rajputs was shaken. Like the Muslim sultans before him, he continued the plundering and destruction of the Hindu temples and killing non-Muslims, particularly Hindus. After his death in 1530, the eldest of his four sons, Humayun, ascended the throne. After Humayun's death in 1556 from an accidental fall, his fourteen-year-old son Akbar ascended the throne.

Akbar the Great became ruler with his uncle Bairam Khan acting as an advisor. Shortly thereafter, he defeated Hemu in the second battle of Panipat in 1556 and established firm control over Delhi and Agra. He was cognizant of the long history of battles with the independent-minded Rajputs and followed a policy of reconciliation with the Rajputs through matrimony. He married the eldest daughter of Raja Bihal Mal of Jaipur in 1562. His son Selim was married to the daughter of King Bhagwan Das in 1584. Akbar was known to be tolerant toward other religions and even started a new religion, Din-i-illahi, expecting it to be pleasing to both the Hindus and the Muslims. However, this politically motivated move was a failure. Off the battlefield, Akbar made many other contributions. He introduced the Mansabdai system that streamlined the civil and military administration. He patronized the arts and literature, and his court boasted the Nav Ratans (nine gems) that included the legendary singer Tansen, poet Mulla-do Pyaza, and administrators like ministers Birbal and Todarmal.

Some historians have contradicted Akbar's image as tolerant toward other religions. According to some historical references, he ordered the massacre of over thirty thousand Rajput Hindus after the battle of Chittod, a fact confirmed by no other than Abul Fazl, the historian in Akbar's own court.

The siege of Chittorgarh Fort is now part of Indian historical lore. Akbar personally led this siege starting with five thousand well-trained Mughal soldiers. The numbers eventually swelled to over sixty thousand in addition to over fifty thousand well-armed and well-trained elephants who were utilized in the Mughal's arsenal to dislodge over eight thousand Rajput soldiers defending the fort. Akbar's cannons were not powerful enough to pierce the fortified walls, but his soldiers dug underground tunnels to lay mines and breach the fort.

Even when the Mughal soldiers gained access to the fort, the fierce Rajput soldiers did not surrender. They worshipped the sun god one last time and fought to the death. Almost all the women committed jauhar (self-immolation) rather than be captured and dishonored. Akbar ordered his soldiers to massacre the Rajput soldiers and display the heads of the dead soldiers throughout the region as a sign of his authority.

Before the siege of Chittorgarh Fort, Raja Udai Singh and the royal family moved out of the fort and settled in the Aravalli Range where he had already built the city of Udaipur in 1559. By the time Rana Pratap Singh succeeded his father, many Rajput chiefs, including Rana Pratap's own brothers, accepted the patronage of the Mughals and even served under Akbar. However, Rana Pratap Singh rebuffed many attempts from Akbar to enter an alliance that would have amounted to accepting subordination under the Mughal Empire.

The enmity was not only based on political differences and the ferocity of Rana Pratap Singh's sense of independence and pride, but was also personal as their grandfathers had fought each other on the battlefield. In June of 1576, the armies of Akbar and Rana Pratap met in the battle of Haldighat. Even though the brave Rajputs launched a frontal attack to take the Mughals by surprise, the sheer numerical superiority and the efficiency of the powerful artillery forced Rana Pratap Singh to retreat to the hills. The folklore about Rana Pratap Singh's beloved horse Chetak carrying him away to safety despite being severely injured has been immortalized in an Indian folk song "O Neele Ghode raa Aswaar" ("O Rider of the Blue Horse").

Rana Pratap fought the Mughals for twenty-one years after he retreated to the hills, using guerilla tactics to make it difficult for the Mughals. Eventually, he reclaimed most of Mewar before his death in a hunting accident in 1597 at the age of fifty-six. Before his death, he made his son and successor, Amar Singh, promise to carry out the eternal conflict with the Mughals. Amar Singh, however, entered a form of alliance and understanding with the Mughals short of accepting total subservience. This disillusioned many members of Rana Pratap's family and other independent-minded Rajput clans, and they moved out of Rajastan and settled in other parts of India, mostly in Haryana and Uttar Pradesh.

Akbar was succeeded in 1605 by his son Jehangir, who never matched the glorious might of Akbar. He was greatly influenced by the charm, beauty, and intelligence of his wife, Nur Jahan, whom he married in 1611, and deferred to her advice in matters of running the country.

Jehangir was succeeded by his son, Shah Jahan, who has been immortalized for building the Taj Mahal, one of the Seven Wonders of the World, in memory of his beloved wife. He also built other monuments that were of great architectural excellence. He ruled from 1627 to 1658 AD. He fought the Portuguese in 1631–'32, and after settling the problems in the Decan, he retired to Agra in 1657 where he was later imprisoned by his son and successor Aurangzeb, who came to power following the war of succession involving his brothers Dara, Shah Shuja, and Murad. Aurangzeb was the last great Mughal emperor who took the Mughal Empire to its greatest heights, extending the borders from Ghazni to Bengal and from Kashmir to the Deccan. He was a religious fanatic who destroyed a multitude of temples and forcibly converted many Hindus after giving them the option of either conversion to Islam or death.

During the seven-hundred-year Muslim rule of India, there were systematic efforts to destroy the religious and social fabric of Hindus and other minorities through an assault on culture and centers of knowledge such as Nalanda University, which was destroyed during the Mamluk Dynasty by Bakhtiyar Khilji in 1197 AD. Thousands of temples and sacred places of worship including Somnath, Mathura, Benaras, Ayodhaya, Kannauj, and Thaneswar were desecrated or destroyed. There was mass slaughter of Hindus and other non-Muslims, yet the Muslim rulers never had it easy. Many independent-minded Hindu kings and warriors resisted fiercely. The Rajputs, Jats, Marathas, and Sikhs led these struggles in North India while in the south this struggle was embodied in the Vijayanagar Empire. The battles between the Mughal emperor Akbar and the Rajput king Rana Pratap Singh live on in the folklore of Indian history. The legendary battles between the great Maratha king Chhtrapati Shivaji Maharaj and the Adilshahi sultanate and the last great Mughal emperor Aurangzeb are also part of Indian folklore. To this day, Shivaji enjoys almost divine status in the hearts of Hindus for his bravery and uncompromising fight against Muslim domination to preserve the freedom of the Maratha Kingdom.

The decline of the Mughal Empire started with the demise of Aurangzeb and several progressively weaker rulers taking the reign, leading to the colonization of India by the British Raj.

There is a widespread perception that the Muslims were a warrior class who spread their influence by means of brute force throughout the world. Even to this date, many Muslims on the fringe believe and dream of establishing an Islamic caliphate based on Sharia law all over the world. This has cast a negative shadow rather unfairly on the entire Muslim religion by extension and association. The developments in Iraq and Syria have added to that perception and led many to deem the Islamic State of Iraq and Syria (ISIS) fighters as terrorists or anarchists who must be stopped. This has created an endless cycle of violence all over the world. The Western world is constantly on the lookout for the next cycle of terror and violence. Sadly, this perception is in sharp contrast to the attributes and core beliefs of the peaceful religion of Islam as reflected in the Holy Quran that contains God's messages for all humanity as revealed to Prophet Mohammad through the Angel Gabriel.

A closer look at the core beliefs and practices inherent in Islam do not contradict those related to other contemporary major religions even though the superficial manifestation and interpretation of each of these core beliefs and practices may look different. The core beliefs of Islam (belief in one god and his angels; his prophets starting with Adam and including Noah, Abraham, Moses, Jesus, and Mohammad; the revealed books of God including the Psalms, the Tawrat or Torah, the Injil or Gospel, and the Holy Quran; the Day of Judgment when everybody will be resurrected to face eternal reward or punishment for their deeds and beliefs; and the divine decree and practices of Islam) and the core practices of Islam (the declaration of faith in the statement, "La ilaha ill Allah wa Muhammad Rasulullah," meaning "There is no deity worthy of being worshipped except God [Allah], and Muhammad is the messenger [prophet] of God); five formal daily prayers to connect to God and seek peace of mind; Zakah that encourages sharing wealth with the poor and needy; fasting from dawn to sunset during the month of Ramadan that teaches self-control and empathy for the needy; and Hajj pilgrimage at least once in a lifetime to the sacred city of Mecca) are all anchored in one universal theme that transcends all religions: lead a life based on righteousness, and maintain the moral order with love and compassion for all fellow beings created by the one supreme god.

No major religion contradicts the essence of any of these core beliefs and practices. All religions believe in one supreme god. All Hindus, Buddhists, Christians, and Jews offer prayers during major religious occasions such as puja festivals, Christmas, Easter, Yom Kippur, and Rosh Hashanah at their respective places of worship such as the temple, church, synagogue, or monastery.

Most Hindu families have a prayer room in their home. All pious persons regardless of their religious affiliation go on pilgrimage to the various holy sites of their respective religion. Christians travel to the Holy Land in Bethlehem and/or the Vatican. Hindus go to many sacred holy sites such as Badrinath, Kedarnath, Gangotri, Yamunotri, Varanoshi/Kashi, Allahabad/Prayag, Haridwar-Rishikesh, Mathura-Vrindaban, Ayodhya, and the holy temples such as the four Peethas of Puri, Rameswaram, Dwarka, and Badrinath among others. The Kumbha Mela (the pitcher's festival) is one of the holiest Hindu festivals that takes place every twelve years.

Buddhists go to Lumbini, the birthplace of Buddha, and Bodhi Gaya, where Gautam Buddha attained unsurpassed enlightenment.

Hindus fast before any puja, and Christians fast in the Lenten period prior to Easter, which often involves an abstinence of some kind such as a favorite food or habit. Helping the needy is part and parcel of all religions. The Day of Judgment is a universally accepted fact of almost all the religions, and the Hindu concept of cycles of death and rebirth based on karma before eternal unity with God through moksha is in line with the concept of the Day of Judgment.

The beliefs and practices inherent in the Quran, Bhagavad Gita, or any other Hindu or Buddhist scripture are not inconsistent with the Ten Commandments of the Jewish, Catholic, or Protestant faiths of Christianity. "You shall have no other gods but me" is the statement about the one supreme god that is believed by all major religions even though Hindus personify God and accept his limitless attributes through many forms. No religion contradicts the essence of any of the commandments: "Honor your father and your mother," "You shall not kill," "You shall not commit adultery," "You shall not steal," "You shall not bear false witness," "You shall not covet your neighbor's wife," and "You shall not covet your neighbor's goods." The Protestant version, however, uses "murder" in place of "kill," and includes "You shall not commit adultery," which is inherent in the other commandments. While the Protestant version does not specifically mention coveting a "neighbor's wife," the commandment "You shall not covet anything that belongs to your neighbor" is all-inclusive of possessions belonging to others. The Protestant version includes the commandment "You shall not make unto you any graven images." Even though there is no specific corresponding commandment in the Catholic version, they do not worship any image or statue as God even though Catholic churches often include many ornate statues of Jesus Christ, Mary, or saints or angels to represent the essence of God just like the pictures or paintings of our family members are inanimate representations of the actual members of our family.

However, some religions take a very strict position with respect to any image of God or their prophets. A few years ago, when a Danish cartoonist created a cartoon picture of the Prophet Mohammad, there was a big hue and cry in Muslim communities across the world. All Hindu temples or Buddhist monasteries include statues of various gods and prophets just to reflect and represent the attributes of the divine spirit, but they do not actually consider these objects as their actual god.

The commandment "You shall not take the name of the Lord your God in vain" probably prohibits bringing disrespect to God by way of swearing in the name of God even though some of us do it out of habit even though no disrespect to God is intended.

I was born in a conservative Hindu family in India. However, for close to thirty years, I was married to a very conservative Roman Catholic whom I met at the Ohio State University while pursuing my graduate studies in mechanical engineering. My wife, Ann Schreiner (later Chakroboty), was a strict adherent of Catholicism, and her guard would go up at the first indication of any deviation from what she perceived as the code of conduct expected from a "true Christian."

On some rare occasions when I have been frustrated, I have screamed or just uttered, "Jesus Christ!" or "Oh my God!" My wife would always frown as I tried to convince her no disrespect was intended. Many Hindus invoke the name of Rama who is an incarnation of god Vishnu in times of distress or adversity. To seek God's blessing, they loudly chant, "Rama, Rama!"

On many weekends, the preachers from various Christian sects such as Jehovah's Witness or the Church of Jesus Christ of Latter-Day Saints (the Mormons) would knock on the front door of our home in California. They would come to talk about their version of the Bible and spread the divine message. Most of the time, they were smartly dressed young boys and girls. Often their parents or other elders would wait on the curb while these young preachers came to the front door. I would always open the door and ask them to come in and gladly participate in the discussion about the Bible and its messages. My wife was always concerned that I would be wrongly influenced in my religious convictions by entertaining any discussion about God and the Bible from anybody who did not belong to the only "true religion," i.e., Roman Catholicism. Obviously, she was a strict and unwavering adherent.

It is believed that Moses, the lawgiver in the Old Testament, received the Ten Commandments from God on Mount Sinai when the Israelites were fleeing Egypt for the Promised Land. The list could also be termed as God's stoplights or "do not do these horrible things" that would decide the person's entry into heaven and the afterlife or banishment into hell, depending on their adherence or lack thereof of these edicts. The lawgiver of the New Testament, Jesus Christ, provides many "mandatory go" lights, which among other edicts include "to feed the hungry, to visit the sick and imprisoned, to give drink to the thirsty, to welcome strangers, and to clothe the naked" (Matthew 25). The adherence to these good deeds ensures entry into heaven, while noncompliance leads to hell. Obviously, all major religions support all the edicts in either the Old or the New Testament; they are just presented or followed in a different form or format. For example, the practice of Muslims to set aside a certain part of their wealth as Zakah is consistent with these edicts about helping the needy.

Unfortunately, the concept of reward and punishment has been misused by many religious zealots. Many young Muslims have been brainwashed by religious fanatics to think that they will be rewarded with seventy virgins if they are killed in action for their religion. In recent years, many unsuspecting young men and women have blown themselves up as part of terrorist activities that have resulted in enormous mayhem and the loss of thousands of children, women, and other innocent civilians. The only surviving terrorist of the Mumbai terror campaign in India in 2008, Ajmal Kasab, told Indian investigators that their handlers in Laskar-e-Taiba, a terrorist group in

Pakistan, assured them these virgins were waiting for them in heaven if they were killed in the terror campaign.

Many of the major religions such as Hinduism, Islam, Christianity, and Buddhism have seen numerous variants resulting from selective interpretations of the core messages of these religions. Even Catholics and Protestants have many denominations or orders that seem to have distinct differences in their approach to the day-to-day practice of faith. Attempts are made too frequently to uphold the purity of one denomination over the other. The Bible-toting Southern Baptist in America might have a different take compared to the Catholics, at least on the superficial level of the gospels and the divine messages.

Religion is deeply and intimately intertwined in every aspect of Indian society. Many social festivities throughout the year are performed as part of religious events. In the Bengal region, there is a saying, "Baro mashay taro parban," meaning "Thirteen festivals in twelve months." In the Bengal region of India, the worship of the goddess Durga, the all-powerful yet the most loving and compassionate goddess who fought evil forces to establish and maintain the moral orders inherent in dharma, is the most significant religious and social festival.

The preparation for the Durga Puja starts many months before the actual festivities. Gifts, mainly of new clothes, are exchanged, and sweets are distributed to mark the festivities. Elaborate platforms known as pandals or mandaps in Bengali are created to house the idols of goddess Durga with ten hands armed with various weapons symbolizing the fighting spirit against the evil forces. The other idols that make up the arrangements include the goddess Laxmi, whom Hindus worship as the goddess of wealth and fortune; goddess Swarashati, whom the Hindus worship to seek blessings for learning and wisdom; Kartik, her warrior son; Ganesha, the remover of obstacles; Asura, who represents the evil demon that goddess Durga destroys; and the ox who carries the goddess Durga. Almost every neighborhood in big cities like Kolkata builds these elaborate mandaps, decorating them with many spectacular artistic arrangements and dazzling lighting that creates a magical nighttime atmosphere.

Millions of dollars are raised through donations from individual devotees living in those neighborhoods or from local political organizations. Millions of devotees stream into the streets and view these elaborate mandaps around the clock.

Too many times I have been asked to explain the caste system as inherent in the Hindu religion. My first reaction has been to state that practically all religions and societies have caste or class systems in one form or another based on the religious sect or family heritage of an individual. Social interactions across these man-made social divides have always resulted in many unpleasant social circumstances. I very much doubt if the royal societies in England or other monarchies hobnob with the commoners as part of their normal social interactions. Unfortunately, there are social divides based on economic, educational, and family background in many societies in the world.

In Japan, the Burakumin, the hamlet people / village people, were discriminated and ostracized in Japanese society for hundreds of years. While the Japanese constitution now bars discrimination based on ethnicity or caste, there is a long history of discrimination of lower-class people like the Burakumin, who were deemed social outcasts. They lived in their own segregated village or hamlet, shunned by the mainstream. While dealing with members of the other castes, they were expected to show subservience with gestures such as removing their headgear. In a court case in 1859 described by author Shimazaki Toson, an Eta was declared to be worth one-seventh of a person! The Burakumin descended from outcast groups like the Eta (meaning literally "an abundance of defilement," or "an abundance of filth") and hinin (literally "nonhuman"). When the social class system in Japan was established at the beginning of the Edo period (1603–1867), the Etas were placed at the bottom of the social rank. They held the menial jobs such as butchers, workers in the slaughterhouse, tanners, and so on. This is similar to the Indian caste system where the lowest caste and the untouchables did the menial work and the upper class such as the Brahmin, the Khatriyas, and Vaishyas were created to designate people based on their ability, expertise, and attributes so as to maximize their potential to become contributing members of society.

The caste systems as inherent in ancient Hindu scriptures were intended to include all segments of the population as valuable and productive members of the society. The Brahmin, the priestly/intellectual class, performed the religious functions and was the standard bearer for uprightness and morality. The Khatriyas were the warrior class that protected society from external aggression and embodied courage, splendor, dexterity, generosity, and lordliness. The Vaishyas were apt in commerce and trade and contributed to the production and distribution of goods and services to the society. The Shudras, the agriculture/labor class, tilled the land, raised the cattle and the crops. Unfortunately, another class, the untouchables, was created to do many menial jobs such as street sweeping and leather tanning. This class was not originally part of the Hindu scriptures that assigned tasks based on attributes and abilities, and have been openly discriminated for hundreds of years even though many national leaders, including Mahatma Gandhi, the Father of Modern India, championed their rights.

With education and enlightenment, the distinct divide that has existed between the different castes is slowly vanishing even though it still exists to a lesser extent. Arranged marriages, organized by parents, which have been an integral part of the Indian social fabric, continue to involve a union among members belonging to the same caste. Only in rare cases have there been marriages across the caste systems when the boy and the girl fell in love and took matters into their own hands by eloping or getting married after winning the approval of reluctant parents. Marriages across the religious divide are quite uncommon and have sometimes created great upheaval in society, such as when it has involved a Hindu and a Muslim.

CHAPTER 8

My Start in America

It was a cold winter day in March 1974 when I landed at the Columbus International Airport in Columbus, Ohio, to pursue my dream in the land of opportunity. I had exactly $9.57 in my pocket. I was completely unprepared for the harsh winter of a Midwestern city in America. I had only a light jacket and was shivering uncontrollably.

My Air India flight ended its route in JFK International Airport. First, I thought I needed to claim my luggage and then recheck into the domestic flight that was to take off from LaGuardia Airport. I did not see my luggage at the baggage claim. I panicked since I'd had some anxiety and premonition about things going wrong in this huge airport particularly after a long international flight. A kind black gentleman helped me sort things out. He took me to the baggage claim office and found out that the luggage was already checked all the way through to Columbus! That was my first encounter with the kindness and helpfulness of the American people, which I continued to be blessed with during my many years in the USA.

The gentleman then took me to the transit area where passengers taking flights from LaGuardia Airport needed to assemble. Obviously, I almost froze on my way to the helicopter that transported me to LaGuardia. My light jacket did not measure up to the task of protecting me from the minus-six-degree-Fahrenheit temperature in New York.

By the time my flight landed at Columbus, it was close to midnight. Again, my anxiety about the luggage came to a head. My luggage had not been transferred to my domestic flight. All my mea-ger belongings and most importantly the paperwork related to my admission at Ohio State University (OSU) were in my checked lug-gage. I needed them before I went to OSU to finalize my admission in the Mechanical Engineering Department for my graduate studies.

I was told that the luggage would arrive on one of the subse-quent flights the next morning, so I decided to tough it out at the airport. I started to get very hungry by morning. It had been at least ten hours since I ate on the flight to New York. I went to one of the fast-food counters. I was struggling to figure out the choices that included items like hamburger, hot dogs, and french fries. Since the hot dog was the least expensive, I asked the young lady at the counter what it was since I could not comprehend that dog meat was part of the American diet. Once I was assured that it was not dog meat, I opted to have it. However, I found out later it was like jumping from the frying pan in to the fire. It probably cost the unsuspecting Brahmin a few divine brownie points for delving into the delicacy of forbidden beef. On the positive side, it put only a manageably small dent in my light wallet! I think I managed my whole meal with less than one dollar.

Finally, my luggage arrived at around 11:00 a.m. The OSU Mechanical Engineering Department chairman, Dr. Donald Glower, with whom I corresponded before I departed for the USA, had arranged temporary accommodation for me at the International Student Center on campus. So I took a taxi to the International Student Center. The taxi driver was a heavyset African-American gentleman in his sixties. When we arrived at the International Student Center, the taxi driver unloaded my suitcase containing just a few sets of clothes and basic supplies such as a toothbrush, a tube of toothpaste, and shaving razor. I opened my wallet to pay the fare and started to count the fare out of my precious remaining $8 or so left after my hot dog meal at the airport.

The taxi driver, an imposing fatherly figure with a deep voice, saw me juggling through my meager funds. Then he asked me if that was all the money I had. Obviously, by that time, he'd figured out that I'd just travelled across the world to pursue my dream of higher studies in the USA. He asked me how much money I had exactly. When I told him, he asked how I was to support myself with so little money. I told him I was to go to the OSU office a couple of days later, on Monday, and they would release some funding to get started before my $280-per-month assistantship kicked in. But then he asked me how I was going to pay for food for the next couple of days until I went to the office. I told him that my understanding was that the International Student Center would allow me to live there for a few days until I found my own place. He was still not convinced that I had the means to sustain myself before going to the OSU office. Then he gave me a long look and said, "Son, study hard. You do not have to pay me." I was taken aback. Despite my insistence, he would not take the fare. "Welcome to America," I said to myself! Another act of American generosity after my experience at JFK Airport that I encountered in less than twenty-four hours of my arrival in America. That was over forty years ago. But that incident has been cast in my heart forever. Over the years, I've thought of that taxi driver often and hoped to meet him again so I could do something special for that wonderful man.

I met the manager of the International Student Center in the lobby. He was actually a graduate student from Brazil. He explained that I could stay there for at least two weeks free of charge, and the other students would share their meals free of charge with me until I found my place. The center had a few students who were staying there for the full academic term. The others were newcomers like me who used this place as a stepping stone before finding a footing elsewhere on the campus.

During my short stay at the student center, I met students from Brazil, Colombia, British Guiana, Mexico, Puerto Rico, India, Dominican Republic, Argentina, and a few other countries. This is where I met Kedar Morarka, a brilliant student from India who would become my roommate a few quarters later.

A few days after my arrival, I went to the Mechanical Engineering Department to meet the department chairman, Dr. Donald Glower. He introduced me to Dr. Seppo Korpela, the professor who was assigned as my academic advisor. Dr. Korpela was from Finland

and had originally gone to the University of Michigan for his PhD. Interestingly I found out later that the University of Michigan and OSU were bitter rivals when they fielded various athletic teams, particularly football teams. During the football season, the Michigan-OSU football game created a carnival-type frenzy.

Dr. Korpela gave me a very good introduction to campus life and some insight into my potential field of studies. My biggest concern at that point was to secure an assistantship that would support my graduate studies. Dr. Korpela indicated that he would offer me an assistantship out of a research grant he had from an American company for research in the field of combustion.

At the International Student Center, while living on the generosity of other students, I was on the lookout to find a place of my own. One of the residents of the center mentioned a rooming house just a couple of blocks away that had a very inexpensive room available. The International Student Center was located on Fifteenth Street off North Main Street, the main street running through the campus. Many sororities and fraternities were located on these streets, and as a result it was a very vibrant part of the campus. The rooming house was located on Thirteenth Street, just a few blocks away.

The rooming house was a typical Midwestern frame house, possibly over fifty years old. I met with the manager who was from Bihar, India, and a graduate student of OSU. He most likely enjoyed a rent discount for doubling as the resident manager.

I signed on to take the small room that had a small twin bed with a dilapidated mattress and a very small desk and wooden chair. The agreed-upon rent of $50/month for the modest room with austere furnishing was possibly befitting a newly arrived foreign student who needed to get by on a $280/month assistantship.

The rooming house had nine rooms that were rented by students from various countries including three from India, two from Romania, one from USA, and two from South America. The common kitchen was in the basement. There was a very small room next to the kitchen that had a tiny window and was almost dark. Normally the room was used for storage; however, the manager, with the consent of the other residents, allowed a young American couple about nineteen or twenty to stay there rent free as they had run out of money to both continue enrollment at OSU and cover their other expenses. They were not receiving any financial support from their parents, which was consistent with American norms whereby children often supported themselves. However, many parents, particularly well-off parents, sometimes helped with the educational expenses of their children as needed. In many cases, the students would take out a student loan financed by the government and pay it off after they graduated and got employment.

The young couple led a very laid-back and easy lifestyle. They played the guitar in the confines of that small dark room. With their long and shaggy hair, they created the image of sixties' hippies. The residents shared the common kitchen with its single refrigerator. Residents would sometimes mark their bags of cooked or uncooked food with their names and count on the honesty of others in safeguarding it. After a while, a few students, including me, realized that some of the food was going missing. First, it was let go, but when it became a recurring theme, we started to be more vigilant about it. The manager asked a few students to take turns in the night to watch from outside the kitchen window to observe the person who was stealing the food. This was to be done after dinner when the residents went back to their rooms. To our shock, even though we suspected so, the young couple who had been allowed to live in the room in the basement were raiding the refrigerator as they did not have the means to buy food on a regular basis. The manager warned them and threatened to expel them if they continued their transgression. They possibly could not handle the humiliation even though many of us took a very compassionate approach in dealing with these two otherwise innocent and lovable young kids who were just going through a rough patch and had no means to support themselves. Many of us offered them meals from time to time and told them they could take our food from the refrigerator if they needed. One day they just moved out without any notice or fanfare. A couple of months later, while we were in the kitchen either cooking or eating our dinner, one of the residents brought in a copy of the daily newspaper. On the front page was a report of a fire that had gutted a dilapidated house in a run-down neighborhood, killing a young couple who were sleeping there—former students of OSU! To our disbelief and horror, we realized the picture was of the couple who had stayed in the basement of our rooming house. I felt horribly sad. Actually, it shook me up very badly, and it took me a long time to get over their senseless losses. Even to this day, after almost forty years, I think about it from time to time.

Most of the residents, particularly those from the Indian subcontinent like myself, had never learned how to cook. We had been dependent on our families and had to learn to put together the ingredients. As we honed our skills, we delved into relatively more involved cooking.

The rooming house was a fascinating and interesting place. The old house had wooden floors. There were four rooms on the ground floor, four rooms on the second floor, and a room in the attic. There was only one bathroom, and there was a heavy demand for its use in the morning before everybody got ready to go to class. The biggest room was not more than ten feet by twelve feet. Each room had a twin bed with a small desk and a chair. The wooden floors would make a loud noise when anybody moved or walked on them. It was funny when the girlfriends of the residents visited their boyfriends. While they had sex, the screaming, groaning, and pounding on the bed would announce their actions in real time for others to enjoy or notice. After a while, it became almost so normal that the residents learned to shrug it off and live with it. Occasionally, some of them would yell in a good-natured and humorous way, "Hey, we are trying to study. We have a midterm tomorrow. Please keep the noise down!"

During the first quarter, I took a heavy load with five courses. That would be considered a heavy load considering I had to perform my tasks for the research assistantship I got from Dr. Korpela. It was also a matter of getting adjusted to the many new situations on and off the campus. My first midterms were mixed successes with good scores in three subjects and average scores in the other two. Even though I was somewhat disheartened, I kept focused and worked hard for better final grades. I got through the first quarter with outstanding final grades in all five courses. Dr. Korpela was ecstatic and elated with his new graduate student.

The first quarter was more or less uneventful. I became good friends with Kedar Moraka, whom I met at the International Student Center. Since we took a few common courses, we shared notes and collaborated on the homework. We would take long walks through the campus to take a break from our studies. At that time, we decided that we would move to a new place and become roommates during the subsequent quarters. We eventually moved to a small two-bedroom apartment in our second quarter in the spring.

Things started to become somewhat more manageable in the spring quarter, which allowed me to get more and more involved in social and extracurricular activities and make new friends. I started to attend a few parties mostly organized by the student organizations on the weekends. My dance moves got progressively refined, and I developed a taste for beer and other drinks. Occasionally my friends and I would go to a number of discotheques such as 2001 and the Castle along North High Street that ran along the campus. This was where I learned how to ask a female stranger to dance, a new concept at the time for somebody from the Indian subcontinent. Occasionally, my friends would be lucky to take some of these girls to their apartment for continued fun and good times!

During my first two quarters, I was mostly confined to the campus area. Like most students, I still did not have a car. Occasionally, Kedar Morarka and I would take the bus to go places such as downtown, which was a few miles from the campus. Then I found out that a Pakistani student who just graduated and was in the process of moving away was planning to call the junkyard to get rid of his dilapidated car. It was a 1963 Buick Special. I offered him $50; the amount he told me he was to get from the junkyard.

One of my fellow graduate assistants in mechanical engineering helped me over a few weekends to spruce it up, installing new spark plugs, adjusting the timing, fixing up the dents, touching them up with paint, and giving it a thorough cleaning and wax job. The car looked remarkably nice and presentable and ran smoothly. This allowed me to move about more freely. All of a sudden, I became very popular and my car was in heavy demand. By that time, I had secured my driver's license in Ohio. Since I had driven before coming to the USA, it was rather easy to secure the license even though I had to pass the written test and driving test like any other new driver seeking their license. Unlike India, almost everybody in the USA learns to drive. High school kids get their learner's permits at fifteen years, which allows them to drive with another licensed driver on board. They get their full license at sixteen.

So whenever somebody needed a ride, to go shopping or out bar hopping in the evening, I would be asked for a favor. Actually, it was quite helpful when any of my friends got lucky during the course of the evening and wanted to bring a new (girl) friend back to their place to continue the jolly good time!

Before I knew it, the spring quarter ended, leading to my first summer break at OSU that would eventually include some life-changing events, such as meeting my future wife, Ann Schreiner, a fellow student in home economics at OSU.

My assistantship did not cover me during the summer quarter, so I took advantage of the little window of time and took off for a long trip across the country with my good friend from Thailand, Shujate, a fellow graduate student in the Mechanical Engineering Department. We covered over four thousand miles and travelled through Pennsylvania, Virginia, North Carolina, South Carolina, Georgia, Florida, Tennessee, Kentucky, Indiana, and Michigan before we headed back to Columbus, Ohio. During this four-week-long trip, we stayed in hotels only three nights and slept on benches in public parks or beaches even though normally it would not be legally allowed. We showered at public facilities where they were available, such as at the beaches, to save our limited money.

Only a couple of times the police told us to move. Once was in Miami Beach and another time when we tried to sleep in one of the buildings on the campus of Kentucky University. Once, when instructed by the patrolling campus police, we packed our sleeping bags and moved away. After driving for about six or seven minutes, we found another building with an open door. We found a corner which was somewhat isolated and not easily visible. We laid down our sleeping bags and went to sleep. We woke up when we saw a flashlight beamed in our eyes. Unbelievably, it was the same campus policeman we had met earlier with another of his partners. Once we told him we were two poor graduate students from OSU with limited money on a quest to explore the country, he took a soft approach. He led us to an adjacent building that had a small room with a couple of sofas used by the campus police on duty. He let us spend the night there and told us where we could clean up or use the shower the next morning. He also told us that we could buy inexpensive coffee and donuts in the nearby cafeteria in the morning. Lady Luck seemed to smile on us. We got a hearty breakfast the next morning that included an omelet in addition to donuts and other bakeries. It felt like a luxury! The policeman came for a few donuts as well and picked up our bills.

When I went back to Columbus, I checked with Dr. Korpela to see if there were any other jobs I could take in the interim before my assistantship restarted in the fall quarter. He told me that there were some openings for hands-on temporary jobs in the mechanical engineering lab. I saw the lab manager who hired me to paint the lab walls and floor at the minimum hourly rate.

This was the first time in my life I experienced the virtue of the dignity of labor. Doing such menial work would be frowned upon in India. Here in America, the children from even the richest families did such work without hesitation to support their education and avoid being dependent on their parents. In many cases, children moved out of home at eighteen to go to school or university and take a part-time job and/or a student loan to support themselves. The positive side is that the children learned to be independent and prepared for life. Before I left for the USA in 1974, this was almost unheard of in India. However, things are changing now. During one of my visits to India in later years, I saw many smartly dressed young boys and girls working in labor-intensive jobs such as in fast-food restaurants.

The job at the lab ended in about three weeks. There was still almost a month before the fall quarter started. So. I looked for something else to do to make some money as well as get some experience in different social settings. I saw an "open position" ad on one of the bulletin boards at the campus. The OSU laundry was hiring temporary helpers. So I went to the laundry to talk to the manager who was a graduate student. I was hired and assigned the task of folding the clean clothes that came out of the dryer. They were mostly bedsheets for the OSU hospitals. I got the job for an eight-hour shift with breaks of a few minutes each.

During one of those breaks, while I was eating my simple lunch that I'd packed and brought from my apartment, I saw a young blonde girl sitting at another table eating an apple. She was the most beautiful girl I'd ever seen. Over the next few days, I made sure to take a chair at the same table where she sat. I simply could not take my eyes off her. Then I shook off my fear and bravely started some small talk. She was just twenty and an undergraduate in the home economics department. She was from a small town, West Millgrove, close to Fostoria and Toledo, about a hundred miles from Columbus. Like most of the workers at the laundry, she'd taken this summer job to support her education. Unfortunately, the manager gave me some bad news after about two weeks. From the paperwork I'd completed, he found out I was on an I-20 student visa that precluded me from holding any jobs other than that of the teaching or research assistantship, so I had to quit the job. Before I left, I bravely asked Ann for her telephone number, and she seemed to give it to me gladly. When I asked where she lived, she even told me the street address of her apartment that she shared with two other girls. I made sure to write it down at the earliest opportunity!

Soon after, I started the fall quarter. By this time, I had started to feel somewhat adjusted with my academic and social life. I got more involved with my research in combustion that was funded by an American company. The research eventually became the basis for my master's thesis. I made top grades in all the courses. Dr. Korpela was elated with my success in the course work and the progress in my research work.

One day during the fall quarter, I stopped at Long's, the main campus bookstore. To my great surprise, I saw Ann there buying some books. She was with her grandmother who was visiting her. She noticed me and came over to say hello. We talked for a while about school. She was happy that I had adjusted to my studies and life in general in a new culture. I told her that she was very nice and it would be great if we could meet again sometime in the near future. She told me she was extremely busy with her schooling and the part-time job she was holding to support her education, but possibly things would change at the end of the quarter. She asked me to keep in touch.

We talked several times over the phone during the quarter. Finally, I convinced her that she needed a break from her hectic life and we should go to a nice dinner one weekend. So after some persuasion, she relented and agreed to go on a date that would ultimately set me on a series of life-changing events.

Finally, we were all set to go on our first dinner date. In the excitement of the moment, I failed to prearrange everything properly, particularly making a reservation at a nice restaurant. I thought I would just pick her up and then we would go to one of the many casual restaurants that were located along North High Street around the campus. I'd worked very hard the previous few days cleaning, waxing, and polishing my 1963 Buick Special. I even sprayed the interior with fragrance! I picked Ann up and then started driving along North High. I asked her which of the restaurants on North High we should go to as we passed by them. Strangely, the first restaurant that came our way was the International House of Pancakes. When I slowed down to ask her opinion, she giggled and told me it was more for breakfast than dinner, but it would be okay if that was where I wanted to take her. I realized my folly. Then I remembered my fellow graduate assistant Thomas had mentioned an elegant restaurant a few miles down the road where he'd taken his wife the week before to celebrate their fifth wedding anniversary. So I started to drive in that direction, and when I pulled into the parking lot, I saw the sparkle in Ann's eyes. Apparently, she knew about the restaurant as it was widely known to be a classy and elegant establishment. Obviously, it was quite expensive beyond the means of a poor student.

We did not have a reservation, so the maître d' had to find a way to get us seated, and fortunately she was able to find a nice booth adorned with candles and fresh flowers. The magical moment came about only because of divine intervention, I thought. We had a lovely dinner. The time flew by, and we were there for close to three hours enjoying the food, talking, and enjoying each other's company. We just hit it off! The bill was slightly over forty dollars, and I had only thirty dollars in my wallet. As ridiculous as it may sound today, I did not even have a credit card. I assumed I could write a personal check. In order to avoid embarrassment on my first date, I went to talk to the waiter by making the pretense of going to the restroom. The waiter was very kind and understanding. He also figured out that the two young lovers were having the greatest time of their lives and he did not want to do anything to sour it. Even though the restaurant did not take personal checks, he told me to go to Kroger, a major grocery chain just across from the restaurant. If I bought something there, I could get some cash back with a personal check. I dashed to Kroger. I had never run so fast in my life.

All this time, Ann was under the impression that I had gone to the restroom. Fortunately, it was past 9:00 p.m. and the checkout line was not crowded. So. I got a nice bag of candy and forty dollars in cash using a personal check. By the time I returned to the booth, a total of twenty minutes had elapsed. Ann asked me if I was okay or if I was sick since I was away in the restroom for such a long time. I told her that I rushed to Kroger to buy a surprise present for her and that was the real reason for the delay and I did not elaborate on my cash flow situation. As I learned later, Ann actually went to talk to the waiter when I was absent for about twenty minutes to make sure I was okay. Apparently, the waiter told her I was up to something good to surprise her. She just pretended that she did not know anything about my trip to Kroger until I told her about it. She was very happy and ecstatic with the presents and the trouble I had gone through to surprise her. I left a hefty tip of eight dollars (a substantial amount for a poor graduate student on a tight budget!).

We drove back to her apartment. I kissed her before leaving. It was an electric moment. I was on cloud nine. My heart was pounding as I drove home. I called her to thank her for a wonderful evening. She told me it was one of the most memorable nights for her. We then started calling each other to talk as we found ways to connect between our busy schedule of schooling and work.

After the fall quarter ended, she went back to her home in West Millgrove to spend the Christmas holidays with her family. Before she left, she promised to come back to Columbus to go to the New Year's Eve party organized by the International Students Association with me. She came back to Columbus the day before New Year's Eve. We went shopping to buy a formal dress for her to wear, my belated Christmas present for her. We drove to downtown Columbus and went to Lazarus, a top department store in the city at that time.

We had a great time at the New Year's Eve party attended by foreign students from many countries in addition to some OSU officers who normally looked after the welfare of the students. It was a very lively and lovely party with a good mix of international food, drink, and dancing. At about 3:00 a.m., we left the party, and since my apartment was closer from the International Student Center, she agreed to come to my apartment and spend the night. This was her first sleepover at my place, and there was no going back from that point. We were in love. She spent the next day straightening my simple room. It was amazing how she could turn that small room into such a nice place with her magical touch.

During the next quarter, we spent a significant amount of time together at each other's place as time permitted. She became acquainted with all my friends, and I became comfortable with her two roommates at her apartment.

By this time, she informed her family she had met an international student. Ann had three sisters, Jane, Martha, and Chris, and two brothers, Steven and Danny. Her mother, Jean, was of German, English and Swiss descent. Her father, Herman Schreiner, was a second-generation German-American. At the time, he was in his early forties. He was socially very conservative even though later I found him to be one of the kindest and most loving persons I'd ever met. Initially, he was obviously very uneasy about his daughter meeting a boy from India. While he did not discourage Ann directly, he was not very enthusiastic about it either. All her siblings and her mother

103

were curious to meet me, so Ann arranged for me to visit her family in West Millgrove during a weekend.

Ann went home on a Friday, and I was expected to drive my 1963 Buick Special the next day to West Millgrove to meet her family and have lunch with them. Unfortunately, something happened unexpectedly on that Friday that did not follow the preplanned script. One of our friends from Japan had a party at his place with an abundance of food, alcohol, and dancing. I suppose my youthful indiscretion took hold of me, and I had way too much to drink. I simply did not wake up until late the next day. By the time I woke up it was too late to drive to West Millgrove by noon as it was at least a two-hour drive. Moreover, I was not in my usual good state of physical health, and I had made a big mess in my room. Undoubtedly this would constitute one of the most irresponsible acts I ever committed even though it was unplanned and it happened at the wrong time and day. Murphy's Law was in action! Ann's father was cooking a whole pig on a rotisserie, among other delicacies in the backyard, and waiting for the arrival of his eldest daughter's serious boyfriend whom he would size up and assess.

Out of desperation, I told one of my close friends to find Ann's family in the long-distance directory and tell her I had fallen ill and she needed to come back to Columbus immediately. This was before cell phones were part of popular culture.

After Ann got the call from my friend, she assumed that I must be seriously sick, otherwise I would not have missed my very first meeting with her family that was so significant for both of us. My friend left out the details of my illness or the cause of it. Ann rushed back and found a great mess in my room that she cleaned up. I had to eventually fess up and tell her what happened. Even though she was very upset at the beginning, she came to terms with it, considering it was something that sometimes happened on campus. I was obviously very sad and remorseful thinking how badly I'd messed up Ann's well-intentioned plan for me to meet her family. Ann covered up for me and told her family I was not well enough to make the trip that day, leaving out the details for obvious reasons.

Three months passed before Ann made another arrangement for me to meet her family. This time she did not leave it to chance. This time, the plan was for us to drive together from Columbus to West Millgrove.

When I first went to Ann's home, all her siblings and her mother were very happy to meet me. I would not say Ann's father was unhappy, but he was trying to size me up. He was working on his vegetable garden at the backyard and occasionally checking on the barbeque he was preparing for a big lunch for the family and the new guest. He was very friendly, and extremely polite and gentle, but was reserved compared to the others. He actually cooked and put together the entire lunch with little help from the children and Ann's mother. It was a very sumptuous and elaborate lunch. After lunch, we all gathered in the small but very elegantly decorated and furnished living room.

Everybody asked me many questions about my family and India. This was probably the first time they'd had a guest from another country in their home. As the day progressed, Ann's dad slowly warmed up to me and the youngest of the siblings, six-year-old Danny, became very attached to me and demanded undivided attention and playtime.

By that time, I had dated Ann for over six months, and the family knew we were in a serious relationship. Actually, I'd moved out of my apartment and started living with Ann at the apartment she shared with two other girls who were also students at OSU.

Ann's dad took me to the backyard to show me his vegetable garden. It was amazing to see so many varieties of vegetables growing in a very small plot, approximately twenty feet by forty feet, such as onions, potatoes, cabbage, tomatoes, and corn, among others. I learned that the garden provided a good part of the vegetables the family used throughout the year. It was the hobby he pursued outside his job at the Chrysler automobile company where he'd worked most of his life. Finally, he asked me a very direct and personal question: What did I think about getting into a relationship with a person who was from a totally different culture and religion? How did I know that it would work? He pointed out that they were devout Catholics, and it was important for them to follow the strict Catholic tenets. I confided that I was in love with his daughter and I would do anything to pursue this relationship. Finally, it was time to go back to Columbus. Little Danny seemed to be the saddest of all to lose his playing partner.

Later I found out Ann's dad, my would-be father-in-law, was probably the greatest handyman I'd ever met and could fix anything! I also found out that smartness was not the result of a college degree alone. He'd never finished college and enlisted in the US Army at an early age and served in Europe, mainly in Germany, before starting his job at Chrysler. He was not rich but an honest, hardworking, and devoutly religious man who never missed going to the Sunday mass at their local church in Fostoria or Tiffin. With his modest salary, he'd raised six children. All of them went to college. They played piano and grew up with good middle-class family values. He was a strict disciplinarian. He needed to be so to raise such a big family with so few resources.

After my first visit, the ice was broken and I started going with Ann whenever she visited her family. The family started to warm up to me, and I started to feel accepted. Ann's dad started to be more accepting, and after a while I noticed nothing but love and acceptance. Danny followed me like a shadow and would get upset if I did not play with him without interruption. Whenever I stayed the night, I shared a small twin bed with him and our body temperature under the blanket kept us warm during the cold winter nights in subfreezing Ohio. I suppose Ann's dad had lots of reservation at the beginning due to his conservative upbringing and the apprehension of the unknown that could result from the union of two young souls coming from two different cultures and upbringing.

Ann and I got engaged in the summer of 1975 and set our wedding date for December 5, 1975. Prior to setting the wedding date, Ann needed my assurance that I would allow our future children to be brought up as Roman Catholics in compliance with the tenets of the Catholic church. Ann and I had to attend a series of classes at the church as part of our spiritual preparation for the wedding. I had very little money to support a big wedding. I spent most of my disposable cash to buy her a beautiful diamond engagement/wedding ring. Ann's family set aside five hundred dollars to cover the costs of the wedding. I did not even invite my advisor, Dr. Korpela, to the wedding. Ann and I booked the date at the St. Wendelin Catholic Church in Fostoria where her family worshiped and talked to Father Ross, a young priest who had just come from Rome. He was very pleasant and compassionate. We met him a number of times to finalize the logistics. Two days before the wedding, Kedar Morarka, my roommate at Columbus, two other fellow graduate students, Omar from Egypt and Glen Steyer from Fostoria, drove with me from Columbus. By that time, I was very close friends with Glen Steyer and he was to be the best man. Glen's family opened their home for us. We stayed there until the day of the wedding. Both Glen's dad and mother were extremely kind and caring. His mother fed us and looked after all our needs and helped us with the details of the wedding.

Ann's best friend from her childhood, Gail Bender, was the maid of honor. With a budget of five hundred, the invitation list was small. In addition to Ann's immediate family, all her uncles and aunts from both her father's and mother's side, and my three friends from OSU attended the small but very beautiful church wedding. Ann's cousin Toby was an accomplished photographer and volunteered to take the wedding pictures as a wedding gift. Father Ross made a very compassionate speech wishing us good luck. After the wedding, the wedding party of about thirty met in the only nice restaurant on the outskirts of West Millgrove for the reception and dinner. Ann's uncles and aunts from his father's side, Howard, Melvin, and Jean; and her mother's side, Rose Mary and Dale; Ann's brothers and sisters, Steve, Danny, Jane, Marty, and Christina; my friends, Glen, Omar, and Kedar; Ann's cousin Toby; two of Ann's college friends; and Father Ross attended the dinner reception. As usual, Ann made sure that the dining room was very tastefully decorated. She had the magical touch that transformed the dining room into a very special place befitting the most important day of our lives.

After the dinner, we went back to Ann's parents' home. That was the first night we shared the same upstairs bedroom in the family home openly. Until that day, I'd shared the bed with Danny.

The next day after breakfast, we drove back to Columbus. We did not have a lot of money to go on an expensive honeymoon, so we decided to drive to Roscoe Village, a rustic town in Coshocton set in the mid-nineteenth century. The village boasted many quaint shops and artisans who depicted life in a nineteenth-century Ohio town. There was a horse-drawn carriage wagon that provided rides through the village. Ann and I took an hour-long ride in the horse-driven wagon through the village in the evening. The coachman, dressed in the nineteenth-century outfit with an oversized black hat, provided a detailed commentary as we rode through the village in the carriage. The coachman went out of his way to make the experience of the newly married young couple a very memorable one. He dropped us at the quaintest restaurant in the village where we had a lovely candlelit dinner. We relaxed and browsed around the village for two days before returning to Columbus on December 9, 1975.

By that time, I'd already earned my master's in mechanical engineering and started my doctoral program. But the reality of the financial crunch hit us as it was a struggle to maintain even a poor-student lifestyle with my $280-per-month graduate assistant's salary minus $60 that I remitted to India every month to support the educational expenses of my two younger brothers. While the lighthearted comments of Ann's siblings about the bald tires on my 1963 Buick Special were jokes, I started to think about it as a gentle poke to change the tires. I decided to take a break from my doctoral program and work in the industry for a while, which would provide me with good work experience in the USA in addition to making a good salary. I interviewed with a number of companies that came to the OSU for on-campus interviews. Union Carbide offered me a position as a plant engineer in their battery manufacturing plant in Cleveland, Ohio, at a salary of $15,000 per year, which was a good living wage for a starting engineering position in 1975.

CHAPTER 9

My Entry into Professional Life in the USA

I decided to accept the position with Union Carbide for two reasons. First, it would free me from constantly having to juggle our limited finances in the aftermath of my marriage. Second, I thought it would give me an opportunity to get some valuable industrial experience. However, it was a gut-wrenching call since my lifelong ambition was always to obtain a doctorate in engineering. I had to convince myself that it was a temporary adjustment to my priorities and that I would eventually go back and finish my doctorate, which I actually did a few years later.

The other challenge was to face my graduate school advisor Dr. Korpela who was so supportive of my personal and academic goals. When I first informed him about my decision to leave OSU to take this position, he was extremely surprised. He was already hurt that I'd gotten married without telling him. Actually, he felt very close to me and was slighted that I had not at least shown him the courtesy of informing him about a major decision that could potentially impact my personal and academic life.

My decision about keeping my relationship with Ann discreet was because I thought Dr. Korpela, or others, might think it was disruptive to my academic pursuits. Also, due to our limited funds,

I could not afford a big wedding and I knew I wouldn't be able to invite them.

After I met Dr. Korpela in his office and informed him about my decision to leave my doctoral program to take up the new position with Union Carbide, he was startled. It took him a while to take in what I had said. He thought I was making a bad mistake, and he expressed his concern that I may become so complacent and set in my job that I might not ever go back to finish my doctorate. I always knew he was deeply interested in my well-being and recognized me as a very good student who simply did not need to squander a precious opportunity to complete a doctorate at a great university like OSU. By that time, however, I had very much made up my mind. He asked me to rethink my decision and meet him again the next day to discuss it further.

In the end, Dr. Korpela relented after securing a commitment from me that I would eventually come back and complete my doctorate. I invited Dr. Korpela and his wife for an Indian dinner we cooked at our small apartment. It was a wonderful and a memorable evening. Dr. Korpela told us about his journey from Finland to the USA for his pursuit of a PhD at the University of Michigan and later how he met his wife who was also from Finland. Dr. Korpela gave me a very hearty and spirited goodbye, handshake, and a hug and wished us luck before departing.

Since leaving Columbus on New Year's Eve in 1975, I have maintained contact with Dr. Korpela and called him whenever there were major changes, accomplishments, and developments in my professional career. Eventually when I went back to school and completed my doctorate in engineering in 1980 from Cleveland State University, or my MBA from the University of California, Davis, he was the very first person I called. I met him again personally for the first time in almost thirty-five years when I went to Columbus to see an Ohio State–Michigan football game. My wife and I took flowers and wine as presents to Dr. Korpela's home and then took Dr. Korpela and his wife to lunch. In 2013 when the OSU recognized me as the Outstanding Alumni for Professional Achievement, I contacted him to give him the good news. He wrote me back saying I was very worthy and deserving of this highly prestigious award. By that time, Dr. Korpela was retired from the OSU and was a professor emeritus. Subsequently, he left Columbus and settled in a small town in Oregon to be near his only daughter's family.

The day I left Columbus was a mixture of sadness and excitement. I felt melancholy as I was leaving the OSU, for which I had developed a deep-rooted sentimental attachment. On the other hand, I was excited and anxious at the same time to start my first full-time job in the USA as a plant engineer and embark on another uncharted journey.

Ann and I rented a U-Haul to take our meager belongings to Cleveland. I joined the Union Carbide plant as a plant engineer on January 5, 1976. By that time, I'd sold my 1963 Buick Special for three hundred dollars, the same car I'd bought for fifty dollars and drove during my entire stay at the Ohio State. We were left with Ann's Volkswagen Beetle, the small car we drove around with while at OSU and travelled extensively through Canada, including Niagara Falls.

It was a very cold day both in Columbus and Cleveland with temperatures dipping below zero. Cleveland, one of the largest cities in Ohio, was located on the shore of Lake Erie, about 150 miles north of Columbus on Highway 71. I knew Cleveland, located in the snowbelt, always had freezing temperatures at that time of the year, but that day brought almost blizzard conditions. We finished our packing late in the afternoon, and then we started to drive to Cleveland. We'd already made a trip to Cleveland about two weeks earlier to secure a one-bedroom apartment in a high-rise, a few miles from the Union Carbide plant along the road that ran parallel to the shoreline of Lake Erie. I drove the U-Haul, and Ann followed me in her VW.

We reached Cleveland around 10:00 p.m. and were desperately trying to locate the apartment complex in that blizzard. We finally found the place and unloaded most of our belongings over two or three hours. It was well past midnight, and we were exhausted and hungry, so we decided to find a fast-food place for a quick meal. We found a McDonald's a few blocks away. After we finished our meal and got into our car, it would not start in that cold weather. The battery cranked feebly for a while before it died. We desperately tried to get the AAA for help, but it was almost two hours before the emergency crew showed up since there was a heavy demand for their service in that blizzard that had caused the malfunction of many cars.

When the AAA finally jump-started our car, we returned to the apartment at around 3:00 a.m. totally exhausted and stressed out. We opened our two sleeping bags and went to sleep. We did not have a bed or mattress yet. What a way to start our first day in our new place just before starting my first industrial job in the USA!

We did not get up until late the next morning when Mr. Moatz, the manager of the apartment complex, knocked on the door. He came to check if everything was fine with his new tenants. When he glanced around and saw the sleeping bags on the floor, he asked when our furniture was due to arrive. I told him we were not expecting any other furniture but we would be buying furniture in a few days. He felt bad about the sad state of our affairs and said he needed to do something to help. He left and came back within half an hour with a young man who helped him carry a twin-size mattress to our one-bedroom apartment on the sixth floor. He introduced the young man as his grandson. My wife and I told him it was not necessary; however, we thanked him profusely for his generosity.

This apartment was our home for the next two years while I worked at the Union Carbide plant. It provided us with a nice and cozy place to start our lives together. Slowly we acquired basic furnishings including the bedroom and living room furniture, a television, kitchen utensils, and so on. We got to know a few of the other tenants, and some of them became our friends. Most of the tenants were young with the exception of a few older ones. There was a ruckus one day involving our next-door tenants, a young professional couple who were newly married like us and an older lady who lived on the floor below them. Apparently, the older lady came to confront them and complain that their moaning and pounding on the bed at night were too disruptive for her to sleep!

I joined Union Carbide and found myself in a very challenging situation. As a plant engineer, my role was to guide or lead a number of blue-collar personnel tasked with ensuring the day-to-day operation and maintenance of the high-speed production lines for the Eveready batteries. This was my very first industrial job in the USA. At the beginning, it was an uphill task to get full support and helpful cooperation from many of these conservative blue-collar personnel. I'd expected a lack of acceptance of a young Indian with brown skin and a heavy accent in a somewhat conservative city in a Midwestern state like Ohio, but when I faced it directly, it was very deflating. On many occasions, I would come home and Ann would wonder why I looked so tired and dejected. However, I kept my focus and worked hard. Slowly but surely, I started to build rapport with all the floor personnel, and I got nothing but full support, acceptance, and cooperation from them. I also developed close friendships with a number of other fellow engineers and managers at the plant. One of them, David Masarin, and his wife, Cathy, eventually became our lifelong friends.

During this time, our first child, Milan, was born. The day of his birth provided us with several dramatic moments in our lives. Ann went into labor unexpectedly a few weeks before the due date. I took her in the car and started to race toward our hospital. It was the month of January, and we had to drive through Cleveland in a snowstorm. The traffic literally came to a full stop after we had been driving bumper-to-bumper for over an hour. There was no way to get around the other cars that were backed up for miles. It was a frightening situation as Ann was getting closer and closer to the delivery. The cars around us became aware of our situation, but they were helpless. One guy and his wife in a car next to ours told us they were both nurses and were ready to deliver the baby in the car if necessary. There was no room to pass and drive around other cars to go to the hospital. We were still about half a mile from the closest hospital, Mount Sinai, which was not even the hospital we'd originally planned to go to.

Somehow, I developed the courage to park the car on the edge of the road and told my wife to get out of the car and follow me. The kindhearted and helpful nurse who'd offered his help earlier followed us on foot in case we needed help, leaving his wife to fend for herself in the car in that blizzard. Even to this date I think of him as a God-sent angel. It was the most frightening situation I have ever encountered in my life. We walked half a mile in the blizzard, and Milan was born half an hour after we got into the hospital. We brought him home a couple of days later. Subsequently, Milan was baptized into the Catholic church. David and Cathy were his godparents.

I completed my course work for my doctorate in engineering at Cleveland State University and started working on my dissertation. This was a time before laptops. I would come home from my job and work on my dissertation sometimes late into the night. On many occasions, Milan would wake up and I would put him in my lap while continuing to work on my dissertation. This was multitasking at its best. But I must say that those were some of my fondest memories that to this date invoke the deepest sentiment and nostalgia for me.

After I obtained my doctorate, I felt that I needed to move to a new job befitting my academic credentials. The plant engineer's job provided me with a very valuable industrial hands-on experience in a tough work setting. I grew up fast in my first industrial job in the USA and learned many valuable lessons in interpersonal skills that would be immensely helpful in later years. One thing became clear to me from that point on; over and above any academic qualification, social skills and building rapport and trust with coworkers were as important, if not more, to be successful in any professional endeavor.

I joined Babcock & Wilcox Company, one of the largest power generation companies in the world, in 1980 in its Barberton, Ohio, facilities, located near Akron about thirty miles from Cleveland. I joined as a senior engineer in the nuclear equipment division that designed and developed nuclear propulsion systems and components for the US Navy.

CHAPTER 10

My Professional Life

My professional career has taken many turns and twists for better and worse since I graduated in mechanical engineering from a reputed engineering university on the Indian subcontinent. A substantial part of my professional life during an eventful career has been in numerous major aerospace and defense companies in the USA as well as in academia as an adjunct professor at several prestigious universities. I was privileged to be accorded with great responsibilities and trust in several high-profile space and defense programs. It is a testament to American society that I was provided, as a first-generation immigrant, so many opportunities to make a significant mark in the scientific world.

My latest job at Northrop Grumman, one of the key defense and aerospace companies in the USA, was noteworthy in many ways. As the chief engineer of numerous enabling technology development programs for the pursuit of several multibillion-dollar NASA space programs, I was privileged to play a vital role in the development of some of the most exciting cutting-edge space technologies. It also allowed me to interact with a plethora of extraordinary personalities in American society. Many of these projects were related to the NASA programs for crewed and uncrewed missions to the moon, Mars, and beyond. The successful flight demonstration of an Autonomous Lunar Landing System, the development of a Multi-Disciplinary Design and Optimization (MDO) program to design and optimize the spacecraft for missions to the moon and Mars were some of my most remarkable achievements.

My tenure at Northrop Grumman was capped twice with nominations for the president's award, the highest award for technical and management excellence. I authored and presented many technical papers for a number of national and international conferences such as the Space 2009 in the USA, and IAF conferences in Hyderabad, India (where Dr. Abdul Kalam, the ex-president of India who was affectionately recognized as the missile man for his pioneering work in the Indian Missiles and Space Launch Vehicles programs, was the keynote speaker); Cape Town, South Africa; and the Global Lunar Conference in Beijing, China.

An interesting incident involving the American attendees occurred during the conference in Beijing. The Chinese government extended great hospitality to the space scientists who travelled from all over the world to attend this conference and went out of the way to showcase their space program. They offered to take the scientists to visit some of their facilities involved in their space programs. On the day the trip was scheduled, the American delegation was notified that some of the American scientists would not be allowed to visit one of the sensitive installations. They singled out a few of the scientists including me. They informed that the companies these scientists worked for sold weapons and did business with Taiwan, a country that seceded from China. At the time I was the Chief Engineer of the Space Segment of Northrop Grumman Aerospace Company, one of the major defense and aerospace companies in the U.S.A. The Peoples Republic of China (PRC) claims Taiwan to be an integral part of its territory and has been in a perpetual feud with it since its secession. Consequently, some of the American attendees were barred from visiting any sensitive government facility and were given the option of visiting other installations that were not sensitive. Following a brief meeting, the American delegation decided to boycott the visit if all of those originally scheduled to visit the sensitive installations were not allowed to go. The entire delegation then just went to other facilities where no restrictions were imposed.

Another interesting incident occurred when we visited the facility that was involved in their lunar project. A lady journalist who was covering the visit was very audacious and was asking many critical questions pointing out the flaws and inadequacies of the Chinese program. It came across as a set up. Probably it was a deliberate effort by the Chinese government to show that its news media enjoyed the uncensored freedom to operate and criticize the government programs and policies.

My experience at Northrop Grumman was enriched by my close interactions with some extraordinary personalities. I reported to Carl Meade, one of the most remarkable people I've ever met. He was a colonel in the Air Force and flew some of the advanced fighter jets like the F-16. He was a test pilot and graduated at the top of the class in the Top Gun Test Pilot school. Then he went on to become a NASA astronaut and flew several space missions in the space shuttle. After he left NASA, he joined the industry first at Lockheed-Martin and then at Northrop Grumman.

The qualities that separated him from the rest were his simplicity, humility, and respect for all his colleagues regardless of their pecking order in the company. If somebody did not know about his impeccable and exemplary background, nobody would ever imagine him to be a man of any significance. He was unassuming and down-to-earth, yet he conducted himself in such a dignified and professional way. He commanded deep respect from everybody. He did not have to demand it, and more importantly, he did not need to prove anything to anybody about his credentials or credibility.

If I went to see him at his office and he was on the phone, he never failed to come back to my office immediately after he finished his call. On one such occasion, he told me he was on the phone with the company president and that was why he was not able to hang up and talk to me right away. He just did not want me to feel slighted and disrespected. The fact of the matter was that most of the other bosses in similar situations would just wait for the other person to come back. If I ever left him a telephone message, he would return the call at his earliest opportunity. These are very simple personal qualities, but at the same time they were the very same attributes that commanded so much respect and adulation for this extraordinary man.

One day when he returned my call very promptly, I mentioned that my call was not that urgent and he did not have to get back to me so promptly. The answer he gave me is still fresh in my mind. As a matter of fact, it gave me some new perspective in dealing with others. He explained that whenever somebody called him he considered it as a mark of relevance and respect for him. Obviously, somebody had needed his opinion, advice, direction, or help; otherwise why would they call him? There were over six billion people in the world, and he was the one somebody had called, so he felt he needed to respond promptly and respectfully to acknowledge the gesture and privilege accorded to him.

One thing I took away from my interactions with Carl Meade was that being respectful, considerate, and humble did not in any way detract from somebody's stature and importance. Most successful and internally secure people have nothing to prove to anybody. They have inner strength and neither an inferiority or superiority complex. Those who were genuinely accomplished were sure about themselves and did not have to put up an artificial aura about their self-perceived and inflated sense of importance. All six of the direct reports of Carl Meade including me were highly accomplished. Three of them were former astronauts, and all were former pilots and held master's or higher academic degrees. Carl commanded unquestionable loyalty and respect due to his low-key, yet towering personality built around simplicity, humility, mutual respect, sincerity, and fairness.

At one time when I was telling one of my Indian friends about Carl Meade, he said, "Oh, really. It seems that he does not suffer from the God syndrome" unlike other highly successful people who sometimes behaved arrogantly and looked down on others.

I learned many lessons from my observations of great individuals like Carl Meade. First and foremost would be the virtue of being respectful and sensitive to others. I also learned the virtue of being helpful to others. Once I complimented a colleague for always being very helpful to others. What he said in reply remains vivid in my memory: "There are many obstacles that nature would throw in our way whether we want them or not, and we don't need to add to the woes of others if we can help it. Share your blessings without any expectations, and it will come back tenfold." Another great quality I have observed and learned from my interactions with extraordinarily successful individuals is their reluctance to speak ill of others in their absence or behind their back. They get ahead in life on their own merit and not by minimizing or demonizing the worthiness of others in their absence. Parasree-katorata (a Bengali word for "speaking ill of others") is normally not part of their vocabulary.

Most successful people are humble, and their every action reflects a great sense of humility. They never show off. Only insecure people attempt to project an aura of arrogance and a self-perceived sense of inflated self-worth about themselves. Their attempts to be what they are not do not bring them any accolades and almost always fail sooner or later. Successful people never miss an opportunity to thank others when somebody helps them, and they never fail to acknowledge or compliment the accomplishments of others, while many insecure people find it hard to compliment or acknowledge the accomplishments of others as if doing so would take the shine away from themselves!

Successful people are goal oriented and are focused to achieve their goals with hard work and determination. Their work ethic is built around hard work. One of the greatest inventors of all time, Thomas Edison, once defined genius as "1 percent inspiration, 99 percent perspiration." Thomas Edison, with only three years of formal schooling, had 1,093 patents for inventions in his lifetime and changed the way the world functions today with his invention of the electric light bulb and phonograph, and his improvement of the telephone, typewriter, motion picture, and so on. My extraordinary astronaut boss, Carl Meade, was always one of the first people to arrive at work and the last person to leave. Thomas Jefferson once said, "I am a great believer in luck, and I find the harder I work the more I have of it"

Successful people manage their time properly to achieve their goals and live their lives to the fullest. They never say there are too few hours in a day, rather they find a way to utilize every available hour to accomplish their goals or simply enjoy their lives.

Most of the successful people that I have encountered and admired radiated positive energy and shunned any unconstructive negativity. There is always an advantage to be gained by associating with people with positive energy. A motivational speaker once told me lightheartedly, "Always learn to rub elbows with people with positive energy to get recharged. Associating with people with negative energy will drain or short-circuit that energy." I have taken that advice to heart.

I have also observed that successful people have an unlimited patience in their ability to listen to others and their differing views. They only advocate their ideas with sound justifications and rationale. They never attempt to impose their ideas by force. I have seen so many bosses and managers fail miserably because they ruled by creating fear and imposed their unjustifiable ideas, autocratically misusing their power. Respect cannot be demanded or forced, but needs to be earned by one's actions or code of conduct.

My close friendship with Dr. Omar Abutalib at Northrop Grumman was remarkable in many ways. Dr. Abutalib came to the USA from Egypt for his PhD in mechanical engineering at the University of Southern California, before becoming one of the top experts in imaging technology in the world. He was in my team for several high-profile space projects. We traveled together to many NASA meetings and for other related business. We jointly authored and presented a plethora of technical papers at numerous national and international conferences. Every time there is a backlash against Muslim immigrants by a few self-serving and bigoted politicians in the aftermath of scattered terrorist acts in the USA, I always remember Dr. Abutalib and thousands of others like him who are model citizens and have made outstanding contributions to the security needs of our beloved adopted nation.

One of the highest privileges during my professional career was to serve the National Academy of Science (NAS), the highest scientific body in the United States (possibly similar in status to the Royal Society in England) that advised the president and the Congress of the United States on many scientific issues of national significance. Most of the members were nationally and internationally recognized scientists, including numerous Noble laureates. The highlight of my involvement with the NAS was to serve on the NAS committee on space exploration that reviewed all the NASA technology programs related to space exploration and the vision for future missions to the moon, Mars and beyond, particularly, President Bush's initiative, "Vision for Space Exploration (VSE)." Most of the fellow members were highly accomplished and nationally recognized aerospace scientists, former astronauts, top managers or directors of national laboratories, and well-known professors at major universities such as the Massachusetts Institute of Technology (MIT). Dr. Ed Crawley, the chairman of Aerospace Engineering at MIT, and Dr. Bonnie Dunbar, the former space shuttle astronaut, cochaired the committee sessions. The committee members would fly into Washington, DC, from their jobs in different parts of the USA and meet at the NAS located across from the State Department building. Some of the committee members such as Dr. Ed Crawley subsequently served on the Augustine Commission put in place by President Obama to further explore the options for space exploration.

My committee members and I went to various NASA centers at Houston, Langley, Cleveland, Pasadena (where the Jet Propulsion Laboratory [JPL] is located), and Washington (headquarters) and held meetings and interviews with many NASA senior engineers, scientists, and directors. The committee eventually submitted its final report, and the findings were eventually briefed to a congressional committee.

More than the scientific involvement, my NAS involvement provided me with an opportunity to interact with an extraordinary group of individuals reflecting many diverse ideas and personalities, giving me a treasure trove of fond memories to cherish forever.

When I went to my first meeting at the NAS, I checked into my hotel and took the elevator to go to my room. There were up to ten other people in the elevator who had just flown in for the same meeting scheduled for the next day. As soon as the elevator started to ascend, I heard somebody with a gravel voice asking, "Now, you have to tell me how you got to fly a Mig 25. I do not believe India has ever had any Mig 25." When I looked behind me, the gentleman introduced himself. He was Dr. Ed Crawley, the cochair of the committee I was to eventually serve. Apparently, he had noted I had listed my flight experience in a Mig 25 in my resume. I explained that my experiences with the Mig 25 had nothing to do with India. I told him I was an FAA-licensed pilot and did the flight in Russia while I was there for my cosmonaut training at the Gagarin Cosmonaut Training Center. Then one of the ladies in the elevator greeted me in Russian. I was startled. It was none other than Dr. Bonnie Dunbar, the former NASA astronaut who was the cochair of my NAS Committee. Later I found out that Dr. Dunbar spent a good amount of time in Russia when she was an active NASA astronaut and involved in a joint US-Russian space mission. That was when she learned to speak Russian. Obviously, I replied to Dr. Dunbar's greetings in Russian, which I had learned while in Russia for my cosmonautic activities. Subsequently, I had many other opportunities to talk to Dr. Dunbar about our experiences in Russia.

On another occasion before a NAS meeting, both of our flights to Washington, DC, were delayed and we did not get to our hotel until close to 9:00 p.m. Both of us were hungry and walked around trying to find a restaurant that was open at that late hour. I was very impressed with her as I came to know a lot about her extraordinary credentials and achievements. Incidentally, Dr. Dunbar later became the president and CEO of the Museum of Flight. Interestingly, when I mentioned Dr. Dunbar to Carl Meade, who himself was a former NASA astronaut, he told me they were contemporaries and once on the same space shuttle mission. It is a small world indeed.

Another of my involvements with NASA would represent one of the greatest highlights of my professional career. It was a great honor to be a panelist at the Go Lunar Landing Conference where I presented my paper that reviewed the technologies used in the Apollo Lunar Landing program and how such missions would be accomplished in the future with the current state-of-the-art technologies. Some of the surviving Apollo astronauts participated in the conference and served as panelists. It brought back memories of my university days in the Indian subcontinent when Apollo 11 astronauts went on a worldwide goodwill tour immediately after their historic lunar landing in July 1969. During their stops on the Indian subcontinent, I was among the millions who lined up to get a glimpse of the Apollo astronauts Neil Armstrong, Dr. Buzz Aldrin, and Michael Collins. I still cherish the black-and-white pictures I took of the astronauts and their wives who were riding in an open motorcade. My bragging rights were that I actually touched the hands of both Neil Armstrong and Buzz Aldrin! And here I was almost forty years later in America as a panelist with the surviving Apollo astronauts at a conference sponsored by NASA. This was an amazing coincidence that could happen only in America, the land of opportunity that allowed an immigrant like me to prosper personally and professionally and make a significant mark in the scientific field.

A few years later, Dr. Buzz Aldrin came to Northrop Grumman to explore a business collaboration involving his small aerospace company, Star Buzz. A peculiar but interesting circumstance preceded the meeting. On the day of the meeting, Debbie Handrich, our department admin, reminded me about the meeting with Buzz Aldrin that Bob Davis, the director of Space Business Development of Northrop Grumman, and I were scheduled to support. It never sank in that I was scheduled to meet with the legendary astronaut and thought it was just another visitor with the name of Buzz. About an hour before the scheduled meeting, Bob Davis came to my office and jokingly asked if I'd brought my camera to take a picture with Dr. Aldrin. Only then it hit me that I was about to meet Dr. Aldrin, the legendary Apollo 11 astronaut.

Bob Davis and I, in my capacity as the chief engineer in the Space Segment, along with another Northrop Grumman director Michael Lembach, met with Dr. Aldrin in a small conference room. He presented many interesting and exciting design options for lander configurations for future missions to the moon and beyond. I must admit that I was somewhat in a state of awe thinking that I was actually in a business meeting with Dr. Aldrin. I remembered staying up all night during my undergraduate years to listen to the radio commentary of the Apollo landing! One funny comment he made during our meeting was about his concept for future lander configurations. These would incorporate two hatches at opposite ends to allow the deployment of ladders from both sides so two astronauts could come down and land at the same time. I could see a wry smile on his face when he mentioned it. Even though it was included as part of the serious discussions about competing lunar lander configurations and architecture, I wondered if it was his attempt at a self-deprecating joke alluding to his status as the second man to land on the moon a few short moments after Neil Armstrong. Possibly, the epoch "small step for man" needed to be cemented in history as "small step for men!" as a more equitable justice for fair recognition.

With Apollo astronaut Dr. Buzz Aldrin during the break at the AIAA dinner meeting in Los Angeles (2008)

After our meeting, I reminded Dr. Aldrin that I was among the millions of people who lined up on the streets to see him and the other Apollo 11 astronauts during their tour of the Indian subcontinent after the moon landing. He clearly remembered those special moments in history. He said that even though it was very special to experience the unprecedented enthusiasm and excitement of the crowd, it turned out to be somewhat scary when the crowd swarmed toward the motorcade to get a glimpse of and touch the astronauts.

I have always enjoyed keeping my association with academia as an adjunct professor, and I have taught various courses in engineering at different universities close to my industrial job at the time, first at the University of Akron in Ohio when I worked for Babcock & Wilcox Company, a major nuclear company, then at the California State University in Sacramento when I was the chief engineer at the Aerojet Propulsion Company. I taught control systems at the University of Akron and thermodynamics and other courses in the mechanical engineering department at the California State University, Sacramento. During my years at Northrop Grumman in Los Angeles, I was an adjunct professor of astronautical and aerospace engineering at the University of California, Los Angeles (UCLA), and I taught two advanced courses, Space Mission Systems Engineering, and Spacecraft Design and Analyses.

The teaching experience at UCLA was rewarding for a number of reasons. I found that Americans have an insatiable motivation for continuous learning. Most of my students at UCLA were working engineers, scientists, and managers in the major aerospace and defense companies in the greater Los Angeles area, such as Boeing, Lockheed-Martin, Northrop Grumman, Hughes Aerospace, Raytheon, Aerospace Corporation, JPL, and Los Angeles Air Force Base among others. Many of these students even held PhDs and were involved in the design, analyses, and development of many major space and defense programs. Many of them were domain experts in a specific scientific field. They would take these courses to broaden their horizons by acquiring knowledge in technical areas outside of their domain expertise. For example, the spacecraft design course dealt with the design and analyses of all the major systems and subsystems of the spacecraft, such as the propulsion, structures, power, avionics, thermal systems, guidance and control, attitude and orbit maintenance and control, communications, and so on. While the limited time available within a semester was not adequate to get into a high level of detail for each of the systems, the students got the opportunity to develop a working-level knowledge in those areas. They got a graduate degree (certificate) from UCLA in aerospace engineering that enhanced their résumés as well. I must say it was a great privilege to get the opportunity to teach these advanced-level courses at one of the most prestigious universities in the world. It provided me with the opportunity to interact with the aerospace community that broadened my own horizon.

My teaching experiences as an adjunct professor ran parallel to my entire professional career in the defense and aerospace industry. As a matter of fact, I can count thousands of engineers who took my courses during that period. On many occasions, their paths crossed with mine, sometimes in very interesting settings and circumstances.

A very interesting situation occurred during NASA's Dr. Von Braun's Memorial Black Tie Dinner. It was attended by many NASA senior engineers and scientists, and its top hierarchy, including the NASA administrator General Charlie Bolden, who was himself a former fighter pilot and an astronaut with *The Right Stuff* credentials.

With NASA Administrator, Lt. Gen. Charlie Bolden
at Dr. Von Braun Memorial Dinner (2009)

There were a few tables that accommodated major aerospace prime contractors such as Boeing, Lockheed-Martin, Northrop Grumman, Aerojet, and Ball Aerospace among others. Each of those tables accommodated various senior technical and management staff and reserved two seats for a senior NASA manager or a director and his/her spouse. I was not seated at the Northrop Grumman table but accepted the invitation to sit at the table of Ball Aerospace, one of our major subcontractors that supported a few of my NASA projects. At my table, eight of the industry attendees were already seated when one of the senior directors at a major NASA center and his wife arrived to take the two seats slated for them. We all introduced ourselves to the honored NASA director and his wife. When we were all getting ready to start our dinner, the NASA director looked at me and asked me, "Are you Dr. Chakroborty, my old professor at the University of Akron? I think I took your Control Systems course in 1983." When I confirmed his recollection, he stood up and shook my hands again and introduced me to his wife as his former professor. Interestingly, when General Charlie Bolden was giving away various awards to NASA scientists and administrators for outstanding performances, the NASA director at our table mentioned that the recipient of the award just announced was also a student of mine in the same Control Systems Course.

A few years later, a similar incident occurred. I was presenting a paper at a technical forum where a senior director of the Air Force Research Lab (AFRL) was the session chairman. After the session was over, he asked me if I was the same Dr. Chakroborty from whom he took a course some years ago. I confirmed this and we shook hands. Once a professor, always a professor, I suppose.

Before Northrop Grumman, I had three long-duration stints at three other defense and/or aerospace companies, at Babcock & Wilcox Company for five years, Aerojet Propulsion Company for fourteen years, and then at Microcosm for eight years.

After obtaining my doctorate, my first major industrial job after a brief stint at Union Carbide was at the Babcock & Wilcox Company, one of the major nuclear companies in the world at the time. I worked in the nuclear equipment division of the company, which was involved in the design and development of nuclear propulsion systems used by the US Navy. This was my first significant job at a major company in the USA, not counting my two years as a plant engineer at Union Carbide in Cleveland, Ohio, between my master's and doctorate.

An interesting circumstance at Babcock & Wilcox Company was that of a department manager. While I found a common ground to work with him with a reasonable level of congeniality, many other engineers struggled with his autocratic management style. His mode of operation might have worked in countries like Japan, India or other Asian countries years ago due to a culture that automatically puts the boss on an altar as someone to be unconditionally revered and listened to. Obviously, an American workplace was not a good fit for this style of management. One thing I have learned over my professional career is that the success of a manager is largely related to his/her ability to inspire or motivate and create a sense of trust and comfortability. The employee needs to feel that the manager is on the same side of the fence and an ally rather than a ruthless dictator.

One of the most important things I have learned over the years is how invaluable it is to network and build rapport with fellow coworkers. Having the relevant domain expertise is obviously essential, but equally, if not more important, is the need to get along with fellow coworkers. Having allies and supporters, particularly those in positions of power in the company, can make a difference when trying to negotiate the slippery paths of the corporate world. I have sadly witnessed the demise of many brilliant scientists and managers simply because of their inability to get along with their fellow coworkers. They failed to understand that mere technical competence without a reasonable level of people skills did not constitute a recipe for success in the corporate world.

Babcock & Wilcox was located in Barberton, Ohio, near Akron about thirty miles from Cleveland. This was where my wife, Ann, and I bought our first home in America, a cozy Cape Cod–style house with just three bedrooms and a single bath in a quiet neighborhood. My son, Milan (Marty), who was born in Ohio, was just two. My daughter, Tandra (Tanie), was born within a year after we moved into our new home. She was born in our family physician Dr. Schneider's home, which doubled as his office. This was a time when some family doctors still practiced out of their homes and sometimes made house calls! It was amazing that we brought her home only a few hours after her birth.

My office was about a mile and a half from our home. It was a challenge during the severe winter season to shovel knee-deep snow from the driveway before being able to drive to work. The work was exciting. I worked on a number of projects related to the US Navy. In addition, I got an opportunity to work on the Clinch River Breeder Reactor Program until it was discarded by President Carter.

My office was near a small lake located in the middle of the small city center. During the lunch break, I would take a walk around the lake, a routine practiced by many of my health-conscious colleagues to squeeze in some exercise and physical activity in their mostly desk jobs. At the end of my walk, I would pick up a single rose every day without exception from the florist shop located near the lake for my wife during the entire five-year period I was in Barberton before moving to California.

Growing up, my children took a deep-rooted liking to several elderly neighbors who in turn loved the little ones. Dr. Brandt, an optometrist in his seventies, was one of our next-door neighbors. Every time Tandra saw Dr. Brandt going for a walk, she would look through the window and ask in her sweet little voice, "Dr. Brandt, can I go walking with you?"

Two other elderly couples were also our neighbors; Tony and Emily, in their seventies, lived behind our home, and Clarence lived across the street. My daughter would dress (her mother would actually dress her) like a ballerina and go to visit Tony and Emily with whom she became very attached. One time I was watching from my window and saw Tony dancing all around the backyard with Tandra in her little ballerina dress. It was so exhilarating to see this innocent little girl and her doting old friend enjoying those precious moments, and the fond memories are etched in my heart forever. Milan was very attached to Clarence, a widower in his eighties, and went to his house to play with him almost daily. Clarence responded with love and care. Milan could not pronounce his name yet and called him "Kenarnence!" Unfortunately, Clarence passed away, and it was difficult to explain to Milan what had actually happened and why he could no longer play with Clarence. After we left Ohio for California, we were sadly informed that both Dr. Brandt and Tony passed away.

Another neighbor, Carlos Ferrari, and his wife, Linda, were close to our age. They were originally from Argentina and had three daughters who were close to our children. The children played together either at our homes or our driveways and learned to ride their bikes. Carlos was a general surgeon at Barberton Hospital. I played tennis with him several times a week. We joined a local amateur soccer league where we played competitive soccer for our city team. Carlos subsequently moved to Houston, Texas, and developed a very successful medical practice there. During the later years, I visited them during my many business trips to Houston.

On one such occasion, I went to visit them after a daylong business meeting. Linda made a nice dinner that included my favorite empanadas, a Latin American delicacy similar to an Indian samosa that I have always loved since the days when we were neighbors in Ohio. Carlos and I had a common liking for Scotch, and whenever we met, we had a good time over a few drinks. On this occasion, after a nice dinner that was attended by their visiting daughters who were then in college, we shared a few more drinks. When I left to go back to the hotel, I convinced myself that I was in a safe state of mind to drive to my hotel. I was driving on the highway and missed the exit that would take me to the hotel. I was going at about seventy miles an hour and applied the brakes. Then I started to backtrack to the exit while the cars on the busy freeway were whizzing by at over seventy miles an hour. It was probably a very reckless and irresponsible decision on my part, but I simply did not want to drive to the next exit and get lost at that late hour of the night. I was operating on a perceived notion that I was not impaired by alcohol.

It was then I noticed the flashing lights of the police car through my back window. The highway patrol officer had noticed my dangerous maneuvers on the shoulder near the exit. When I stopped, he appeared at my window and requested to see my driver's license.

Knowing I was in deep trouble particularly if I was given a sobriety test for alcohol, I went with my gut instincts and was honest and frank with this young highway patrolman who was probably in his midtwenties. I told him I was on a business trip from California and had missed the exit to my hotel so I was reversing back to it as I was worried about getting lost if I drove to the next exit. He may have figured out I'd had too many drinks and sensed my state of physical well-being or the lack thereof. He looked at me, paused for a while, and told me to follow him. He put on his siren and escorted me to my hotel. After I parked and got out of my car to thank him, he just said, "Just go straight to your room and do not drive any further." An honest and sincere confession brought out the best of this good-natured young policeman. Even to this date I wonder what would have happened if he had booked me with driving under the influence (DUI). Texas had a very strict DUI law in place at the time.

I joined the Aerojet Propulsion Company in 1985 and moved to Sacramento, California, to avoid the harsh winter of Ohio. I had spent my first eleven years in the USA in Ohio since my arrival in 1974. There was also another major reason that prompted my decision to move to California. The nuclear industry at the time had been in a tailspin since the 1979 nuclear accident at the Three Mile Island nuclear power plant in Pennsylvania that involved a partial nuclear meltdown. At that time, Babcock & Wilcox Company had many confirmed multibillion-dollar contracts to build new nuclear power plants. Each of those contracts was canceled due to the worldwide backlash against nuclear power. So I decided to reorient my career in a different industry. I looked to the sunshine state of California where I had always wanted to go. California was also the hub of the aerospace industry. I started to look around. Finally, one day I got a call from a heavily accented gentleman by the name of Ted Fleishman who was a manager at Aerojet Propulsion Company in Sacramento. Aerojet was one of the largest and most prestigious rocket propulsion companies in the world. It provided the rocket engines for practically most strategic and tactical nuclear missiles and many major space programs dating back to the dawn of the space age. I came to Sacramento to talk to Ted Fleishman and other managers at Aerojet.

I fell in love with Sacramento, a tranquil city located between San Francisco on its west and the Sierra Mountains on the east. Aerojet gave me an offer as a senior engineer and arranged for me and my wife to fly to Sacramento before we made the final decision.

I joined Aerojet in Ted Fleishman's organization and began a long and rewarding career in the aerospace industry. Later, I came to know about the remarkable background, particularly the childhood of Ted Fleishman. He was originally from Hungary and came to the U.S.A as a 10-year old boy after surviving in Auschwitz concentration camp in Poland during WWII. He still worked with a limp due to the injury inflicted by the German guards during his painful internment at the concentration camp where most of his other relatives were exterminated. I remain very appreciative and grateful of the fact my eventual career in the aerospace industry started with a simple call from him while I was trying to transition from the nuclear to the aerospace industry and move away from the harsh winter of the Midwest to the sunshine state of California. I used to visit him regularly when he retired and was living in an assisted-living facility before passing away due to prolonged cancer-related illness. My fourteen-year experience at Aerojet was eventful. Eventually, I achieved the rank of chief engineer and had the privilege to play a pivotal role in several major defense and commercial space programs. I achieved the rank of technical fellow as a rocket scientist, the highest technical designation achievable in American companies. I received the president's award at Aerojet twice, the highest such awards given for outstanding technical and management excellence.

America is my adopted country where I have prospered personally, professionally, and spiritually, and my indebtedness and loyalty to America runs deep. Thus, the very fact that I was privileged to be in a position to make a significant contribution toward the security needs of my beloved adopted country gives me a great source of pride and joy.

I played a key role in numerous major missile programs such as the Peacekeeper, SICBM, and the Minuteman Strategic missile programs. At one point, when the Peacekeeper Missile program was experiencing a host of complex technical issues that shut down the program, I was privileged to be tasked to be the leader of the Technical Tiger Team comprising of some of the brightest minds in the rocket industry in the USA. The program was back in operation due to the innovative technical solution devised by the Tiger Team. It is testament to American society that it accepted a first-generation Indian-American like me with open arms and gave me the enormous opportunity to lead the effort in one of the most important missile programs in the history of the USA at that time.

I was regarded as one of the top proponents of solid rocket motors, the type of rockets used in many strategic and tactical missiles and as the boosters or rocket propulsion systems for many space launch vehicles. I authored a book on solid rocket motors, which could not be published in the public domain because of the detailed technical contents but was used as part of the training for rocket scientists in the company and for many Air Force officers who came to Aerojet from time to time for training.

Subsequently, I spent many years in the launch vehicle programs that used the liquid propulsion system. The most eventful involvement I had in liquid propulsion systems was in the commercial Kistler K-1 Launch Vehicle as the chief engineer for the propulsion systems. The main concept was the recovery and reuse of the rocket engines after the stipulated burn duration and separation of the first stage that used three Russian NK-33 liquid rocket engines. This would have been a sharp contrast to many other traditional expendable launch vehicles that were used for just a single launch, costing hundreds of millions of dollars. This concept of reusability of the first stage was adopted by SpaceX founded by Elon Musk many years later in their Falcon Launch Veficle.

The Kistler program was remarkable in so many ways. For starters, it was one of the first efforts in the USA to acquire and use Russian rocket engines. The NK-33 and NK-43 engines were part of the Russian N-1 Launch Vehicle of their lunar program when they were competing with the USA to be the first to land a human on the moon. After they lost the moon race, they mothballed some of these engines. After the Cold War was over and the Soviet Union was disbanding and its republics becoming independent states, Aerojet was one of the first US aerospace companies to collaborate with the Russian Space Agencies and the various Russian rocket companies with direct encouragement from the US government and the State Department. At the time, this type of collaboration stemmed from the direct involvement of a high-level joint team that included Al Gore, the vice president during the Clinton presidency, and the Russian prime minister Victor Chernomyrdin. The Gore-Chernomyrdin Commission was established following a summit between President Clinton and President Boris Yeltsin in Vancouver in 1993 to facilitate economic and technical cooperation between the two countries. It was a widely accepted notion that the intent of the American government was to stop the spread of missile and nuclear technology, hardware, and scientists to rogue nations such as North Korea, Iran, and other volatile nations and promote a transition that would allow a peaceful and productive use of these valuable technical assets and personnel.

Russia was facing serious economic hardship, and so it was possible to acquire many of these assets at a fraction of the cost of their development. The NK-33 and the NK-43 engines are probably some of the best LOX-Kerosene engines ever built based on the thrust-to-weight ratio. It would require billions of dollars to design, build, and flight-test such engines. Aerojet acquired these mothballed engines for just a few million dollars each.

The use of the NK-33 and NK-43 engines required complex modifications for adaptation into the Kistler K-1 Reusable Launch Vehicle. The Russians used them as fixed engines, and the gimballing was performed by thrust magnitude control of its multiple engines used in the launch vehicle configuration. The K-1 Launch Vehicle modified these engines to be used as vectorable gimbaled engines so that the first stage with a three-NK33-engine configuration could fly back to its launch site after staging and separation from the second stage (the orbital vehicle that used NK-43 engine with a bigger nozzle expansion ratio compared to the NK-33 engine).

Many of the engineers from my organization went to Russia, and many of the Russian engineers came to our Aerojet facilities while we were in the process of redesigning and retesting these engines. Several of the Aerojet engineers came back with Russian wives, giving a new meaning to *From Russia with Love*.

The Kistler K-1 Launch Vehicle program was led by Dr. George Mueller, the former NASA associate administrator who headed the Apollo program during the lunar landings in the 1960s. The program pulled together several major aerospace companies such as Boeing, Lockheed-Martin, Northrop Grumman, and Aerojet among many others as associate contractors. Eventually, I became the chief engineer for all the propulsion systems for the K-1 Launch Vehicle. It was a privilege to work with so many legendary personalities in addition to Dr. Mueller, such as Dick Coors, Aaron Cohen (who had leadership roles in the development of some of the major defense and aerospace programs such as the B-2 Bomber and the NASA Space Shuttle), and former space shuttle commander Dan Brandenstein. The leadership meeting at the Kistler facilities in Seattle was chaired by Dr. Mueller, and the major associate contractors were represented by their senior-level staff with the ranks of the chief engineer, directors, or vice president. I would represent Aerojet after I took over the position of the chief engineer from Bob Starke, a remarkably successful rocket scientist and program manager. It was such an exciting time to be part of this pioneering program. It was a great honor to work so closely with the legendary Dr. Mueller.

I travelled to Melbourne, Australia, in 1998 to present a technical paper on the development of the propulsion systems of the K-1 Launch Vehicle at the International Astronautical Federation (IAF) Conference. The conference was opened by the governor general of Australia. He began with an apology for the inconvenience caused by the explosion of the gas supply network that supplied natural gas to Melbourne. We were not even able to take a hot shower in one of the most expensive hotels in Melbourne, the Crown Plaza Hotel, during the entire week of the conference. Even the restaurants had great difficulty in preparing the food due to the interruption of the gas supply.

Dr. George Mueller held a reception at the Crown Plaza Hotel where many of the attendees of the conference were staying. The attorney general of Australia, in addition to a few other high officials of the Australian government, attended the reception. I talked to the attorney general for quite a while. I found him to be quite interesting, easygoing, and certainly not stuffy. A jazz enthusiast, he inquired about the Sacramento Jazz Festival, one of the major jazz festivals held in the USA every year. At the time the Australian government was showing great interest in developing the space sector and extended the welcome mat to attract major aerospace companies to help develop or expand their nascent presence in Australia. At the time Kistler was playing with the idea of launching the K-1 Launch Vehicle from Woomera, which already had launch facilities for sounding rockets. Aerojet had a presence in the Woomera launch facilities.

On my way back from Australia, my wife and I and Craig Judd, one of my IPT team leaders, and his wife, Sheri, took some time off to visit New Zealand, Tahiti, and the French Polynesian Moorea Island before returning to Sacramento. New Zealand remains one of the most beautiful and tranquil places I have ever visited.

The Kistler K-1 Launch Vehicle went on for another few years. Unfortunately, after spending hundreds of millions of dollars, the program started to falter mainly because of the problem of raising the hundreds of millions of dollars from private investors. It turned out to be a monumental task even though the concept was pioneering and the program involved many legendary who's who in the aerospace community and some of the biggest aerospace companies in the USA. The list of the investors was incredibly diverse. It even included a Middle Eastern sheikh who was an astronaut in one of the space shuttle flights commanded by Dan Brandenstein. Obviously, Brandenstein's connection may have played a role in securing a substantial investment from him! He was a vice president of Kistler, but he focused mainly on raising funds rather than getting into the minute technical details of the design and development. Once it failed, Aerojet and other associate contractors subsequently had great difficulty getting reimbursed for the substantial funding they had already committed or spent in good faith.

Craig Judd was one of many colleagues with whom I have developed a great friendship in and out of the workplace. In addition to working collaboratively as fellow managers at Aerojet, Vaughn Shell, who was the project manager of the Minuteman Strategic Nuclear Missile Program, turned out to be a great friend socially. We played tennis regularly. He helped me become reasonably good at downhill skiing, and we went on outings to various ski resorts in the Sierra Mountains near Lake Tahoe and Reno. We shared a deep loyalty to Ohio State University and particularly its storied football program. Vaughn was originally from Ohio, and his father, a high school principal, was an Ohio State alumni. Vaughn was an outstanding multisports athlete and could have attended OSU on an athletic scholarship, but opted to attend the University of Colorado on a baseball scholarship. Subsequently he was drafted as a pitcher for the New York Yankees, the storied Major League Baseball franchise. After his short professional sports career, he acquired his master's degree in engineering and received an MBA before embarking on a successful career in the defense and aerospace company. We collaborated in many missile programs, and he was the person who submitted the nominating papers for my Outstanding Alumni for Professional Achievement Award from the Ohio State University (OSU) in 2013.

Commercialization of space programs has been challenging. Until very recently, space endeavors were mainly spearheaded by NASA with government funding and the participation of major aerospace companies under contracts with NASA like Northrop Grumman, Boeing, Lockheed-Martin, Aerojet, and Orbital Science among others. In more recent times, NASA has undertaken many initiatives to open the door for the commercialization of space programs. Upstart aerospace companies in Los Angeles, Space X and Orbital Science, received NASA funding to develop the launch vehicles to supply the International Space Station (ISS) after the Space Shuttle program ended as part of NASA's Commercial Orbital Transportation Services (COTS) program. Space X and Orbital Sciences have successfully developed the Falcon and Antares Launch Vehicles, and the cargo missions on board these launch vehicles have successfully delivered the cargo supplies to the ISS. Unfortunately, after a few successful missions, Orbital Science's Antares Launch Vehicle had a catastrophic failure immediately after the launch.

The subsequent investigation identified the NK-33 Russian engines from Aerojet as the cause of the failure. These were the same Russian engines that Aerojet during my tenure as the chief engineer tried to use in the Kistler K-1 Launch Vehicle. The engines seemed to have a home in the Orbital Science's Antares Launch Vehicle after the demise of the K-1 reusable vehicle program. Orbital later took measures to incorporate a different Russian engine that would replace the decades-old NK-33 and NK-43 engines.

Space X had a number of successful cargo supply missions with their Dragon Cargo Capsule launched with their Falcon 9 launch vehicle until a catastrophic failure destroyed the launch vehicle and the Dragon Cargo Capsule within a few seconds of the launch. Within a short span of the failures of the Space X and Orbital missions to the ISS, the workhorse Russian Progress Cargo spacecraft failed on the way to the ISS. These three failures, in such a short span after many successful missions to the ISS dating back to its construction phase and subsequent operation by a multinational space crew, bring to light the fact that space exploration is still a highly sophisticated, yet dangerous proposition. However, it has never stopped the human desire to explore space beyond the far reaches of earth's gravity. Russia sent another Progress supply spacecraft to the ISS shortly after the failure. Subsequently, Space X and Orbital Science also resumed their missions to the ISS. Space X also successfully brought back the first stage after staging for a soft landing and subsequent reuse that would dramatically reduce the cost of space launches. Subsequently, SpaceX successfully launched the Falcon Heavy reusable launch vehicle which used the Falcon 9 core with two additional Falcon 9 as strap-on boosters making the Falcon Heavy launch vehicle with 27 rocket engines the most powerful rocket in use today. The other resupply missions to the ISS include Japanese Kounotori and HTV, and the European Automated Transfer Vehicle (ATV).

As part of the NASA initiatives for commercialization of space programs, Space X and Boeing were awarded multibillion-dollar contracts through a fiercely competitive process involving many other aerospace companies to develop crew capsules that would transport astronauts.

Prior to the awards to Space X and Boeing, Lockheed-Martin was already contracted to develop the Crew Exploration Vehicle (CEV) that would be used for the crew transportation in space programs. However, the CEV program was not part of NASA's space commercialization program and had direct NASA oversight. I was very heavily involved in the CEV program while I was one of the chief engineers in the Northrop Grumman–Boeing joint team. It was a formidable team and was in a strong position to win the multibillion-dollar program. Boeing had been involved in practically all the human space programs as the prime contractor. Northrop Grumman built the lunar lander that landed the first humans, Neil Armstrong and Buzz Aldrin, on the surface of the moon in 1969. Yet, after a fierce competition, the CEV contract was awarded to Lockheed-Martin. From the post-award briefing, we learned our technical proposal was outstanding but our cost was hundreds of millions of dollars higher than that of Lockheed-Martin. It was a heartbreaking loss for Northrop Grumman with a devastating impact on the company's continued involvement in the NASA space programs.

The progress of Space X from a very humble beginning with a handful of employees handpicked by its founder, Elon Musk, is not only extraordinary but should be inspirational to all who aspire to achieve greatness. Elon Musk has gone the farthest as a private entrepreneur in creating the capability for low-cost space launch. I have a remarkable personal connection to Space X. In the beginning, Elon Musk started Space X with just a handful of engineers in a small facility in El Segundo, California. Elon Musk came to the USA from South Africa and pursued his PhD in physics at Stanford University. However, he was destined for a higher calling. He left Stanford to start multiple innovative initiatives. He cofounded Pay Pal, the online billing services which propelled him on a path to be a billionaire when he was still in his twenties. But he set his vision in the space exploration particularly for missions to Mars. Obviously, he gives credence to the idea of dreaming big, and he worked hard to realize his dreams.

At the time, I was working at Microcosm in El Segundo after leaving Aerojet in 1998, and worked there until 2006 when I joined

Northrop Grumman. At Microcosm, we were involved in the development of the Scorpius family of launch vehicles to provide low-cost access to space. The goal was to lower the cost of space launches compared to the existing launch vehicles that were the monopoly of the big aerospace companies. As the chief engineer and vice president of Microcosm, I headed the development of a number of pioneering enabling technologies such as low-cost rocket engines, innovative lightweight all-composite propellant tanks and structures, and an innovative Tridyne-based pressurization systems that were essential to make the pressure-fed Scorpius family of launch vehicles viable.

Dr. Bob Conger, the indefatigable vice president, my colleague, and good friend, worked very hard in securing the government funding to support the development work. The funding mostly came from the Air Force Research Lab (AFRL). Dr. Conger and Dr. Jim Wertz, the founder and president of Microcosm, worked with the high-powered congressional lobbyists in Washington in pushing for the congressional plus-up money to support the development of the Scorpius family of launch vehicles. I made a few trips to Washington, DC, with Dr. Conger and Dr. Wertz and witnessed the fascinating wheeling and dealing of Washington power brokers in action. On one occasion, when we met at a restaurant across from the US Capitol, I watched a stream of them as they passed by. Dr. Conger tried to identify and point some of them out to me. It was a fascinating experience for someone like me who was not a routine visitor to this type of seat of power.

Dr. Conger was the consummate deal maker. A handsome man with a very engaging personality, he was extremely successful in bringing in the funding by tirelessly working with the various government entities. All we had to do was to give him some ideas, and he could package it and sell it to anybody. He had developed a wide network of acquaintances, including many generals and admirals, and did not seem to have any problems in getting access to them. There was an inside joke at Microcosm, "Bob could sell ice to the Eskimos!"

A four-star general who took a civilian job in an aerospace company after retirement became part of the IPT team for a DOD program that I was managing at Microcosm. I must admit it was a strange feeling at the beginning to sit at the head of the table to hold my weekly staff meeting with a retired four-star general in attendance as a team member representing his company SAIC, one of our subcontractors for the program.

For me personally, Bob was a great friend. We traveled together several times. We spent many long hours together at Microcosm's remote engine test facilities in Socorro, New Mexico. We supported each other while dealing with our difficult government customers and program managers. I provided him with essential technical support that allowed him to bring in new funding to keep the rocket operation going. Bob and his wife, Nancy, invited me to their beautiful home in Palos Verdes many times, which had a majestic view of the Pacific Ocean from the backyard. Every time any of my relatives visited me from India, Bob and Nancy always invited them to their home for a lovely dinner and drinks.

Dr. Wertz was also very successful in bringing new contracts and funding. He was a nationally recognized space scientist. He authored many books on space technologies that were used as textbooks in practically all the major universities. As a matter of fact, I used his books as the text for some of my courses when I was an adjunct professor of astronautical and aerospace engineering at UCLA. He also taught courses in Space Mission Design and Analyses at the University of Southern California (USC) and offered these courses in the form of short courses to aerospace communities in the USA. His stature was quite helpful in advancing Microcosm's interests, although I must say his autocratic micromanagement sometimes resulted in unwarranted and unnecessary circumstances.

In the end, it became increasingly challenging to secure funding to support the Scorpius program. Normally, the Air Force brass would not support this type of funding with congressional plus-up. If there was any program they needed to champion, it would be part of their budget they solicited from the Department of Defense (DOD). The Scorpius was almost a competing proposition and in essence became a source of annoyance for them. However, by the time I left Microcosm in 2006, we had developed most of the enabling technologies and successfully flight-demonstrated two suborbital rockets from the White Sands rocket facilities in New Mexico. We built another suborbital vehicle made with mostly all-composite lightweight propellant tanks and structures and incorporated other enabling technologies. Unfortunately, by the time I left, we simply could not secure the funding to cover the launch costs.

It was a disappointing setback and letdown for me. I left the chief engineer's position at Aerojet, a highly prestigious rocket propulsion company, to join Microcosm, a relatively small company, because it gave me an excellent opportunity to play a significant role in creating the capability for the low-cost access to space. Some of my most trusted and loyal engineers, Arden Edwards and Lee Malany, who reported to me at Aerojet, followed me to Microcosm. Arden led efforts in the Thrust Vector Control (TVC) systems and cryogenic valves, and Lee Malany led the efforts for the pressurization systems. They were instrumental in the integration of the two suborbital rockets before their successful launches from the White Sands rocket launch site in New Mexico. Then, there were other extraordinary and dedicated engineers like Jim Berry, my predecessor as chief engineer at Microcosm, and Dr. Thomas Bauer, who reported to me as the director of systems engineering. In the end, the lack of funding turned out to be the backbreaker, and I eventually left Microcosm to join Jim Berry, who had earlier left Microcosm to join Northrop Grumman to work on a number of NASA's space exploration programs.

Dr. Thomas Bauer was one of the most interesting people at Microcosm. He got his undergraduate engineering degree from the University of Michigan and then did his PhD at the California Institute of Technology (Caltech). For his deep expertise in space technologies, I used to refer to him as the walking encyclopedia. Unfortunately, he decided to stay at Microcosm while practically all other engineers involved in the rocket operations left. Dr. Bauer was one of my most trusted and loyal colleagues and a friend, even though I was his boss. I got to know Donna, his lawyer wife, very well, and we did many things socially. Thomas and I golfed after work occasionally. Paul Graven, a Stanford- and Harvard-educated program manager, a remarkably pleasant and bright man, would join us on our outings at nearby golf courses. Afterward, we would meet at a local restaurant or bar for drinks and dinner and had a good time. Paul Graven also became a good friend and an ally.

I always wondered why Dr. Bauer, who had a distinguished career at NASA and Aerospace Corporation before joining Microcosm, did not explore other exciting opportunities when Microcosm's rocket operations almost came to an end. He had a simple answer: the commute to work was very manageable! He rode his bike to work from his home in Redondo Beach, just a couple of miles away.

While Microcosm's pioneering bold efforts in lowering the cost of space launch sadly came to a near halt, Space X achieved progressively greater success in their mission to provide low-cost access to space, starting with a humble beginning. Obviously, funding was not a hindrance at the beginning with a self-made billionaire leading the charge. Starting in 2001, I started to lose many of my key engineers and managers at Microcosm to Space X. First it was Dr. Hans Koenigsman, who reported to me as the manager of avionics. Hans was from Germany where he received his PhD from a prestigious university. He was an extremely bright engineer with a hard drive and extraordinary work ethics. One day he asked for a meeting to discuss some important issues. I thought he wanted to discuss some technical- and personnel-related issues. He came to my office and closed the door. He said he had some bad news. He then said he was leaving Microcosm to join a start-up company, Space X, down the road from Microcosm. At that time, Space X was hardly on anybody's radar. Obviously, the thought of losing one of the key players in the Scorpius team was a big shock, but I also had a great level of respect for Hans's capability and future. He was like a friend to me. Both being licensed pilots, we even did recreational flying together. On occasions, we would rent a small plane and take off from nearby Torrance Airport and fly to Catalina Island, which had a small airport and runway on the top of a cliff that was always fun to land on. We would eat our lunch that often included a buffalo burger and then fly back to attend to the rocket business.

I thought Hans was taking a big risk going to an unproven small rocket company. I reminded him that a number of millionaires who'd invested heavily in developing a rocket company in the past had achieved very little success. It would be another fly-by-night company that could seriously disrupt the career of an extraordinarily bright engineer. I knew little at the time about the company that came to be known as Space X, but Hans was steadfast. There was no amount of persuasion on my part or others such as Dr. Wertz that would hold him back. Hans joined Space X as a vice president at a time when it was still a company with a handful of engineers. Soon, Ann Chinnery, the manager of operations of Microcosm, another of my direct reports, left us to join Space X. Then some of the brightest and most competent technicians, machinists, and other floor personnel started to leave Microcosm and join Space X.

During this time, I interviewed Tom Mueller, a highly respected propulsion engineer at TRW (an aerospace company that was subsequently acquired by Northrop Grumman) for the position of the director of propulsion at Microcosm. This was my previous position before becoming the chief engineer. I'd known Tom Mueller for quite a while. I helped him test TRW's LOX-Hydrogen rocket engine at Microcosm's engine test facility in a remote mountainous area near Socorro, New Mexico. Tom Mueller at the time worked for Bob Saquaim, who subsequently went on to become the head of propulsion at NASA's Marshall Center in Huntsville, Alabama. Microcosm provided this help as a friendly gesture to Robert Sackheim, who had a very cordial relationship with the Microcosm leadership, including Dr. Conger and Dr. Wertz. After the interview, I decided to make an offer to Tom Mueller. I took him to lunch at Cozumel Mexican restaurant, and we agreed on a joining date. I received a call from him two days before his joining date. He'd decided not to join Microcosm and opted to join a "small start-up company Space X!" Where did I hear about that company, I asked myself in exasperation. Tom Mueller joined Space X as the vice president of propulsion. He brought his expertise in Pintle rocket engines that he'd acquired at TRW. These Pintle engines ultimately became the core of the propulsion system for Space X's Falcon Launch Vehicles.

Eventually, Gwen Shotwell, the head of business development and the space segment, left Microcosm. Her career took a meteoric rise, and she went on to become the president of Space X. After some initial failures of their first few launches, which is to be expected for any new company in this field, Space X established itself as one of the main players in the launch vehicle arena in the USA. It was not just the deep pockets of the billionaire entrepreneur that became the success story of Space X; it was Elon Musk's visionary goal and sheer determination to succeed that made him so successful in so short a time where many others, even those with deep pockets, had failed. Space X put itself in a position that created a huge backlog of satellite launch contracts with several other commercial and US government customers and a few international customers. Elon Musk even challenged the monopoly of ULA (an alliance of Lockheed-Martin and Boeing that launched the Delta 4 and Atlas V launch vehicles) to launch DOD payloads. After a series of legal challenges and other complex negotiations, Space X positioned itself to secure the certification required to share the launch of the DOD satellites with the ULA.

Space X eventually turned out to be in the forefront of NASA's efforts for the commercialization of space. It appeared that everything Elon Musk touched turned into gold. He became the CEO of the electric car company TESLA, which became one of the most sought-after electric cars both in the USA and in international markets. He is widely recognized as an environmental champion, particularly for his pioneering effort in the clean energy revolution including the utilization of solar energy through his Solar company. His pioneering vision for high-speed mass transportation with the hyperloop technology has received worldwide attention and application. It has been widely reported that he resigned from President Trump's Industrial Advisory Board after President Trump decided to pull out of the Paris Climate Agreement which was championed by President Obama and signed by close to 200 countries. It is only fitting that Elon Musk is often referred to as the modern-day Henry Ford or Thomas Edison.

CHAPTER 11

Contrasting Cultures—
Eastern versus Western

It was an overwhelming experience for the young man in his early twenties to step out of the Air India flight at JFK Airport in New York on March 18, 1974. It was an "Alice in Wonderland" experience, and the grand setting and pure spectacle of JFK Airport left me with a feeling of awe and wonder. No two countries or cultures are the same, and a new visitor to any country is expected to experience cultural shock in one form or another. I do not believe that even after over forty years, I have stopped marveling at or exploring the beauty and dynamics of the American way of life with its many contrasting social aspects, compared to the Indian way of life that I was born into and in which I was raised.

Obviously, the first thing I observed immediately after landing at the JFK Airport was the fast pace of life. Everybody seemed to be so focused and disciplined in their activities. The other startling new observation was the open show of affection in public. When I finally arrived at the OSU campus, I saw lovers openly holding each other and kissing intimately in public. This would be almost scandalous in India and in many other Eastern cultures. As a matter of fact, Indian movies received approval from the censor board just recently to include intimate love scenes and kissing.

The open show of love is ingrained in daily American life. The phrase "I love you" is very commonly and openly used when expressing one's love or affection for loved ones, whether it is used between a parent and a child, husband and wife, or two lovers. It is very rare to hear "Ami tomakay bhalobashi," the Bengali version of "I love you," openly in any family or social settings in Kolkata or an equivalent greeting in any other regional language in any part of India. It would be scandalous and bring about immediate public outcry and consternation if two people of the opposite sex were seen kissing in open public places.

Many Indians or immigrants from Eastern cultures tend to maintain their strict conservatism when it comes to showing emotion or loving gestures in public, even after living in the USA for many years. Several years ago, while still a graduate student at Ohio State University, I went to visit a Bengali family for dinner. My future wife, my fiancée at the time, Ann, a white Caucasian girl with whom I was engaged, had accompanied me. The host had been in the USA for over five years and had just completed his PhD in mathematics and was preparing to go back to India to take up an academic job at a university. During dinner, while the hosts were complimenting that we looked good together and looked like two persons in love, I turned to my fiancée and planted a soft kiss on her cheek almost as a natural reaction to the comment. It seemed that the hosts (both the husband and the wife) were startled. After dinner, the man told me that my open show of affection was probably not proper in front of their six-year-old son as it would set a bad example for him. Their son was born in the USA, and I was certain he had witnessed similar displays of affection in the past. But the parents seemed to have held on to their conservative values and beliefs even after spending over five years in the USA.

The open show of intimacy is prevalent in Western societies but rather frowned upon in Indian or other Eastern cultures. When I was working as an engineer on the Indian subcontinent before coming to the USA, my girlfriend used to visit me at my apartment every now and then. She was in her final year at the medical school and on the verge of becoming a medical doctor. The very fact that an unmarried couple spent so much time behind closed doors in the confines of their own home caused uproar in the neighborhood, and on numerous occasions I was taken to task by a few uptight neighbors and lectured about not having the right moral compass. It's unlikely that the meeting of two twenty-something adults in a relationship would even get noticed in Western society. Possibly, it would be quite normal even if it involved two junior high school students. Social dynamics are now changing somewhat in India, and the premarital interactions between a boy and a girl are now less scandalous, particularly in cosmopolitan areas.

While a couple of the opposite sex holding hands in public is very common in America, two men or two women holding hands or kissing in public is not, even though same sex marriage is now legal in most of the states. However, the issue of same sex marriage has been the subject of bitter debate and disagreement between conservatives, who would go to any length to maintain the traditional way of life built around the union between only a man and a woman, and liberals, who are more welcoming of same sex union. Obviously, in India, anyone holding hands in public, be they a same sex couple or of opposite sexes, would probably raise an eyebrow.

I experienced one of my first cultural shocks a few months after my arrival at the Ohio State University (OSU). This happened during the football season. Football is followed by the Ohio State football fans with almost religious fervor and uncompromising devotion. The annual football game against archrival Michigan creates a carnival-type frenzy. When OSU beat Michigan in 1975, thousands of loyal fans streamed into the streets to celebrate. Then to my surprise and shock, I saw over twenty totally nude male students running up and down the Fifteenth Avenue where many of the fraternities and sororities were lined up on both sides of the street. A large number of girls, many of them with bare tops, were cheering the nude revelers from the rooftop of the sororities. I was bewildered as I have never seen anything like that growing up in the relatively conservative Indian subcontinent. So, I asked somebody cheering those naked revelers what was going on. He said they were streaking to express their extreme joy in the OSU victory over Michigan. So, my vocabulary got enriched with the new word "streaking" I learned on that day.

A few years ago, I took one of my relatives visiting from India to my tennis club. He was utterly shocked to see many completely nude men taking showers together in the common shower of the tennis club, a concept or scene that is not common in India.

The other remarkable and stark difference between the two societies relates to how marriages or serious relationships develop. Both sides raise their eyebrows at the way the other does it, be it arranged marriages in India or in other Eastern cultures, or marriages without parental involvement in Western societies. Both sides find the other bizarre, inappropriate, and unacceptable.

After a life of deep-rooted experiences in both cultures, I continue to ponder the good and the bad of the two distinctly contrasting approaches. The very fact that both systems have stood the test of time for thousands of years warrants a neutral scrutiny rather than outright rejection of one by the other.

In an Indian-arranged marriage, the parents are heavily involved in locating and selecting the right matrimonial match for their eligible unmarried child. Normally one of the very first things they would look for is the caste of the family. A Brahmin (highest caste) would invariably look to another Brahmin family. Barring extremely unusual circumstances, they would not generally consider matrimonial arrangements with families of a lower caste such as the Kayastha, Vaisha, or Shudra. For a family belonging to a lower caste, it would be more acceptable to find a match in a higher caste. However, this type of union would be unlikely unless the boy and girl met and fell in love and either eloped or were able to get the permission of the parents.

Parents would also look into the family background in terms of economic and social standing; the academic, professional, and extracurricular achievements; the hobbies; and the likes and dislikes of the boy and the girl. If they were at par or compatible with each other, they would then look into the personality traits, physical features, and other attributes. The more beautiful the girl is or the more handsome the boy is, the proposal becomes more saleable. Sometimes, one factor might be slightly compromised if another attribute is over-whelmingly superior. For example, if the girl was extremely beautiful, possibly there would be willingness to compromise somewhat on the other aspects, such as the education or the family status.

Unfortunately, there is a strong preference or bias toward the fairer complexion in any marriage search in India. The fairer-skinned girls have relatively easy sailing in the marriage stakes compared to darker-skinned girls. Similarly, the darker-skinned boys sometimes are found to be less desirable. While getting a tan is a multibillion-dollar industry in the West, skin color is a puzzling variable in the Indian marriage equation. Most of the top heroines of the Indian film industry or those competing in the beauty pageants have very fair skin. Any actress with relatively darker skin finds it difficult to secure a major leading role in the film industry and succeed.

Astrology is also given consideration by parents in India during the search for a bride or groom. The astrological signs are compared and matched. In more recent times, the evaluations of the astrological compatibility (based on the birth and the astrological signs or rashis) have been done with sophisticated computer programs by an astrologer hired by the family. One of my close family members recently found an extraordinary match for his eligible son who was very handsome and accomplished with a PhD in genetics and many other eye-catching attributes and qualities. The prospective bride was also highly accomplished in music, education, and came from a very respectable family. But the astrologer came back with his computer analyses that threw off any chances of a matrimonial union. Their astrological signs and attributes were not compatible! More specifically, the astrological analyses pointed out that there was a strong possibility that the girl would suffer from serious illness some years down the road even though she was perfectly healthy at that time. Their compatibility score was only nine out of a possible score of thirty-six. My relative grumbled that if the score was at least twenty, he would have been more willing or agreeable, so he backed out.

Obviously, this incident was an extreme case even in India, and Western society would see it as ridiculous. Hardly any major decision made in Western society is based on astrological analysis even though there was some documentation about First Lady Nancy Reagan's dependence on her astrologer's advice while setting up President Reagan's activities and schedules.

Sometimes, it can seem like the parents finding the match are also in it for themselves. It is rare the boy or girl is involved during the initial search. In recent times, there has been more willingness on the part of the parents to arrange and allow a get-together between the boy and the girl in a place of their choosing after the parents felt comfortable in the strength of the compatibility.

Recently, there are more and more cases of the boy or the girl finding the match on their own, many times from their classmates, coworkers, or through mutual acquaintances just like in Western societies. In many of those cases, love overrode other considerations in physical beauty, family background, and caste among other factors. In some cases, the parents would consent, while in other cases the parents would refuse and cause a serious rift with their children who would follow their hearts and go their separate ways. Recently, the crown prince of Nepal, a mountainous kingdom in the Himalayas region, killed his parents, the reigning king and the queen, in a rampage after they disapproved his selection of his future wife. There have been a few well-publicized cases in many conservative Eastern cultures where the parents went as far as killing their own children or their love interests to protect the family honor, particularly if they married somebody belonging to a lower caste or a different religion. For example, any marriage between a Hindu and a Muslim would evoke a very deep-rooted emotional reaction and societal frown.

However, in most cases, the Indian system based on arranged marriages facilitated by the parents or the families has worked for thousands of years despite of the mostly negative way it is perceived in the West. Extensive effort goes into matching the compatible attributes of the boy and the girl and their families, thus enhancing the chances of success after the union. Practically all my siblings were married through arranged marriages. They were all happily married for a long time. My parents were married for over sixty years before they passed away. That does not mean there were no issues, arguments, or problems. However, there was an overwhelming inclination to make it work, and there was no rush to see the divorce lawyers for every little argument. However, recently there have been relatively more cases of divorce compared to the past.

Normally, the husband was the breadwinner and the wife was the homemaker in India. However, more and more women are joining the workforce, and much of the younger generation with college degrees opt to hold jobs while the parents, grandparents, or other elder relatives help take care of the children, particularly if they are cohabiting as part of a joint family.

The unique feature of the Western system is that the boy and the girl work out what they like for themselves. After all, the decision affects their own lives and is a lifelong commitment. No one makes the selection on their behalf; however, parents are not totally excluded. Normally, when the dating has proceeded to a certain point and there's a reasonable level of confidence in the relationship, the boy or the girl brings their partner to the family to meet the parents and other family members. The boy or the girl then participates in many family events that allow them to be more and more involved with the future in-laws and other family members leading up to the wedding.

The Western system based on dating often fails to bring out all the issues of incompatibility. They are not fully explored during the dating period, particularly if the premarital encounters are of short duration. Both are generally on their best behavior to impress each other, and there's little or no due diligence done by the parents or their friends. Consequently, many of these marriages fail in a very short time, in extreme cases in a matter of days. However, just like the Indian system, the dating concept has survived the test of time even though some of the cases do not turn into a long-term marriage and the divorce rate in the USA is reported to be over 50 percent. The number of remarriages in Western societies is significantly higher compared to India.

There is a certain level of spirituality built around an Indian marriage. In ancient times, this was taken to extremes, and women even burnt themselves alive on the pyre during their husband's cremation in a ceremony called satidaho (meaning "sacrifice of the pure woman") until the evil ritual was banned through the progressive movements spearheaded by Raja Ram Mohan Roy, considered the Father of the Indian Renaissance by many for his leadership in bringing about numerous socioreligious reforms through the Brahma Samaj movement he cofounded with Dwarakanath Tagore in 1828.

Contrary to the Western myth that Indian women are subjugated by men, Indian women often run the family affairs and command respect from all. It is different in rural areas where women are more dominated by the men, but in urban areas, women are equal partners in every facet of life. Many corporate CEOs and high government positions are held by women. It is not uncommon to see an all-women crew fly a commercial airplane or fighter jet or command a military unit while maintaining a balanced family life. During the Republic Day parade in 2015 when President Obama was the chief guest, the smartly uniformed and confident Indian women officers commanded the various defense units during the parade. As a matter of fact, a female Indian Air Force officer commanded the all-services guard of honor for President Obama. On a number of occasions, President Obama profusely lauded the increasing roles of Indian women in all spheres of society as contributing to the progress of India.

However, there are still large sections of the Indian population that hold a stereotypical, old-fashioned, and outdated view of the role of women in the society. After several high-profile rape cases, some Indian male politicians made public statements directly or indirectly blaming the women or the victim of the rape. They opined that the right thing for the women to do was to stay at home and take care of the household chores and tend the family, playing the traditional role of a housewife. They blamed the suggestive dresses worn by women, staying out late into the night, partying and drinking with friends among other factors causing these unfortunate rapes.

Recently, the lawyer for the rapists who raped a highly educated woman in a moving bus in New Delhi that resulted in her death opined:

"We have the best culture. In our culture, there is no place for a woman."

"A female is like a flower."

"In our society we never allow our girls to come out from the house after six thirty or seven thirty or eight thirty in the evening with any unknown person."

"You are talking about man and woman as friends. Sorry, that does not have any place in our society. A woman means, I immediately put the sex in his eyes."

"That girl was with some unknown boy who took her on a date."

"If very important ... very necessary ... she should go outside. But she should go with her family members like uncle, father, mother, grandfather, grandmother, etc. etc. She should not go in night hours with her boyfriend."

The lawyer was reported as saying, "If my daughter or sister engaged in premarital activities and disgraced herself and allowed herself to lose face and character by doing such things, I would most certainly take this sort of sister or daughter to my farmhouse, and in front of my entire family, I would put petrol on her and set her alight." When asked at a later point by a journalist who interviewed the lawyers for a BBC documentary if he stood by those comments, he replied that he did.

While the Indian government banned the documentary, fearing public resentment and unease, there was huge outrage in India demanding the lawyer be censored and punished. Unfortunately, there are areas in Indian society that are more outdated and where an old-fashioned school of thought is subscribed to; however, the overwhelming majority of Indians do support the full participation of women in all phases of society. That does not mean a woman can't play the role of a traditional housewife if the family dynamics or personal choice leads to that role. Even in Western societies, there are many women who prefer to play the role of homemaker and take a big role in rearing their children. For India, it is absolutely necessary to utilize the resources of the entire population in the national effort toward becoming an economic and cultural superpower.

India was ruled by a democratically elected prime minister, Mrs. Indira Gandhi, for close to twenty years. Indian women have held positions of supreme court justice, speaker of the parliament, state chief minister, leaders of major political parties, and so on.

Another sharply contrasting approach in Eastern and Western cultures is in the way older generations are dealt with and treated. In Eastern culture, elders are respected. The older generations are taken care of by the children during their golden years. Even the separation by a single year sets the pecking order in terms of respect. While addressing a person even a year older, "da" or "di," which is the abbreviation for "dada" or "didi," meaning "elder brother" or "elder sister" in Bengali (one of the many languages in India), is used after the name. Bobby will be addressed as Bobbyda, and Rina will be addressed as Rinadi. Older people would be addressed as "kaku" ("uncle") or "mashi" ("auntie") in Bengali. Younger people normally get up from their seats in a crowded bus or train to make room for elders and women, although these unwritten social rules are some-times broken here and there by disrespectful urchins.

At home, the elders, particularly the parents, uncles, aunts, and elder siblings, are revered and listened to. The parents normally com-mand unconditional respect from their children and are involved in every phase of their lives, including their education from high school to college, marriages, and so on. The children seek blessings from their elders before taking any major decisions, e.g., taking a test, going for a job interview, and so on.

The concept of the extended or joint family has been ingrained in Indian society for ages. Sometimes three or four generations live in the same house under the same roof for a mixture of cultural and economic reasons. In many cases, the younger generation live and share the house with the parents, grandparents, uncles, and aunts and commute to work from home. If their wives are not working, they take care of the household chores, including the cooking and cleaning, even if the family has domestic help. They also tend to their elderly in-laws and relatives.

In recent times, more and more of the younger generation are branching out on their own since the affordability of a flat and other amenities is much more improved in India with the newly burgeon-ing economy. However, it is very uncommon to see elders, particularly the parents or grandparents, being told to be on their own and sent to a nursing home or assisted living home. The concept of the nursing home or the assisted living facility is catching on in India now even though it is on a much smaller scale compared to Western societies, particularly the USA.

Even when the parents are housed in nursing homes or assisted living homes in the USA, the children, friends, and relatives regularly visit them and look after their well-being. The frequency of these visits obviously varies depending on the family dynamics. Many working American families save up for their golden years to cover the costs of such assisted living when they may be incapable of taking care of themselves. These homes also provide the social outlet for many lonely elders who might not have any children or close relatives to visit them frequently.

In America, the children normally graduate from high school (twelfth grade) at eighteen. In many cases, they are expected to move out of the parents' home to go to college and support themselves. Often, the children get a part-time job and/or take a student loan to support their education. While some Eastern societies may frown on the idea of putting the kids on their own at such an early age, the positive aspect of it is it teaches them responsibility and independence from an early stage of their lives.

This does not mean that the parents totally wash their hands of helping or supporting their children when they turn eighteen. While many wealthy families may decide to pay for their children's education entirely, many middle-class families start saving for a college fund for their children right from the time they are born. So the extent of parental support for children's education in America can range from 0 to 100 percent, depending on the financial strength and dynamics of each family. Apart from financial support, American parents are as deeply involved, loving, and supportive of their college student children as any other parents anywhere in the world while still allowing the children a tremendous amount of freedom and independence to become self-reliant.

In India, parents seem to shadow their children from childhood and all the way through their adulthood. It is all built around love and care even though from the Western perspective it may be perceived as overbearing. The parents of one of my close relatives who came to the USA to pursue his PhD would call their son almost every day, sometimes multiple times, and share every detail of their daily life through Skype. The parents kept up to speed with every detail of their son's roommates, friends, professors, academic progress, as well as daily menu for meals. Some neutral observers might argue that this was overbearing and would inhibit independence even though it was done out of love.

There is a stark contrast in the two societies in terms of adhering to punctuality. Indians, particularly the Bengalis (my ethnic group), are notoriously lax in maintaining punctuality. While they are compelled to be punctual in attending official appointments, and office meetings, they are notoriously late or lax in coming on time for social get-togethers and are often late by one or two hours. When my wife and I gave a party at our home, all our American friends would show up almost on the exact hour of the scheduled starting time while the Indians would trickle in over a long period, some of them being late sometimes by an hour or more.

My wife and I are normally sticklers about being punctual. On many occasions, we would go to the weekend parties hosted by our Indian friends right on time, but we would be the first people to arrive, and sometimes it would be awkward as if the hosts were not even expecting us so early. In some cases, we would wonder if we had even gone to the wrong address since we could not see any other cars parked in front of our destination. We would always be two of the very first guests, then the others would start coming in at various times. It is almost the norm to be late. In one extreme case, an Indian couple called us to ask for directions to our home for a sit-down dinner that had started two hours earlier. They were highly educated and respected professionals and had been living in the USA for over thirty years. I had to work hard to pacify my wife so she did not show her anger, disappointment, or frustration openly when the guests finally arrived. After all, she had worked very hard to cook a nice and elaborate dinner and was afraid it would be ruined by reheating.

Americans are generous with their compliments when reacting to the accomplishments of their friends, coworkers or family members. "Congratulations," "Keep up the good work," and "We are proud of you" are just some of the many complimentary remarks given in American society to somebody's accomplishments. It would be extremely unfair and may amount to stereotyping if I made a blanket statement to say that Indians are comparatively miserly in dispensing their complimentary or congratulatory vocabulary as it may support the false myth about many Indians being driven by jealousy (parasreekatarata in Bengali). Rather, I think the difference in the number of compliments is possibly a cultural issue, similar to the open show of love.

The obsession with English medium schools seems to be deeply imbedded in Indian society and possibly a legacy of the British in India. In the past, it was almost a status symbol for elite families to send their children to English medium schools from early on. In recent times, it seems more like an imperative even for middle-class families. Many of these schools were established by various Christian missionaries. The logic behind the tendency toward English medium skills is built around the perceived advantage they are supposed to provide for children to get work in the global economy. Many of these children are pushed or encouraged by their parents to set their goals from early on to one day fly across the Atlantic or the Pacific for career opportunities and the greener pastures of Europe, Australia, or the USA. In recent times, they have also found work opportunities in multinational companies operating in India or call centers that support overseas companies. This has meant learning to speak with little or no accent, and to understand the accent of English-speaking clients is of the utmost importance. Many of these workers attend "accent reduction" classes. Those who support American companies learn to Americanize their accent.

I have never been convinced that the emphasis on English medium schools is the differentiator in career success. It is a mixed bag in my family. Those who opted for Bengali medium schools with English as a compulsory language course in the curriculum rather than the entire mode of instruction did equally well or sometimes even better than those who went to English medium schools from the get-go. I went to Bengali medium primary and high schools before going to study engineering in a university which used the same text books as American or European universities and where most of the instruction was in English. This was not an impediment for me in earning my PhD or MBA at prestigious American universities and later becoming a successful professor at UCLA or chief engineer at several major aerospace companies in the USA. I have often been good-naturedly referred to as the man with more degrees than the degrees on a thermometer. Needless to say, I still carry a moderate accent even after living in the USA for over forty years, just like millions of others who learned English as a second language taught by teachers who went through traditional Bengali medium schools like me.

Most of the non-English-speaking advanced countries such as China, Japan, Germany, France, Italy, and Russia have done well without making English the backbone of their educational systems. In a lot of ways, their advancement may arguably be attributed to a reliance on their mother tongue in every aspect of society. While a heavy accent can be an impediment to good communication, the relevant job skills are more essential compared to language-related barriers. During my long career in the USA, I had the privilege to work with many outstanding engineers and scientists from many countries including China and Japan. Many of them were invaluable contributors, not because of their aptitude in English, but for their expertise even though they probably would not be invited to be a speaker at the local Toast Master's club. However, if the accent is heavy enough to the point of being incomprehensible, it does affect communication and impact career progress in certain workplace settings. Americans are mostly tolerant, but there are some who lose patience in dealing with people with accents. Sadly, many Indians spare no time in pointing out the heavy accent of the Indian guys next door while touting their own flawless or elegant version! During a social get-together I attended a few years ago, somebody was mimicking the heavy Indian accent of Mr. Pranab Mukherjee, the then president of India. To his consternation, somebody reminded him that Mr. Mukherjee's English was good enough to be the president of a country of over a billion people, while his mastery of English had only given him a job writing software in a not-so-glorious eight-to-five-PM job. I doubt the presidents of China, Russia, or France would fare any better than Mr. Mukherjee in demonstrating their fluency in English in the IT expert's opinion.

During one of my recent trips to India, I saw a talk show program where a leading Bollywood heroine was being interviewed. In response to the questions of the Hindi-speaking talk show host, the actress replied mostly in mixed languages, switching back and forth between Hindi and English. It came across as an attempt to create an elitist persona. I doubt if a German or a French national would switch between German or French and English under similar circumstances.

The reuse and resale of almost anything in working condition is part of the American way of life. Parents save the toys and clothing of older children and reuse them for the younger ones growing up. Some of these things are even passed down to the next generation, and children may even reuse their parents' old items. It is very common for parents to pass on their older cars to children when they get their license at sixteen years. It was startling to see so many young people behind the wheel when I first arrived in the USA in 1974. It would be an unusual sight to see so many high school kids in India arriving in their own cars.

The yard sale is very much part of American culture. It is common for a family to put out used household stuff such as clothing, furniture, and appliances in their front yard on a weekend for anybody looking for a bargain. In some cases, a neighborhood may arrange a larger neighborhood yard sale when several families have things to sell. This way the stream of prospective buyers can go around the neighborhood to get useful items for a bargain. Most of the time, the prices are negotiable.

One of my nephews who came to do his PhD in computer science at the University of Cincinnati called me one weekend after he arrived in Cincinnati and informed me excitedly that he had bought a desk and a chair for only fifteen dollars—perfect for a student who did not have a lot of money. He said that even though they were not new, they were in very good condition. He had been walking by a church near his campus and seen all kinds of used items in the parking lot with bargain price tags on them. That was his first introduction to an American yard sale.

Neighbors or visitors come and buy these items if they have need of them. The price depends on their condition but is normally a fraction of what the item would cost new. In Indian culture, buying secondhand stuff is sometimes a prestige issue and can be frowned upon as it may be deemed to reflect the poor financial health of the person or the family. It is still not a very common or socially acceptable phenomenon in India.

My first introduction to a used item involved my first car in America, a 1963 Buick Special which I bought for fifty dollars about six months after my arrival at OSU. It needed a thorough tune-up and a few other small details that the crafty hands of my mechanic friend, a fellow graduate student, sorted out. I spent probably another fifty dollars to spruce and shine it up. So my initial investment of one hundred dollars gave me a car that drove like a charm for over two years without any significant major problems before I sold the car for three hundred dollars when I left the OSU and moved to Cleveland. My wife and I then bought a relatively newer and more dependable car to withstand the harsh winter weather of Cleveland.

Another big difference between East and West is in the way people clean themselves after going to the toilet. While India and many other Eastern countries mainly use water and soap to wash, Western societies use toilet paper. Each side is wary about the effectiveness of the other method or the lack thereof. While the Western system would be deemed as insufficient or incomplete in terms of a thorough cleaning, the Indian or Eastern system is considered messy or dirty. Also, Indians or Easterners who have been accustomed to relieving themselves in a squatting position on a ground-level system have to learn to transition to the Western system that provides a more natural sitting position on a commode to achieve the same goal. Many Indians have struggled with the issue when they return to India after years of living in the USA, particularly if their families have maintained the old systems.

Another major difference is in the way people address each other in Eastern and Western culture. In America and most Western societies, people are addressed mainly by their first name, irrespective of the age difference or generational gap. Even a five-year-old may call an eighty- or ninety-year old person by their first name. When we lived in Ohio, our three-year-old daughter and five-year-old son would visit or be visited by three of our septuagenarian neighbors who lived next door. It was so amusing to hear our toddlers calling them by their first names—Clarence (which my son pronounced as "Clarnence"), Bill (Dr. William Brandt), or Tony.

In an office setting, CEOs are generally addressed by their first names in the West even by an entry-level person. This would be unthinkable in India where a "Mr.," "Dr.," "Ms." or "Mrs.," "Sir," or "Madam" is added when addressing somebody older or in a higher position in the workplace. In India, a person would be offended if a younger person addressed them only by their first name, rather than addressing them respectfully such as Bobbyda (older brother Bobby) or Sujatadi (elder sister Sujata).

In America, "uncle" and "auntie" are commonly used for different relationships while distinctions are made in Indian culture, depending on the type of relationship. A mother's brother in Bengali is a "mama," but the father's brother is a "jetha" (if older than the father) or a "kaka" (if younger than the father). A mother's sister is a "mashi" while a father's sister is a "pishi." A mother's mother is a "didima" while a father's mother is a "thakurma," and so on.

One social interaction that was somewhat new to me was how Americans exchange greetings or pleasantries when their paths cross. Strangers meeting while taking a walk around the park or in any other open public place may exchange a short and simple "hi," "good morning," or "how are you?" with a smile. These innocent, friendly gestures in the West would be a strange concept in India. As a matter of fact, trying to smile or exchange pleasantries with a stranger in India would probably be met with surprise or elicit an awkward reaction.

Americans tend to put a higher importance on privacy. It would be very unusual for somebody just to knock on somebody's door for an unscheduled meeting or a visit. In India, it is very common to simply show up at a friend's or relative's house unannounced. If it is lunch, dinner, or teatime, they would be expected to join in. The offer of "come and visit us any day" is not literally followed in America. Normally, a visit will be prearranged or agreed upon. Also, personal and private matters are not pried into or poked at in America. In India, people may sometimes, if not always, ask about the other person's age, finances, health, and other personal matters very openly. While it is not totally discouraged in America, people would normally use discretion to make sure they were not poking around in somebody's personal affairs.

Americans are usually very casual in every aspect of their day-to-day life as compared to the rigid way of life in India. The dress attire in an office setting in the USA can include tennis shorts and other very casual attire, which would be almost unthinkable in India. In the past, a professional in America would be expected to come to the office dressed in a suit or other professional attire, but more recently the dress code has become increasingly casual. With the exception of a formal meeting with external visitors or valued customers, suits have given way to more casual attire.

People can go out in practically any casual outfit to any day-to-day outing without attracting any attention or frown. In India, people are more conscious about their dress and attire in public settings.

Some years ago, I had a visitor from a European country. She was in the fashion industry and normally dressed up in chic and elegant attire. When I took her to different touristy places such as Disneyland or Hollywood's Universal Studios, she was amazed how casual Americans were in their interactions, gestures, and dress codes with many of them in shorts. It was an attention-grabbing new experience for my guest. She joked that even though America was a rich country, they did not seem to have sufficient money to afford anything other than shorts.

Many industries in the USA, particularly high-tech industries, cultivate a culture where the office setting is anything but formal.

Closed hierarchical offices are giving way to doorless cubicles where even the CEO may be in a cubicle next to other low-level employees.

The interaction between the boss and the employee in an American office setting is not normally built around fear and intimidation. In America, an employee reading a report with his/her legs up on the desk is not always expected to reposition themselves in a more uptight position to greet the boss. While the fear and respect for the boss is a universal phenomenon, the Indian system demands it to be the norm. In India, employees are generally expected to rise from their chair out of respect when the boss shows up. In the classroom, when the teacher or the professor enters the room, the entire class rises from their chair as a mark of respect. I think it is a legacy left over from English colonial times when reverence was openly shown for higher authorities.

When I first returned to India ten years after leaving in 1974, I took my wife with me. This was her first visit to an Asian country. We stayed in my brother's lavish residence provided by his company. My brother was a high-level senior executive in a major company in India. He took us to his company's New Year's Eve party. The party was held on the beautifully decorated lawn of the company complex. The president of the company was the chief guest. As soon as he arrived, the entire audience of over two hundred people, including all the executives and their wives, got up from their chairs as a mark of respect. After ten years in the USA, I just did not think fast enough or react in time to get up from my chair. My wife was just staring at me with a look of bewilderment since she did not know what was going on. My brother was standing next to my chair and almost panicked, probably thinking his brother was inadvertently about to send a message of open disrespect to his boss, which would not be a good thing for his reputation and image in the company. I saw a concerned look on his face and immediately stood up from the chair and nudged my wife to do so too. It was not that we were deliberately trying to be disrespectful or rebellious, but we just did not acclimatize with local social norms fast enough.

Life is very fast in America compared to India. It is almost a rat race. Americans tend to work hard during the week and use the weekend to relax with many social and sporting activities on the weekend. Americans often undertake home improvement or other jobs on the weekend. They tend to be handier and opt to do home repairs or improvement jobs themselves rather than call for professional help. It is not entirely driven by the need to save money; it's just built into the American psyche. Many of my American friends built their own homes with help from other friends or relatives, turning only to professionals as necessary. In India, homes needing a paint job go unattended for years. It is not because of money all the time; it's just not a priority in the Indian mind-set. It would not be unusual to see an American painting their home with help from their young children. In India, these types of menial jobs would be frowned upon and would possibly become a prestige issue.

Americans tend to be more athletically active. They get involved in a variety of athletic activities such as walking, jogging, biking, and swimming and team sports such as soccer, tennis, golf, baseball/softball, football, and so on. They regularly take membership in gyms, tennis and golf clubs, and go bowling, and so on. Employees in workplaces also arrange leagues that play after work. There are many company-sponsored golf, tennis, bowling, baseball/softball leagues after work hours. Over the years, I have played in company-sponsored golf and tennis leagues. I have gone to ski outings with my office colleagues. This camaraderie built around social and athletic activities helps to develop great friendships and, in many cases, creates a healthy and friendly work setting.

American families tend to get the children involved in many extracurricular activities right from a very young age. Young boys and girls get into soccer, ballet, piano, scouting, softball/baseball, martial arts, tennis, golf, and other activities in addition to the pursuit of academic studies. Many parents volunteer to coach the youth soccer, baseball, and other leagues where their children participate. I coached both my son's and daughter's soccer teams during their early school years. My daughter took piano for many years. My son was in martial arts and achieved the rank of black belt and was in the Boy Scouts, achieving the highest rank of an Eagle Scout during his early high school years before both graduated from the University of California and started their careers in teaching.

Many parks and neighborhood playfields come alive during the weekends with hundreds of youngsters playing in different Little League sports with the direct and caring involvement of their parents. Many families go camping in various state parks with their children for quality family time in a natural setting. Barbequing on open grills and hiking natural trails provide lifelong memories and joys. My children still fondly remember helping their daddy set up the tents and going for long hikes on the trails or along the beach if the campsites were near oceans or lakes.

While youngsters in India participate in various sports, they don't always receive grassroots participation or the active support of parents. To this date, Indian parents place an uncompromising emphasis on academic pursuits and often discourage other distractions out of well-meaning intentions to safeguard a secure future career. "Lekha pora koray jay, gari ghora choray shayee," a Bengali proverb in Bengali means, "He who studies hard gets to ride the horses and fancy cars" and still drives the family dynamics in most cases. Many Indian parents push their children to achieve the best grade. If they receive a B+, the children are often asked why it was not an A with the suggestion that next time it should be. If they get a score of 95 percent, there will be questions about the other missing 5 percent. While there is nothing wrong about setting lofty academic goals, excessive pressure sometimes results in negative consequences.

In America, second-generation Indian children have achieved great success in academic as well as in many other extracurricular fields. Many Indian-American children go to top universities like Harvard, Stanford, or other Ivy League schools on full scholarship. The second-generation Indian children are also perennial winners of the National Spelling Bee, National Geographic, or National Science contests. In most cases, the deep and loving involvement and encouragement of their parents are the main reasons for these remarkable successes.

It does not mean that American parents slight the academic pursuits of their children. They are equally interested in their academic pursuits. Even though individual efforts and independence are encouraged after the children turn eighteen and start their college education, many parents, particularly middle-class families, start a college fund right after the children are born. Often, the children get all-paid athletic scholarship to support their education if they excelled in any sports during their high school.

In many Eastern societies, particularly in India, hosts try very hard to show their hospitality. In Bengal, sweets and tea are almost always an integral part of any visit. An answer of no is hardly acceptable even if the guests are full, have no appetite, and have politely declined any food. Sometimes, the hosts can appear unhappy if the guests do not consume all or most of the food on the plate. This is normally done out of the intention to show great hospitality, but can sometimes become uncomfortable both physically and mentally. While visiting an American friend or family, the host might ask, "Would you like to have a drink, how about a beer or a wine?" but if the guest politely declines the overture for one reason or another, normally this would not offend or hurt the sentiment of the hosts.

Family dynamics regarding taking care of children is different in America and India. Indian women generally stay at home even if they need to give up their career to rear children. In joint families, children might be taken care of by the grandparents or other elders while the women pursue their career. In America, many career women work almost until a few days before the delivery and then go back to work shortly after the birth. One of my female colleagues delivered her baby while on a business trip to Washington, DC. She was rushed to the hospital when she went into labor during a presentation in a big conference room! In America when a baby is born, the parents often depend on day care centers or babysitters who are normally the teenage children of neighbors or friends trying to make some extra money. However, recently more and more American women are opting to stay home to rear their children as many employers provide maternity leave for extended periods. My daughter opted to quit her job as a teacher to take care of her firstborn son and plan for the next child. Many of these women eventually rejoin the workforce once the children grow up, the timing depending on the family situation and the psychological makeup or family values of the mother.

Other obvious differences are in dinner table manners and the way Americans or other Westerners eat their meals compared to Indians. Americans normally use forks and knives to eat most of their meals while Indians still eat mostly with their hands. It is a centuries-old custom in India to eat with the hands even though some Westernized families occasionally venture into using forks and knives. From a practical point of view, some Indian foods and delicacies such as curries and naan are more effectively handled with the hands. During one of my visits to India, I took many of my family members to a five-star hotel for an elaborate dinner. The restaurant was very modern with a Western setting, and there were many Western tourists dining there. Most of my family members were highly educated, modern, and successful professionals. Some of them had travelled widely. But it did not take them long before they all abandoned their forks and knives and started using their hands. It even got my attention, and my wife was wide-eyed. However, both of us understood the local norms and habits; there was nothing wrong about it, just a different way of doing things in a different sociocultural setting.

No social events bring out the distinct differences in how American and Indian societies celebrate more than weddings. A typical American wedding may last just a day or two to include the actual wedding rituals in a church or a similar setting, followed by a reception with dinner, dancing, and other festivities in a banquet hall on the same day. If there are 150 to 200 guests, it would be considered a big wedding in America. On the other hand, an Indian wedding for a middle-class family could last for a few days with many religious rituals and festivities. The homes of the groom and the bride are elaborately decorated with flowers and lights. The invited guests could range from many hundreds to even many thousands. Big wedding halls are reserved to accommodate the huge gathering. An elaborate spread is provided with many delicacies to satisfy the culinary desires of the guests. All family friends, close and distant relatives, and their entire families are invited. Attempts are made not to hurt the sentiment of any friend or relative by their omission from the guest list.

While the wedding rituals and festivities vary from one region to another, the enormous excitement, craziness, chaos, confusion, joyful mood, and family togetherness are all prevalent in any Indian wedding for any middle-class and well-off family. Different rituals consistent with the religious and social customs of the region are performed on different days. In a Bengali wedding, there will be a day when the bride is decorated with turmeric in an event called guyeh hollood. The bride and her friends are also painted by experienced henna artists depicting elaborate and intricate floral arrangements on visible parts of the body, mainly the hands and the legs. There will be another day that celebrates the last official day of bachelorhood of the groom, which is like a bachelor party in America, except it is done in a family setting with religious rituals and feasting as compared to the groom's friends in America sometimes taking him to nightclubs (and sometimes strip clubs) for lighthearted bashing, roasting, and drinking. In some parts of India, sangeet day is set aside for singing to celebrate the auspicious event. Family and friends from all over India, or even from outside of India, come for the wedding. Arrangements for the accommodation and transportation of everybody from all the venues often create serious logistical challenges.

In India, neighbors make their extra rooms available, and people do not mind sleeping on the floor; in fact many of them staying in the same room gossip and reminisce about old family events throughout the night. Every time I took my wife to India to attend the wedding of any of my relatives, she would comment in jest that the fun-filled experience bordering on chaotic madness reminded her of what was depicted in the Indian movie *Monsoon Wedding*!

Many parents sometimes overstretch their financial capabilities just to put up a good and impressive show for the wedding of their children. Until recently the dowry system, which has now been legally banished, was a big impediment for the parents of many poor girls who would be under pressure to provide jewelry, cash, and other gifts to the groom's family. The amount of dowry would depend on the attributes of the groom such as the family background, education, type of job, or position. The groom's family might compromise on the amount somewhat if some other intangible factors such as the physical beauty, extracurricular attributes (such as in music), and family status were out of the ordinary. If the bride was not pretty, it would be more problematic and difficult to find a suitable match and meet the associated larger dowry demands. It can often be difficult for parents with eligible, unmarried daughters to meet huge dowries. There have been many reported cases of the new bride being subjected to humiliation and torture by the groom's family if the promised dowry was not fully delivered to their satisfaction. There have also been reports of parents committing suicide if they were unable to marry off their daughters. In recent times, the Indian government has made dowry illegal, but parents still find ways of showering their children with many gifts to give them a head start as they embark on their new life together. This is also true in America and other societies.

Another big difference is the credit card culture that is prevalent in America. Indians mostly try to live within their means, which may mean austerity in day-to-day life. Americans sometimes fail to live within their means and sometimes borrow an exorbitant amount of money to support extravagant lifestyles and expensive tastes. In many cases, they fail to pay off their debts in time, and in extreme cases they are forced to declare bankruptcy. The widespread use of the credit card is now slowly creeping into Indian societies, particularly newer generations of young professionals and the nuevo rich. Hopefully they will use the benefits and convenience the credit card offers and not fall into the trap of living beyond their means.

One of the first things I observed about Americans was the way younger generations were taught to be hands-on in fixing things. Many American kids can come across as lacking even rudimentary knowledge in geography and world affairs, but are very proficient in fixing gadgets and other mechanical things like cars. From childhood, they are brought up in that culture. They help their parents fix their cars or do home remodeling projects. They are very much at ease earning some extra money mowing the neighbor's lawns or babysitting or taking other menial side jobs even if they are from wealthy families.

Most Asian children, particularly Indian kids, are encouraged or sometimes pressured to excel in academics. Most of them would not be as competitive with their hands-on aptitude as their American counterparts. On the other hand, many American kids would fail to answer even very rudimentary questions about American history or world affairs. While there are many exceptions, in general that seems to be the case.

Adult Americans are also adept at doing hands-on work. Most of them try to fix or repair things that go wrong around the home such as plumbing, electricals, cars, landscaping, or painting. That does not mean that plumbers, electricians, auto mechanics, or landscapers are not sought-after, but in general Americans resort to self-help unless the complexity or conflict with other higher-priority projects forces them to seek outside help. It would be more common for the Indians to seek outside help right away or simply live with the problem until it absolutely had to be fixed. Again, there are many exceptions to this general observation.

Partly because of the misinformation about the current state of affairs in India, many Americans have the wrong perception of India. While the emergence of India as a wealthy, prosperous, and highly developed country with one of the largest economies of the world and an expanding huge middle class is widely acknowledged, until recently, India was perceived simply as a backward country with abject poverty. Many years ago, when India launched a space satellite successfully, one of the American news broadcasts showed a stray cow running through the street while reporting this highly successful milestone for India. When India successfully launched the Mangalyan Mars Spacecraft that ultimately reached the Mars orbit, a highly educated lawyer sarcastically opined to me that India and a Mars mission seemed more like oxymorons. I reminded him that it was more of an issue of ignorance and arrogance on his part to make such a foolish comment.

One difference that would be quite visible to any newcomer from India would be the absence of people on the streets or other public places in America. While the teeming millions in India are always on the streets commuting to and from work, walking to various destinations or crowding the many shops along the streets, most Americans use personal cars to go places. The huge population of India and the relative prosperity of the two countries have something to do with this situation. A few years ago, one of my Indian friends brought his parents to the USA for a visit. They were always wondering where all the Americans were as they hardly ever saw a big crowd beyond the occasional walker or jogger, unless they were in a school, shopping mall, athletic event or concert.

Americans are more attentive to their physical fitness and are athletically involved. Recently, there has been increased participation and interest, particularly by the emerging middle class in India, in getting into healthy lifestyles and exercise. It is now common to see many Indians, both young and old, crowding the walkway of parks or the tracks of the neighborhood housing complexes for long strolls.

Unhealthy fast food-centric habits have resulted in a serious obesity problem for both younger and older generations in America. Recently there has been a greater awareness of this problem leading to many projects, such as the one led by the former First Lady Mrs. Michelle Obama who championed healthy diets and lifestyles.

Another major difference in day-to-day life is the extent of domestic help. Domestic help is readily available and used by many middle class and wealthy Indian families. Almost all wealthy family and many middle class families employ domestic help or servants to do household chores such as cleaning, cooking, gardening, and laundry. Those who own cars might also employ part-time or full time chauffeurs. This cheap domestic help might be perceived as the exploitation of the poor masses, however for many of them it provides a minimum level of income. On the other hand, these servants exist within a perpetual cycle of poverty that may have lasted for generations. In American society, it would be unthinkable or unaffordable to hire domestic help and a chauffeur unless the family was ultra-rich. As a matter of fact, Americans tend to rely on self-help in all aspects of their day-to-day life.

The general state of cleanliness in India is in sharp contrast with that of America. While the huge population of India has something to do with this, it is also in the mind-set. In India, it is common to see people relieving themselves in public places or by the side of the road. One of my American friends who travelled to India once showed me a picture he took of over twenty people on a railway platform relieving themselves at the same time into the rail track while standing on the platform. He jokingly referred to the action depicted in the picture as the Indian fire brigade in action. Needless to say, my deep-rooted Indian sentimentality got bruised by the lighthearted but crude joke of my friend, and I made sure to point out it was tasteless. One of the pictures that recently went viral on the internet was that of a high-level minister in a state government relieving himself on a wall in public while a number of his gun-wielding security guards were standing back just a few feet away. As they say, when you got to go, you got to go. However, it is also true that a similar act on a railway platform in America would have resulted in serious charges, including heavy fines. In India, there are often open drains in public places that breed flies and mosquitoes and result in a very unhealthy environment. There are very few, if any, public toilets or wastebaskets. Objects are just discarded without any fear of legal repercussions. Recently there has been an increased awareness about cleanliness. One of the major initiatives after Mr. Narendra Modi was elected as prime minister was to launch the Swachh Bharat (Clean India) campaign for a cleaner India. Initiatives are being taken to provide public toilets in all villages and clean the dirty water of some rivers.

The traffic on Indian roads provides a sharply contrasting picture compared to American traffic. Even though there are traffic laws, very few people seem to actually follow them. Drivers constantly make their own lanes and weave in and out of the traffic. Horns are the most used part of the car. Many outsiders would be fearful of the way Indian drivers maneuver their vehicles at the very last minute to avoid head-on collisions at such high speeds. There are hardly any divider marks for lanes, and the number of lanes constantly changes as drivers try to utilize all available open space in either direction. Consequently, the number of lanes in one direction can change from one to five in the matter of a very short time. Surprisingly, there are not too many accidents resulting from these crazy and chaotic conditions. Drivers get very accustomed to dealing with these situations daily. They also routinely ignore traffic lights. On rare occasions, the police stop the violators and cite them. In some of those situations, a little bribery may save the day for the violators.

Another major difference in the two societies is in American gun culture and the ramifications resulting from easy access to guns as guaranteed by the Second Amendment of the US Constitution. One of the major problems in American society is violent crime, thanks to the easy access criminals have to guns. Attempts to control the sale of guns through legislative actions have failed due to the strong lobbying by the National Rifle Association (NRA) and other hard-core defenders of the Second Amendment that guarantees citizens the right to own or bear arms to protect their lives and property. The downside is that guns are easily available to anybody, sometimes with a minimum level of background check. Many mentally ill individuals have found a way to acquire guns and use them. Underage children often have easy access to guns, too, sometimes through the collection of their parents.

Twelve students and a teacher were killed in Columbine High School in Littleton, Colorado, by two deranged teenage students in April 1999 before they killed themselves. Twenty children and six staff were killed at Sandy Hook Elementary School in Newtown, Connecticut, by twenty-year-old Adam Lanza. He had killed his mother with her own gun before going to the school. In one of the deadliest school massacres in the world, seventeen people including mostly students, a coach and a teacher were shot and killed on 14 February 2018 at Marjory Stoneman Douglas High School in Parkland, Florida by 19-year old Nikolas Cruz who had a long history of mental illness, but was still able to acquire an automatic rifle legally. Recently there have been a number of shootings in movie theaters and other public places, many times by individuals with mental illness who should not have been permitted to own guns in the first place.

Many urban population centers are hotbeds of rival gang members who are often responsible for violent crimes, including homicide. Many of the gang members own sophisticated and deadly automatic weapons. Home invasion burglaries, bank robberies, and other acts of violence committed by gun-owning miscreants cause great concern, yet the efforts by many well-meaning public officials and legislators continue to be pushed aside by the defiance of the powerful gun lobby. The extent of violence and the casualties resulting from easy access to guns in the USA is now considered astronomical compared to other civilized Western societies.

Sometimes these crimes are committed for reasons that can at best be termed as insane. Recently, a few graduate students from India ordered some pizzas. When the delivery man arrived at their campus apartment, he killed them and ran away with just a few dollars. The Indian students had only been in America for a few months! On the other hand, there have been instances where the pizza delivery person was robbed and killed. The list and type of crimes involving guns in America are varied and long.

CHAPTER 12

India and Its Uniqueness

While living in America for most of my adult life, I have observed the stark difference between Indian and Western culture with keen interest. At the same time I have been increasingly intrigued and fascinated with India's remarkable uniqueness. I have visited India many times over the years since I left in 1974. My American-born wife has accompanied me on several of these trips. Every time, it has been a new experience for me. I have enjoyed and marveled at India's majestic natural beauty as displayed in its majestic mountains and beautiful beaches, and its cultural diversity and history with countless sites proudly displaying the grandeur of Indian civilizations that date back thousands of years.

During my most recent trips, I have seen a new and emerging India that is increasingly prosperous and self-confident, yet inching unmistakably toward Western norms that can compromise and contradict its age-old cultural and spiritual heritage. It seems the youth now prefer Starbucks, McDonald's, KFC, and Pizza Hut to local cafes or roadside dhabas, and Western chains have mushroomed in every nook and corner. Nursing homes are now increasingly replacing the centuries-old concept of the joint family that in the past accommodated three or four generations under the same roof.

The opulence that exists within the walls of five-star hotels in metropolitan cities like Mumbai, New Delhi, Kolkata, or Chennai can match or even exceed the material grandeur in any other part of the world. Sadly, as soon as I exited these glitzy hotels, the abject poverty was painfully visible. While the sight of countless Mercedes, Porsches, and other exotic luxury cars is now common enough, so too are mothers with malnourished children knocking on car windows for help—a painful reminder of the great divide between the haves and the have-nots. On one occasion, my wife and I took our family in Mumbai to the Marriot to splurge on a fabulous lunch buffet. The buffet was as sumptuous and elaborate as can be expected in any American five-star hotel; however, we could not help but feel guilty eating so much food when we exited the hotel and saw scores of hungry people just outside the door.

Many foreign visitors sometimes take away a negative image of India as a consequence of seeing the rampant and widespread poverty. They take issue with uncleanliness and run-down ghettos, but I have learned to see and appreciate India and her immense beauty through a more colorful lens that bring the myriad positive aspects of India such as her vibrant culture to the forefront. America is a very large and prosperous country, so there are plenty of resources to spread out among the populace. On the other hand, India has the second largest population in the world but not enough land and resources to house and feed its teeming masses.

Focusing on the majestic natural beauty; the friendliness of the people; the peaceful coexistence (most of the time) of diverse populations spanning many religions, languages, and cultures; and the emergence of a new modern India in the shadow of the old one help put things like the nation's poverty into perspective. India has made great strides in lifting up the downtrodden and now boasts an ever-expanding middle class. However, there are many miles to traverse before a minimum level of economic well-being reaches the multitudes that still languish in poverty.

I have a few funny memories from my trips to India. During one such trip, my wife and I were traveling to Agra to see the Taj Mahal in a luxury bus that we had taken along with other Western tourists from the Hyatt Regency in New Delhi. Obviously, I was soaking in the views of the country from the bus windows. At each stop, snake charmers or monkey handlers would knock on the windows asking us if they could showcase their tricks for a few rupees.

The snakes would slither out of the small basket and strike against the bus windows or sway their heads rhythmically to flute music played by the snake charmers. It was a very dramatic and fascinating experience for my wife.

When we were driving toward Agra, my wife noticed women trying to paste a round-shaped patty that looked like a hamburger onto the mud walls of their homes. When she asked what they were doing, one of the tourists laughed and explained it wasn't something to be eaten but cow dung that would be used as fuel in the earthen ovens once it had dried in the sun. On the positive side, he opined that this primitive yet effective process helped to cut down India's dependence on foreign oil and was an environmentally friendly source of energy!

Another interesting experience for my wife was her first encounter with the non-motorized Indian van. During our visits, Kolkata and Barasat (a city on the outskirts of Kolkata where my parents lived) were always part of our itinerary. Usually the family car and chauffer were available to take us around, but on one occasion my sister-in-law Ratna took my wife to the local market in Barasat in a hired van. They were going to buy a few ready-made blouses and skirts to go with the saris that had been presented to her by various family members. So my wife was waiting on the balcony of the second floor of the sprawling family home in Barasat for the van. I instructed her from inside the house to go downstairs and Ratna would meet her at the van that was waiting outside on the road in front of the home. She told me there was no van as she was expecting to see a motorized four-wheeled version. While she was on the balcony, she noticed an old man sitting on the seat of a three-wheeled cycle that was attached to a wooden flatbed at the back. He was making a funny loud sound by pumping the hand-operated rubber horn to make his arrival known to his passengers. Finally, having figured out her confusion, with a mischievous smile, one of my nephews asked her to go outside. She now also realized the van and the chauffeur had indeed arrived and it was time to go shopping! Between my two sister-in laws and my wife, the chauffeur had to deal with close to four hundred pounds. It was astonishing to see how this skinny and feeble old man pedaled away at a remarkable pace negotiating his path through buses, cars, rickshaws, bicycles, stray cows, dogs, and the sea of humanity that moved in every direction in the absence of any enforceable traffic laws. The return trip after shopping was relatively more luxurious with a cushioned seat and a colorful hood in another version of an environmentally friendly three-wheeler, the classic cycle rickshaw. The fare was eight rupees or just twelve cents at the exchange rate at that time.

For my wife, those experiences have added to the mosaic of increasingly fond memories presented by the mystical and magical land of India. She always looked forward to her next trip, anticipating new and exciting experiences.

CHAPTER 13

America—The Melting Pot and the Land of Opportunity

America is the melting pot. People from all over the world have left their countries of birth to pursue the American Dream. The reasons and justifications for these endless journeys of immigrants to America extend far beyond the wealth and material prosperity that America offers. It is the lure of a land that has provided hope and opportunities to an endless stream of immigrants since the days of the early European settlers.

When Columbus embarked on his sailing adventure as part of the Spanish expedition to find a new trade route to the Far East, he inadvertently stumbled on the Americas in 1492. Two other voyages followed, and Spanish colonization of the southern Americas got under way. Many other European expeditions followed, including that of John Cabot of England in 1497. Portugal colonized Brazil while the French began visiting North America in the sixteenth century and colonized part of Eastern Canada, founding Quebec and Montreal; they also founded and colonized New Orleans, Baton Rouge, Detroit, Saint Louis, Green Bay, and the areas around them.

The first British settlement is documented as Jamestown in the colony of Virginia in 1607. The first recorded African slaves of about fifty men, women, and children were brought by a Portuguese slave ship in 1619 from the West Indies and worked in the tobacco fields as indentured servants (Wikipedia). Subsequently, more African slaves were brought in by European colonists to provide similar indentured labor. Many of these slaves worked in the cotton fields of what would become the Southern states. The South depended on them to work their plantations, and at slavery's peak, there were four million slaves in the South. The polarization on the issue of slavery ultimately led to the formation of the Confederacy after the Southern states seceded from the Union. Abraham Lincoln won the presidency in 1860 on the platform of no new slaves. After a protracted and costly civil war, slavery was formally abolished by the Thirteenth Amendment to the US Constitution in December of 1865. American blacks, many of them direct descendants of the slaves of early white settlers, have come a long way since the abolition of slavery.

In addition to the early European settlers, many people of other ethnicities subsequently came and contributed to the development of America. The western portion of the Transcontinental Railway by the Union Pacific Railroad was laid mostly by Irish immigrants while the western part of the Central Pacific Railroad was built using Chinese labor after President Lincoln signed the Railway Bill in 1862.

America is unique in terms of the way it has opened its doors to millions of immigrants from all over the world. I doubt if there is any other country in the history of mankind that matches the enormous magnanimity of American society in accepting and assimilating immigrants from all corners of the world.

Some years ago, I was invited by Rotary International to speak at their dinner meeting in Sacramento to talk about my personal and professional accomplishments in the USA. Some of the leaders of Rotary International knew me personally or had read my story of how I had come to the United States with $9.57 in my pocket and gone on to serve the National Academy of Sciences among many other extraordinary personal and professional achievements.

When I started to think about the theme or title of my presentation, I thought of talking about America as the melting pot, or as the land of opportunity. I settled on "America, the Beautiful" as the title of my talk. I have always firmly believed it was not only the diverse and majestic natural beauty of America that makes it one of the most beautiful countries in the world, but rather that America's uniqueness lies in the magnanimity of its people to accept anybody from any part of the world with open arms. These immigrants in turn have contributed to the development of America and what I see as the greatest country on earth.

While the success stories transcend all ethnic groups in America, I specifically pointed out the remarkable success stories of many first- and second-generation Indian immigrants. I believe these types of successes would be almost impossible to achieve in any other country. First-generation Indian immigrants like Dr. Hargovind Khorana, Dr. Chandrashekhar, and Dr. Amartya Sen received the Nobel Prize. Many first-generation immigrants became CEOs and presidents of major companies and universities like Bikram Pandit of Citi Bank, Ronen Sen of United Airlines, Ajaypal Singh Banga of Master Card, Satya Nadella of Microsoft who took over the helm from Bill Gates, Sundar Pichai of Google, Indra Nooyi of PepsiCo, and Renu Khator of the University of Houston. It is very common to find Indians among the prominent faculty members or department heads of major universities and among the foremost physicians or surgeons of major hospitals, medical centers, or medical universities. First-generation Indians who came here either as students or budding entrepreneurs have succeeded and made an indelible mark in practically every professional or business field into which they have ventured.

Dalip Singh Saund was the first Sikh-Punjabi Indian to be elected to the United States House of Representatives in 1957 and served until 1963. Subsequently, there have been many other remarkable successes by a number of second-generation Indians. Bobby Jindal and Nikki Haley, the son and daughter of Indian immigrant parents, were elected as governors of Louisiana and South Carolina, an astounding achievement in two conservative Southern states. Bobby Jindal was also elected to the House of Representatives, and Nikki Haley also served as the American ambassador to the United Nations. Dr. Ami Bera and Ro Khanna from California, Tulshi Gabbard from Hawaii, Raja Krishnamoorthy from Illinois, and Pramila Jayapal from Washington were also elected to the House of

Representatives. Kamala Harris became the first Indian-American to be elected as United States Senator from California.

Two Indian-Americans, Kalpana Chawla and Sunita Williams, went on to become NASA astronauts. Kalpana Chwla died along with six fellow NASA astronauts during her second space flight when the Columbia Space Shuttle was destroyed in flight. Sunita Williams became a naval officer as a helicopter pilot and later flew a number of space missions as a NASA astronaut, including one as the commander of the International Space Station. At one point, she held a number of records, including that of the longest single space flight (195 days) and the maximum number (7) and time (50 hours, 40 minutes) for a space walk by a woman.

There are many other notable second-generation Indian-Americans in other fields. Preet Bharara, the district attorney for the Southern District of New York, successfully prosecuted many high-profile Wall Street executives. Sri Srinivasan was nominated by President Obama and confirmed by the US Senate by a vote of 97-0 as a circuit judge of the United States Court of Appeals for the District of Columbia Circuit. It has been widely assumed that this was a stepping-stone that may eventually lead to his position as a justice of the United States Supreme Court. There have been many other cabinet-level positions including that of Dr. Rajiv Shah, the son of Indian immigrant parents who served as the administrator of the United States Agency for International Aid (USAID). Vivek Murthy was nominated by President Obama and confirmed by the US Senate as the surgeon general of the United States.

Richard Rahul Verma, the son of immigrant parents from India, was nominated by President Obama and confirmed by the US Senate to serve as the United States ambassador to India. During President Obama's second official visit to India, it was very interesting to see Ambassador Verma sitting next to President Obama as part of the US delegation during an official meeting with the Indian delegation headed by Prime Minister Narendra Modi sitting on the other side of the table

There have been many successful inventor/entrepreneurs like Vinod Dham, who is considered as the Father of the Pentium

Processor, and Vinod Khosla who cofounded Sun Microsystems that created Java programming and became a billionaire venture capitalist. Vivek Ranadive, the principal owner of the Sacramento Kings of the National Basketball Association, came to the USA with less than $100 in his pocket before graduating from MIT and Harvard and later founding TIBCO, a billion-dollar-a-year software company. The list of such success stories is long and extensive.

While both first- and second-generation Indians have succeeded in numerous academic and professional fields, many of them also ventured into various businesses. There have been a large number of successful IT and software businesses founded by first- and second-generation Indians. Many others, particularly those from Gujarat, have become very successful in the hotel industry. Nearly half of the motels in the USA are owned by Indian-Americans.

So many of the "rags to riches" stories among the immigrants have been made possible by the limitless opportunities that America provides. The life story of President Obama embodies two of the greatest aspects of America: that it is indeed the melting pot and that it is the land of opportunity where anybody has a chance to realize their goals if they make a genuine effort to achieve them. Obama's father came to America from Kenya and met his mother, Stanley Ann Dunham, a white American studying at the University of Hawaii. President Obama's father returned to Kenya when Barack was still a young child. He was raised by his single mother and white maternal grandparents in Hawaii. His mother went on to obtain a doctorate in anthropology and made a name as an anthropologist while Barack Hussein Obama went to Harvard Law School before being elected as a United States senator and then the president of the United States of America.

The ethnicity of an American is sometimes lightheartedly characterized as Heinz 57, which refers to the fifty-seven ingredients of the Heinz brand of popular ketchup. American immigrants have frequently married outside their own ethnicity such as an Italian marrying a German or a Frenchman marrying an Irish woman. My first wife's father was of German ancestry while her mother was of English-German-Swiss ancestry. Both of my second wife, Paris's parents trace their ethnic lineages to a number of European countries. My children have an East Indian father and a white Caucasian mother. My neighbor across the street is a white American man who is married to a Chinese woman. Another neighbor is a white American man who is married to a woman from El Salvador. The children from these interracial marriages are then further integrated with other children with different ethnic lineages. America is truly a mosaic representing practically all the ethnicities from all over the world.

CHAPTER 14

Race Dynamics in America

I am forever grateful for the blessings and acceptance I have enjoyed in America. However, I have also painfully observed or occasionally experienced racial bias and prejudice that are not in keeping with the ideal of a color-blind American society.

Race relations in American society have a long and troubled history. Many social upheavals have resulted from issues related to racial discrimination and inequality that run contrary to the great ideals on which America was founded. Obviously, American society is not unique in terms of its imperfections in race relations. No other country or society can boast of an unblemished record in all aspects of its society.

The race dynamics in America are complex. American society has evolved from its early history of slavery to an egalitarian society where any form of discrimination based on caste, creed, color, race, religion, or national origin is illegal. That does not mean that discrimination in one form or another has not raised its ugly head in many facets of American society from time to time. There are legal remedies for discrimination and harassment in the workplace due to race, gender, or sexual orientation, yet many individuals have suffered at the hands of bigoted and racially biased individuals who show no reservation in misusing their power to do so. At the end of the day, America is still in large part the beacon of light and hope for millions of minorities and immigrants.

The history of American blacks has taken many turns and twists since the days when slavery was abolished with the Thirteenth Amendment in 1865 following the Civil War. However, racial segregation continues to be part of American society. Only recently has the segregation of schools and neighborhoods along racial lines given way to a more integrated social order.

December 1, 1955, is a great milestone in the history of race relations in the USA. On that day, Rosa Parks refused to give up her seat in the colored section of the bus when the white section had filled—normally she would be required to vacate her seat. This act of courage and defiance by Rosa Parks and the subsequent Montgomery Bus Boycott became the spark for the ensuing Civil Rights Movement. It was not until 1964 when the Civil Rights Act and its subsequent expansion of scope were enacted during the presidency of Lyndon B. Johnson that the fundamental rights of a great segment of society, including black Americans and other minorities, were adequately protected by the law. This new law helped fulfill the promise of equal protection found in the Fourteenth Amendment of the US Constitution. The Title VII of the law created the Equal Employment Opportunity Commission (EEOC) to implement and enforce the law that barred any discrimination in hiring, promoting, or firing based on color, race, religion, sex, disability, age, or national origin.

America has come a long way since the turbulent years preceding the Civil Rights movement of the 1960s when African-Americans (i.e., black Americans), particularly in Southern states such as Alabama and Mississippi, were routinely persecuted, harassed, and sometimes lynched. African-Americans had to sit in designated sections in public buses, use separate public toilets designated "only for blacks," keep their distance from areas designated "only for whites," and attend segregated schools and universities. Some of these racial biases were similar to those that were practiced during the apartheid era in South Africa and Rhodesia (now Zimbabwe). The infamous speech of Governor George Wallace in 1963 at the University of Alabama, "Segregation Now, Segregation Forever," to protest the admission of African-American students and desegregation orders of the federal courts prompted President John F. Kennedy to make his civil rights speech, which eventually heralded the way for the Civil Rights Act in 1965 during the presidency of Lyndon Johnson. Since then, segregated schools, neighborhoods, and other vestiges of open racism have slowly given way to a more accepting society.

The government encouraged many affirmative action programs to provide an extra incentive to the segment of society who had been historically discriminated and pushed back. President Lyndon Johnson eloquently stated in 1965, "You do not take a person who, for years, has been hobbled by chains and liberate him, bring him up to the starting line of a race and then say you are free to compete with all the others, and still just believe that you have been completely fair." The basic premise of the affirmative action was to break down the visible or invisible racial barriers in society that existed in the checkered history of racial discrimination in American society and create a level playing field for everybody to compete and succeed. However, the use of government-mandated affirmative actions in employment, university admission, or as a consideration for awarding government contracts to minority- or female-owned companies has been fiercely debated. There have been accusations of reverse discrimination when an otherwise equally qualified white candidate has lost his or her opportunity for a job or a university admission.

There have been a number of legal challenges to the affirmative action, and in some cases, the court has ruled to affirm the claim of reverse discrimination. One of the most publicized cases was filed by Allan Bakke, a Caucasian student who twice applied for admission in University of California Davis School of Medicine but was denied admission. The university at the time reserved 16 percent of the seats for minorities. Allan Bakke argued in his court filing that his qualifications were superior compared to some of the minority students who secured admission. He contended that his civil rights of equal protection as guaranteed in the Fourteenth Amendment of the US Constitution had been violated. The US Supreme Court sided with Bakke and ordered the University of California to admit him as a student. However, the court also opined that the university could continue to use race as one of the criteria for admission, thus legalizing the use of affirmative action. However, the use of affirmative action continues to evoke intense arguments from both sides of the issue. Some states have severely curtailed the scope of the affirmative action.

Despite all the laws in place to discourage or bar discrimination in employment or in any other segment of American society, however, the ugly head of racism has cast a negative shadow from time to time on an otherwise largely egalitarian society. Some people from extremely conservative or extremist sections of society still hold deep-rooted conviction about their race supremacy. While the Ku Klux Klan (KKK) or other white supremacist fringe organizations would go out of their way to blame all social ills on the blacks or other nonwhite immigrants, the overwhelming majority of Americans are in general open-minded and accepting of the need to provide equal opportunity to every segment of society. There have been many instances when an extremely qualified black or immigrant candidate has lost to a white candidate with fewer qualifications, decisions which at least on the surface seem to be race driven by a biased decision maker.

Obviously, there are many documented cases of reverse discrimination as previously stated. There have been several instances of successful legal challenges to those discriminatory actions through the EEOC or a court of law, but the deep-rooted prejudice and racial bias by a small fraction of American society has cast a shadow on the greatness of this open-minded society. Many believe a minority has to be much smarter, more qualified, and work much harder to get the same recognition automatically accorded to a white worker. This might be an overly exaggerated view. The argument also seems to be weak, considering the fact that minorities and first and subsequent generations of immigrants now hold many top positions in practically every corporate and government sector. However, despite enforceable laws or the good intentions of the great majority of American society, the path of a minority and a racially biased decision maker often cross with a less-than-ideal outcome.

There are some Americans representing a very small minority, including prominent personalities like William Shockley (a Nobel

Prize winner who coinvented the transistor that ushered in the modern electronics age), who have unabashedly advocated for racial eugenics. They hold the belief that African-Americans and other nonwhite races are inferior and not as genetically endowed with the intellectual capacity of white Americans. They have openly expressed their concern that the quality of the human race would be degraded if the inferior segment of the human race was allowed to breed in numbers superior to their white cognitive-elite counterparts, warranting actions to stop the inferiors from breeding.

The mainstream scientific community and the intelligentsia in general rejected the racist views of William Shockley who was heckled by student protesters during public appearances in his post–Noble Prize era. Sadly, the view of William Shockley is not a singular aberration in the tranquil equilibrium of race equality in American society. There are many Americans who live on the fringe with a race-based superiority complex.

There have been many well-documented attacks on the places of worship or homes belonging to minority communities. A Sikh gurdwara in Wisconsin was attacked in 2012 by a white racist who gunned down six worshipers. A young white supremacist gunned down nine African-Americans in a black church in Charleston, South Carolina, in 2015. The nationwide outrage and demonstrations in the aftermath of the shooting in Charleston led to the removal of the flag of the Confederacy, a symbol of the inglorious history of slavery from the grounds of the South Carolina State Capitol. Ironically, the removal of the flag of the Confederacy was spearheaded by Nikki Haley, the then governor of South Carolina who was the daughter of Indian immigrant parents. This fact is indeed a bright example of the great progress in race relations in America.

As a successful immigrant with a rewarding professional career, I cannot cite any form of real hindrance to the pursuit of the American dream; however, I have faced and overcome a number of unpleasant situations when my path crossed decision makers who were less tolerant toward the interests of persons of color without regard to their extraordinary qualifications or credentials.

In the immediate aftermath of the 9/11 tragedy when Al-Qaida engineered an aerial attack with hijacked airplanes to destroy the twin World Trade Center towers and damage the Pentagon, there was a backlash against many immigrants resulting from the raw sentiments created by these heinous and cowardly acts. There were attacks on many minorities and their businesses. Some Sikhs were mistaken as Muslims by some ignoramus vigilantes due to their beards and turbans. Actually, I felt uncomfortable going out, particularly after dark. My wife would call me from Sacramento when I was working in Los Angeles at the time to tell me to be careful. Similar advice came from my many American friends who were concerned about my safety.

Then something happened that was a very startling and a pleasant surprise. The president of the company, Dr. Jim Wertz, called me to meet him at his office. I had never felt threatened in my job, and I had an excellent relationship with Dr. Wertz based on mutual respect. I was a very critical employee who headed all the technical operations of the rocket division of this aerospace company. However, the hugely negative and frightening circumstances in the aftermath of the 9/11 tragedy were weighing on my mind. I must admit I felt anxious when I went to meet Dr. Wertz. To my shock and surprise, Dr. Jim Wertz asked me to join him and his wife, Alice, the chief financial officer (CFO) of the company, at a concert that evening at the Hollywood Bowl where they had a box. While they were driving me there, Dr. Wertz dropped the ball. "Shyama, as you know, Jim Berry, our chief engineer, has left the company to join Northrop Grumman. I want you to take over the operations of the rocket division as the vice president and chief engineer." I had been suffering from anxiety arracks after the 9/11 tragedy, and now the immigrant with dark skin and heavy accent from the Indian subcontinent was being offered the opportunity to head the operation of a rocket company. This was an extraordinary moment for me, and I believe it is just one of countless other instances where color-blind decisions have enriched the core of American society.

However, it would be less than truthful to I say I never faced any hurdles or unwarranted obstacles in my personal or professional life in the USA. From time to time, my path crossed with people who always operated on the theory that "you do not look like us and talk like us, so you cannot be up to par of the job at hand!" There have been some occasions when I missed out on a number of well-deserved opportunities due to my outsider status. I have always strived to take them in stride with a philosophical angle, believing that the missed opportunities were not meant to be. After all, everybody faces obstacles in life in one form or another, and everything happens for a reason. So I learned to train my mind to count the positives and many blessings I received while blocking out the negatives as inconsequential aberrations. What I have learned dealing with those situations it was imperative to never play victim. With patience, conviction in the supremacy of truth and hard work, and a determination not to lose faith in the fairness of the American society, I have always succeeded in rising above the poisonous cloud of prejudice. While my extraordinary academic and professional credentials have helped my upward mobility through the corporate ladder, it would not be totally uncommon for members of the minority or immigrant community to face unnecessary and unfair hurdles created by the egregious actions of those driven by bias and prejudice.

The issue of immigration has been a very contentious topic and has dominated the political discussions at both the local and national level for a long time. The fact of the matter is that America is a land of immigrants. America has prospered by drawing on the hard work and talents of millions of immigrants from all parts of the world. While that fact is generally recognized, there have been rumblings from conservative circles about the continued flow of both legal and illegal immigrants into America.

In recent years, there has been a huge influx of immigrants from various South American countries, particularly from Mexico. Millions of Mexicans continue to cross into the USA through its porous border by avoiding the watchful eyes of the border security personnel. There was a backlash against this influx of illegal immigrants who were assumed to be a huge burden on local resources. There have been attempts to push for legislation to create a path to citizenship for millions of illegal immigrants, the overwhelming majority being from Mexico and other South American countries.

While the Democratic Party seems to be more vocal in pushing this legislation, the Republican Party has taken a firm stand about the need to secure the border. After many years of stalemate in Congress, President Obama issued a number of executive orders to stem the forced deportation of illegal immigrants and create opportunities for a path to citizenship, drawing further consternation of the Republicans. On the other hand, one of the major pillars of Donald Trump's presidential campaign in 2016 was to build a "beautiful, tall" wall along the entire southern border of the United States with Mexico with a vow to force Mexico to bear the cost of building the wall.

Many of these immigrants work illegally in menial, low-paid jobs such as landscapers and hotel maids. There are very few whites in those jobs, so the moral arguments have been to accommodate and integrate those in society who till our farm land, make our beds, maintain our lawns, and provide many other essential services. According to the 2013 census, there were fifty-four million Hispanics, constituting 17 percent of the US population, making them the largest ethnic group in America. The Hispanic population in California is poised to overtake the white as a majority. The startling demographic shift is now playing a major role in all aspects of politics at the local as well as the national level. The immigration issue played a very dominant role in the presidential election in 2016. Donald Trump masterfully played the issues of illegal or undocumented immigrants and unsecured borders, arguably creating an atmosphere of fear and anxiety and ascended to the seat of the most powerful position on earth, the presidency of the United States of America.

Despite the new reality about this demographic shift, there is high-level resentment in some white and conservative segments of society about the unchecked number of illegal aliens crossing the border. The path to assimilating these immigrants into American society is more tortuous than that of European immigrants. The children of Indian immigrant parents will still look very much Indian even if they were born and brought up in the United States. With the exception of their close friends, most in the mainstream would see them as outsiders. Generations of African-Americans continue to struggle in the tortuous process of integration and acceptance into American society long after the abolition of slavery and many well-intentioned government programs to facilitate their assimilation.

The issue of integration and assimilation of dissimilar societies in terms of religion, ethnicity, and cultural lineage is not unique to America. It has been always a matter of great complexity everywhere in the world. In 2015, the world witnessed a huge influx of migrants from the turbulent regions of the Middle East into Europe. Millions of people were displaced from their homes as a result of the civil war and atrocities committed by ISIS in Iraq and Syria. Hundreds of thousands of these migrants have made daring treks covering thousands of miles on land, or attempted to cross the turbulent seas in small boats, in their desperate attempts to reach the shores of Europe. A few thousand have tragically lost their lives in these attempts. The sad image of three-year-old Syrian boy Alan Kurdi lying facedown on the shore of a Turkish resort during the 2015 refugee crisis was heart-wrenching and captured worldwide attention. Some European countries have struggled to cope with this unprecedented influx of refugees due to the severe strain on their economic resources as well as apprehension of the impact Muslim migrants may have on the European way of life. It was deemed by many conservatives in Europe as a cultural invasion. Some countries built fences and took heavy-handed measures to stop these migrants from entering their countries. Eventually, some relented, and wealthy countries like Germany, with Chancellor Angela Merkel's direct support, and France, agreed to accept tens of thousands of them. The United States agreed to accept ten thousand Syrian refugees even though it created an unprecedented level of backlash from various political circles because of the fear and anxiety caused by the attacks of Muslim terrorists in Paris and San Bernardino in 2015. The assimilation of these refugees and others before them into European and American societies has been and will continue to be challenging at best.

African-Americans had been subjected to rampant racial profiling in the USA more often than not. There have been many highly publicized cases of harassment of African-Americans by law enforcement personnel. They are stopped disproportionately more for traffic offences and arrested for arguably trivial pretexts. In 2015, an African-American female motorist in Texas was stopped and arrested by police for failure to indicate while changing lanes. She was found dead later in her jail cell. There have been many incidents of heavy-handed treatment of African-Americans by white law enforcement officers, sometimes resulting in violent confrontations. The Watts Riot, Rodney King's beating (captured by video), and the shooting of Trayvon Martin by a white vigilante are some of the incidents that have caused protests across America. The "Black Lives Matter" signs were ubiquitous in those demonstrations.

The cases of many high-profile African-Americans who were subjected to racial profiling came to light and received great publicity in the news media in recent times. Eric Holder, the attorney general during President Obama's presidency, stated he was stopped by law enforcement personnel for a trivial reason when he was a federal prosecutor. The policemen probably were unaware of his true identity and assumed him to be another African-American troublemaker!

Colin Kaepernick, a highly successful NFL quarterback who led the San Francisco 49ers to the Super Bowl in 2013 took a stand against racial inequality and profiling that often involved highly publicized heavy-handed police brutality against American blacks by kneeling down during the playing of the national anthem as a sign of protest before the NFL games. Soon, Eric Reid, a strong safety of the San Francisco 49ers and many other NFL players joined in the protest by kneeling during the national anthem in solidarity with Colin Kaepernick's position. This turned into a highly controversial and polarizing issue with many lauding his brave attempt to bring attention to this contentious social issue and supporting his first amendment right to freedom of expression. Many others including President Donald Trump strongly condemned the actions as unpatriotic and disrespectful toward the national anthem and the flag. President Trump actually urged the NFL team owners to fire the players, or "SOBs" as he called them who disrespected the national flag thus raising up the temperature of the heated debate. Colin Kaepernick who was waived by the SF 49ers remained unsigned by any other NFL teams as the team owners either did not condone his actions or simply were fearful of the potential backlash if they signed him.

Nobody has been subjected to more unnecessary and atrociously unfair scrutiny than President Obama himself. Long into his presidency, many conservative groups and high-profile individuals, such as Donald Trump, have questioned his eligibility to be the president of the United States, claiming he was born in Kenya. Even after producing his birth certificate that established the fact he was born in Hawaii, they continued on this theme. Kenya was the country of birth of his father who came to the USA as a graduate student and later married President Obama's mother who was a Caucasian student. Despite his many remarkable achievements, Obama has not been accorded the recognition he deserves. The Republican Party and many other conservative interest groups continued to throw endless streams of obstacles and roadblocks in his way. When he took over, the economy was in shambles. The banking and insurance industries were about to collapse. The auto industries in Detroit were about to be pronounced bankrupt. Many middle-class families were forced into foreclosure on their homes. The unemployment rate was hovering over double digits. The country was overstretched with two protracted wars in Iraq and Afghanistan.

Obama not only stemmed the downward spiral, but he put the country on a more peaceful and prosperous path. He helped the economy and the stock market turn a corner, and other economic factors rebounded after deep recession in 2008. He ended the war in Iraq and scaled down American involvement in Afghanistan. He provided the leadership in negotiating the Iran nuclear deal to stop Iran from developing a nuclear bomb, and successfully helped enact the trade law that gave him the fast-track authority for the transpacific partnership which was later scrubbed by President Donald Trump. After his futile effort toward immigration reform thanks to resistance from the Republican Party, he issued a series of executive orders to stem the deportation of many immigrants, and proposing a path to eventual citizenship to those who qualified.

Millions of Americans who did not have health insurance became the beneficiaries of the Affordable Health Care Law, which came to be referred to as Obamacare. Until then, the richest country in the world had fallen short in providing the basic minimum health care to millions of its citizens, unlike other civilized Western societies. Many other earlier attempts to legislate universal health care law failed. There were many attempts by the Republican Party to repeal the Obamacare law, but they fell short. They even took it all the way to the Supreme Court, which upheld the major tenets of the law by a majority decision. However, after Donald Trump was elected and the Republican Party gained control of both houses of Congress, Obamacare was slated to be repealed and the process was initiated to replace it.

President Obama still managed to make many remarkable contributions despite the incessant barrage of kitchen sinks that were thrown at him by the Republican Party and the conservative special interest groups. Perhaps history will judge him favorably in the future for the remarkable things he achieved.

Stereotyping is sometimes painfully obvious. A few years ago, while I was the chief engineer of an aerospace company in Los Angeles, we were involved in a major pursuit of a defense program. I was dealing with a number of other companies for teaming arrangements with us to pursue this program. During a meeting with the top executives of these aerospace companies, one of the CEOs seemed to be rude toward me during the early part of the meeting. He probably looked at my Indian appearance and his biased attitude started to come out of the bag. Most of the other executives were well-known to me, and I enjoyed a high level of respect from them as a nationally recognized rocket and space scientist. At one time, the chief engineer of another company, with whom I had a long-standing professional acquaintance, decided to deal with this uncomfortable situation in a diplomatic way. During his turn to speak, he mentioned that our proposed team would be very strong, particularly "with the leadership of Dr. Chakroborty who did cosmonaut training in Russia and was a professor of astronautical and aerospace engineering at UCLA." He mentioned that I was an FAA-licensed pilot with flight experiences in a supersonic Mig 25. This was a program where experiences and credentials in high-speed aircraft and astronautics were of immense importance. It was almost hilarious how the demeanor and attitude of the CEO changed almost drastically. He finally made eye contact with me while talking. He addressed me as Dr. Chakroborty, rather than the customary first name, during the remainder of the meeting. Before he knew my credentials, I was simply an Indian with a brown face and an accent!

On another occasion, I was talking to a highly successful lawyer immediately after India launched their Mars orbiter, Mangalyaan. "Shyama," he said. "I heard India launched an orbiter to Mars. India and Mars Mission sounds like an oxymoron," he said, alluding to the historical notion of India being backward. I was very upset with his ignorance and condescending attitude. I kept my cool and politely told him that he was out of touch with recent scientific developments in India and it was now considered one of the major space powers with the capability to routinely deploy satellites for other paying international customers. They had also successfully sent Chandrayaan to lunar orbit. My lawyer friend did not know how to react or respond once I told him this.

On the other hand, there are many hard-core Indophiles who follow every aspect of India's recent advancements. One day, one of our senior consultants, Dr. Vlad, came to my office with a copy of *Newsweek*. He pointed out an article about how Indian pilots had outperformed Top Gun American fighter pilots in a war exercise code-named Copa India held in India. It had not been a one-time fluke; Indian pilots repeated their extraordinary performance at another aerial combat exercise in Alaska a few years later. This gave me bragging rights, and I always produced these examples whenever the derogatory comments of ignorant and arrogant individuals became too much to bear.

European migrants and their subsequent generations blended more easily into mainstream society, unlike Asian immigrants whose skin color was always noticeable. The assimilation of immigrants into the American society is a complex and often a highly controversial issue. I would be curious to know if there are any values that are uniquely American or European that must be emulated by newly arrived immigrants in the pursuit of establishing their American identity. Most of the fundamental values such as honesty, truthfulness, altruism, and tolerance are universal and are not the exclusive traits of American or European exceptionalism, and consequently, there cannot be any strong argument to exhort the immigrants to change any of their universally accepted moral or social bearings.

Often the immigrants tend to gravitate and settle in their own ethnic neighborhoods. So it is common to see the predominantly Haitian, Jamaican, German, Italian, African, Indian, Chinese, Hispanic, and other neighborhoods or enclaves in many parts of the American landscape. Sometimes, for generations, many immigrants remain rooted in their own ethnic neighborhoods. This tendency might be driven by the assumption that it would ensure a safe and accepting environment for them. While there is nothing wrong in choosing a neighborhood to meet one's family, cultural, religious, or spiritual needs, many of these immigrants remain stuck within their own family and cultural bounds for generations and never make any reasonable attempt to explore the surrounding cultures that could possibly further enhance or enrich their lives without compromising their core cultural or ethnic values.

Over the years, I have gone to many Indian, particularly Bengali, social get-togethers. Most of the time, the invited guests were predominantly Bengalis. There would be very few, if any, guests belonging to the mainstream. Their social world seems to revolve mostly around their own ethnic circle of friends.

There are many views and interpretations regarding the true meaning of assimilation. Does it mean that the immigrants need to change their names to mainstream names? Over the years I have seen many of my Indian friends adopting names like John, William, Steve, Donald, Lisa, Cathy, Susan, and so on. I must say I have somewhat struggled to relate a Sundarajan Ramchandran from India as a Johnny Ramchandran. I do not know if my loyalty to my Indian name, Shyama, has ever put me in any disadvantage, personally or professionally, during my forty-plus years in America. However, I must admit that I get occasionally amused to hear my last name mispronounced in so many different ways by my mainstream American friends. At one time, I took my family to a busy restaurant for dinner. We did not have a prior reservation. So I had to give my name to the maître d' for the waiting list. While she was struggling with the pronunciation and spelling of my name, I just asked her to put down "Sam" for my name, assuming it would be a short and close representation of my first name. My son, who was only seven at the time, looked at me in bewilderment and asked, "Dad, when did you become a Sam?"

Does the assimilation mean that a new immigrant has to put up a Christmas tree inside the home and decorate the yard with Christmas lights during the holiday season? Does it mean that the immigrants need to roast a twenty-pound turkey during the Thanksgiving holidays to entertain the whole family and other social friends? Does it mean that the immigrants have to plant the American flag and barbecue hot dogs and hamburgers during the Memorial Day, Labor Day, or the Fourth of July weekends? Is it necessary for the immigrants to encourage their children (or grandchildren) to go trick-or-treat at Halloween or open their doors and treat neighboring children when they knock on their doors on Halloween night?

Does it mean the immigrants need to show their romance and appreciation for their lovers on Valentine's Day? Does it mean the immigrants must go to the pub or a sports bar to watch and cheer for their favorite NFL, NBA, MLB, or college sports teams over a few hamburgers and cold beers? Do they need to join the office pool for the Super Bowl or go to a raucous Super Bowl party arranged by a coworker or a social friend? Or do they have to intimately get involved in the political process and participate in the raucous demonstrations to show solidarity with their favorite candidates, like Hillary Clinton or Donald Trump, and participate in the demonstration against or support for any foreign war involvement? Would screaming passionately against or in favor of causes like Planned Parenthood, Black Lives Matter, Occupy Wall Street, abortion, and affirmative action in a demonstration be considered as assimilation friendly and a necessary prerequisite for successful assimilation into the mainstream? Who would decide if forgoing the ethnic dresses or religious and social customs such as wearing a hijab would be steps in the right direction to authenticate somebody's proper assimilation? Is interracial marriage conducive to the concept of social integration?

The assimilation or the lack thereof of the African and Muslim immigrants, which constitute close to 8 percent of the French population, has become a major social issue in France. Many of these immigrants live in impoverished and isolated neighborhoods. Many of them are unemployed and linger in poverty with very little prospect of any upward mobility in French society. Many of the recent high-profile terrorist attacks in France have been perpetrated by these disgruntled immigrants of African origin.

Possibly, the objective of any social engineering would be a colorful mosaic of multiple cultures that everyone can learn to appreciate and enjoy. Canada and Australia have made great strides in this regard.

CHAPTER 15

Outside Perceptions of America

America is the most benevolent and accepting nation, having opened its doors to millions of immigrants from across the world, which makes it almost impossible to understand why it is perceived so negatively and its morality questioned in various parts of the world. The image of an ugly American, a term made famous by the 1963 Marlon Brando movie, is so prevalent in some parts of the world that it stands in obvious contrast with the high ideals, magnanimity, and morality that America and Americans represent. This personal observation is based on my firsthand accounts of what I've seen and experienced in this magnificent and glorious country. Many belligerent regimes such as Iran and North Korea have labeled the USA as the Great Satan to justify their open hostility toward America. Are these characterizations totally misplaced? What dynamics of international politics generate this type of unfair characterization?

It is universally accepted that America is one of the wealthiest and most powerful countries in the world. Millions of people from every corner of the world have left their countries of birth and came to America to pursue the American Dream. With the exception of occasional aberrations, America continues to be one of the most welcoming countries to receive these endless streams of immigrants with open arms. The American social fabric is colorful and is comprised of practically all ethnicities and nationalities. Little India, China Town, Korea Town, and Japanese, Ukrainian, Iranian, German, Italian, Mexican or other enclaves are spread all across the United States.

This is a country of immigrants who have aided in its nation build-ing. The "rags to riches" stories in America among these immigrants are countless.

It is not only the poor and have-nots of the world who have been attracted by America's wealth and flocked to its shores for material considerations alone. Even the wealthiest and most powerful people have made their journey to America to soak in its limitless freedom and opportunities to prosper spiritually. It is very common to see the children and close relatives of many foreign heads of states or billion-aires attending major American universities. Actually, many of these heads of state and billionaires at one time or another came to the USA for education and professional enrichment that propelled them to subsequent greatness. Ironically, Adolf Hitler's own extended fam-ily has lived in the Long Island and New York area for several gener-ations now, and the daughter of Soviet leader Joseph Stalin, Svetlana Allilueva, came to the USA and lived there from 1967 to 1984 as a naturalized citizen.

During my undergraduate university days on the Indian sub-continent in the 1960s at the height of the Vietnam War, it was very common to see masses of student protestors on the streets shouting anti-American imperialism slogans. At the end of the day, many of these same students would be found at the USIS or American consul-ates trying rigorously to find out how they could go to the USA for higher studies or to settle there.

Every time there is a natural disaster, war, or famine causing devastating human suffering, America is one of the first countries to come to the rescue. It has fed the poor all over the world. During the early years after independence, India received substantial food aid under Public Law 480 of 1954 that created the Office of Food for Peace. America has always stepped up to defend and protect the helpless from their tyrannical oppressors. It has spilled blood to stop ethnic cleansing time and again in places like the Balkans where Muslims were the victims of ethnic cleansing. They also aided Yazidi Christians in Syria when they were surrounded by brutal Islamic jihadists of ISIS who threatened to behead them if they did not con-vert to Islam. America dropped in food supplies to the starving refugees and used airstrikes to open a route for the Yazidis to flee to safety.

Millions of Americans risked or sacrificed their lives to liberate Europe from the clutches of Hitler's heinous agenda and rebuild it from the ashes of war after WWII. Similarly, it helped rebuild Japan after its defeat in WWII. When the ebola epidemic created havoc and panic in a number of countries like Liberia, America made an all-out effort, including deploying its military, to contain it. The list is long and goes on forever of the things America has done. Then why is America subjected to anything but unquestionable adulation?

There is a view held by many, even though it may be grossly overstated, that American intervention around the world is solely driven by its narrow national and ideological interests and is not entirely based on humanitarian, idealistic, or moral grounds. They contend that America's wars in the Middle East are not totally driven by the need to defeat and crush Islamic jihadists, but also by the need to safeguard the continued supply of oil to feed the rapacious requirements of American and other Western consumers. They contend that America got involved in Vietnam with the sole agenda of defeating the Communists and containing the spread of Communism. Tens of thousands of American lives were lost, and millions of Vietnamese either lost their lives or suffered devastating and life-altering consequences.

Ideologically driven war is not limited to America alone. The Soviet Union subjugated the Eastern Bloc countries with an iron fist. Soviet tanks rolled over Czechoslovakia in 1968 to ensure its continued Communist rule. Russia invaded Afghanistan in 1979 and continued occupation until its forced departure in 1989 due to heavy casualties inflicted by the Afghan freedom fighters with help from the USA. The Soviets and the USA came to the brink of nuclear war over the deployment of Soviet missiles in Cuba. The USA responded to the security concern by establishing a military blockade to prevent further missiles entering Cuba. The Soviet premier, Nikita Khrushchev, reached an agreement with President John F. Kennedy to dismantle their weapons and return home.

During the protracted Cold War in the post-WWII era, America and its NATO allies fought many open and covert wars on behalf of their client states or ideological partners. While North Korea continues its brutal Communist rule with Chinese patronage, America continues to maintain tens of thousands of its soldiers across the DMZ in South Korea. The regional conflict in Georgia and Ukraine has again brought Russian and American troops into the fray on each side.

During the Bangladesh war, India supported the freedom fighters, the Mukti Bahini, who were waging the fight to liberate Bangladesh from the yoke of tyrannical Pakistani rule. At the beginning, India provided material and logistical support in addition to championing the legitimate cause of Bangladeshis in the international forum. The then Indian prime minister, Mrs. Indira Gandhi, traveled to various world capitals to bring the Bangladeshi struggle for independence to the forefront of world conscience. There was worldwide grassroots support for the Bangladeshi people, including a Beatles recording of their famous "Bangladesh" song. There was widespread support among political leaders, intellectuals, and people all over the world. Senator Edward Kennedy became one of the fiercest supporters of the Bangladeshi cause, yet it is a documented fact that President Nixon's administration openly supported Pakistan without getting directly involved. Following many small battles between the Pakistani Army and the Mukti Bahini who were waging guerrilla warfare by crossing the border from their bases on Indian soil, an all-out war between India and Pakistan broke out in 1971.

Henry Kissinger, then national security adviser and later the secretary of state, met with Mrs. Indira Gandhi prior to the Bangladesh war and later exclaimed, "The Indians are bastards anyway. They are starting a war there!" The meeting was also attended by President Nixon, who said, "We really slobbered over the old witch," about the meeting between Mrs. Gandhi and his aides. The USA made a number of maneuvers to project its military might by way of directing a number of its warships and aircraft carriers to the Indian Ocean. India and the Mukti Bahini mostly ignored these gestures and stayed its course in their fight with the Pakistani Army.

Eventually, close to two million Bangladeshis would be killed in the war for freedom. Tens of thousands of regular Indian soldiers were killed fighting alongside the Bangladeshi freedom fighters. India and the Mukti Bahini scored a decisive victory with the surrender of close to one hundred thousand Pakistani soldiers. Millions of Bangladeshis lined the streets of Dacca, the capital of Bangladesh, to greet Senator Edward Kennedy who got a hero's welcome when he visited Bangladesh immediately after its independence. The lack of support from the Nixon administration for its legitimate freedom fight and its open favoritism toward the Pakistani dictatorship did not endear Nixon or Kissinger to the hearts of Bangladeshis. Their actions did not represent the high ideals of America that champion freedom and liberty. Rather they sided with the tyrants and those who were fighting against freedom and liberty. Henry Kissinger said in an interview many years later that his comments needed to be considered in the context of the Cold War, particularly India's close ties with the Soviet Union. He termed those unflattering comments about Mrs. Indira Gandhi as typical Nixon language.

America's wars in the Middle East, particularly those in Iraq, Afghanistan, and Syria, have received widespread scrutiny. Many have argued that America started the war in Iraq based on incorrect intelligence about the existence of weapons of mass destruction (WMD) in Saddam Hussein's arsenal, a claim that was later proven to be false. They argue that this war has brought about the total destruction and disintegration of Iraq as a country and as a society. They contend that even though Saddam Hussein was a ruthless dictator who used chemical weapons against his own Kurdish citizens in 1988, he kept the country together even though he used heavy-handed tactics. They contend that if it were not for the long and protracted American war efforts in Iraq, the Sunni insurgency or the emergence of ISIS as a potent force would not have happened. These critics selectively forget that Saddam Hussein invaded Kuwait, and the USA had to directly intervene to liberate Kuwait.

A similar argument has been raised that Muammar Gaddafi at least kept Libya under control with his ruthless dictatorship. The critics of American involvement in Libya point out that Libya disintegrated and descended into total chaos with many factions fighting to gain control and exert their authority, creating a vacuum for the Islamists to come in and set their foothold. The USA was originally hands-off in this conflict but later got involved. The world cannot close its ears and eyes when atrocities are committed by ruthless dictators anywhere in the world. But the question is to what extent the USA should get entangled in these overseas wars, committing its armed forces that include a great majority of young soldiers, some of them still in their teens, fresh out of high school. Tens of thousands of innocent lives have been lost or destroyed in these wars. So many families have lost a son, daughter, father, mother, or a friend. These are ordinary citizens who have responded to the patriotic urge to fight and protect their country and its moral values. They are simply innocent young men and women who love baseball, apple pie and love to tinker with cars. Most of them do not have a single mean streak in their bones. I will never forget the day when the television news reported a young American soldier in his twenties was killed by a sniper's bullet when he was distributing candy to young Iraqi boys and girls.

There are many in the intelligentsia, political scientists including Senator Rand Paul, or his father Congressman Ron Paul, who have argued against indiscriminate deployment of American soldiers in overseas wars, a position that was also held by America's founding fathers. Their libertarian views have been subjected to criticism from various conservative politicians.

The immediate aftermath of the 9/11 tragedy when 2,977 innocent citizens were killed by the aerial attacks on the World Trade Center and Pentagon by terrorists was tumultuous. The raw sentiment and resentment about these dastardly acts were overwhelming, so the need to attack and destroy the sources of the terrorist beds which hatched and exported these terrorist plots was deemed to be a national priority. The Bush Doctrine "that the United States had the right to secure itself against countries that harbor or give aid to terrorist groups," including preemptive strikes as a defense against any immediate perceived threat against the United States, was the basis for the invasion of Afghanistan in 2001. The 9/11 plot was hatched with the direct involvement of Osama Bin Laden from his base near Kandahar, Afghanistan. America had the legitimate right to protect its land and its citizens from its enemies wherever they may be.

It is an irony that most of the terrorists of the 9/11 tragedy were enjoying the freedom and unconditional privileges accorded by America. They even received training in America to fly the Boeing 767 commercial planes they hijacked and used as weapons to attack the World Trade Center towers and the Pentagon. If it were not for the heroics of a few brave Americans on board who said "Let's roll" and attacked the hijackers of another plane, Flight 93, the US Capitol or the White House could have been other potential targets. Flight 93 was forced to crash during the struggle between the hijackers and the passengers.

There are many instances where America has supported and nurtured a number of ruthless dictators who oppressed its own citizens. The likes of the Shah of Iran, Augusto Pinochet of Chile, and many other dictators got direct support and help from the CIA and the US government. In a number of cases, the coup d'état that brought such dictators to power was widely assumed to be directly or indirectly facilitated by the USA with direct involvement of the CIA. The population of the countries these ruthless dictators ruled perceived the USA as the sponsor of the dictatorship that was suppressing them. As a natural consequence, there was a widespread belief that America became involved only to protect its shallow interests by nurturing these brutal dictators and their efforts were not driven by any ideological or moral compass. This is such a travesty. America with all its glorious history of benevolent contributions toward the welfare of humanity gets such a generalized characterization due to a few misplaced government policies. As they say, it takes just a drop of lemon to sour the whole bottle of milk.

I have witnessed America's greatness from very close quarters and have been blessed with the acceptance and kindness of the American people. Only in America can a young man in his early twenties land with a few dollars in his pocket and go on to serve the National Academy of Science. My feelings are shared by millions of others who have made their homes in America. I love America, my adopted country, which gave me the home I never had growing up in Pakistan as part of a persecuted Hindu minority. I do not believe that there has been any other country in history which has done more or sacrificed more to protect life and liberty around the world.

CHAPTER 16

My Adventures—The Sky's the Limit

America provided me with the opportunities that allowed me to undertake many exciting adventures all across the world. Since my childhood, I have been driven by a strong desire to undertake exciting adventures. I was born and brought up in a traditional Bengali Hindu family and culture where the emphasis on academics directly or indirectly discouraged any significant involvement in extracurricular activities. The path to a career in engineering, medicine, or more recently in the IT (information technology) industry that ensured a certain level of future economic well-being was clearly laid out by all our parents from early childhood.

It required some juggling to create a delicate balance between my various athletic activities while minimizing the anxieties of my parents by maintaining a good standing in the classroom. I played cricket, football (soccer in India), and a few other sports for my school and neighborhood teams while focusing on excelling in my academic endeavors that would one day bring me the proverbial fame and fortune. I was the topper, first boy, in every year from first grade until I graduated from high school.

During my early childhood, I read with intense interest the history-making achievements of Sir Edmund Hillary and Tenzing Norgay who were the first to climb Mount Everest; Brojen Das and Mihir Sen, the legendary swimmers from both sides of Bengal (East Bengal, later Bangladesh, and West Bengal, now part of India) who made India proud by successfully swimming the English Channel;

the early adventurers such as Robert Peary and Frederick Cook who attempted and succeeded against all odds to reach the North Pole. And in later years, the achievement of Chuck Yeager who was the first pilot to break the sound barrier, and Yuri Gagarin who blazed the trail for the ensuing space age with his first manned space flight. Those historical events have always inspired me to set lofty goals and work hard to achieve them. It was my destiny that eventually took me through some of the same paths taken by those legendary figures.

While I ran marathons in California and raced an Indy 500 car at the Fontana Speedway in Los Angeles, the site of many professional NASCAR and Indy 500 races, I undertook a number of extraordinary adventures around the world by carefully planning them around my very hectic professional life. I have always believed that many people look for excuses, mainly lack of time, to avoid doing things they would normally love to do. A blend of positive energy and sheer determination to stay the course once a goal is set goes a long way toward eventual success. To a great extent, this has worked for me.

Getting ready to race the Indy 500 car at Fontana speedway

At the finish line of marathon in California

I have managed to slip in and out of the country to undertake a number of grueling and exciting adventures in different parts of the world. I had to work around my demanding job as a top executive with the responsibilities of running the day-to-day operations of an aerospace company involved in various space and defense programs and my job as a professor of astronautical and aerospace engineering at the University of California, Los Angeles (UCLA).

First, it started with a trekking expedition in the Himalayas in Nepal. I arrived in Kathmandu in early April of 2001 to start the trekking expedition as part of my initial goal of reaching the base camp of Mount Everest. This was meant to be an exploratory mission for me to see how I handled high altitude while going through the rigors of climbing to progressively higher altitudes. Then I would train and plan a serious attempt to summit Mount Everest a year later, depending on the outcome of this trekking expedition. Eventually, I would meet and join many other trekkers, including a number of expedition teams from various other countries who were attempting to reach the top of Mount Everest, known also as Sagarmāthā (Goddess of the Sky) to the Nepalese and Chomolungma (Mother Goddess of the Universe) to the Tibetans.

I took a short plane ride from Kathmandu, followed by a helicopter ride through various mountains to reach Lukla, located at an altitude of about seven thousand feet. The plane ride with a very unassuming and shabbily dressed, yet highly proficient Nepalese pilot at the controls involved many sharp turns and twists through the mountains before landing on a very short and impoverished landing strip. This was in itself a somewhat nerve-racking experience. I joined a few other climbers and started trekking toward the base camp from there.

I traversed approximately twenty miles and climbed about two to three thousand feet each day, going from one village to another at increasingly higher altitudes and sleeping overnight in many primitive hotels or rest houses with the bare minimum of modern amenities. While the menus in these so-called rest houses included many entrées named after fancy cuisines from various parts of the world, thanks to the continuous stream of Everest expeditioners from all over the world, dahl, rice, and yak meat would show up in different forms or preparations under the cover of those fancy names.

By the time I reached the base camp, I had met and trekked with a number of Mount Everest expedition teams from Chile, England, USA, Canada, and Australia. An Indian Army expedition team was at the base camp waiting for the weather to break for a final assault on the summit of Mount Everest.

On the way to base camp, I took a detour for a day to reach the peak of Kalapathar, which was 19,200 feet. The base camp is located at approximately 18,000 feet. The breathtaking natural beauty of the Himalayas, the grueling climb to progressively higher altitudes with thinner air, meeting so many world-class mountaineers who were attempting to achieve the crown jewel of mountaineering, and the good-natured and highly skilled Sherpas whom I fondly started calling mountain monkeys for their agility on the steep slopes of the Himalayan mountain ranges are vivid in my memory.

Before I left Nepal, my Sherpa Furbo gave me the title of Sherpa Shyama Dorjee. It was supposed to be a compliment for my strong showing. He exhorted me to come back next year for an attempt to climb Mount Everest.

At the base camp of Mount Everest.

After I came back from Nepal, I started contemplating my options of either going back to Nepal for an attempt to climb to the summit of Mount Everest or do something that would be totally different but equally if not more challenging. During this time, I learned about an expedition to the North Pole by an international team. This was a truly international team with participants from Germany, France, Austria, England, Italy, Denmark, Poland, USA, Turkey, Iran, and a few hard-core Russian paratroopers. The logistical support included the use of Russian Antonov cargo planes to take us up from Siberia to Base Camp Barneo. I was fortunate to be accepted as part of this nineteen-member expedition team and arrived in Moscow in early April of 2002 to meet with the rest of the team and start the expedition. Soon, I became aware that the complexities and the logistics of trekking to the North Pole was not any easier than going to the summit of Mount Everest. Statistically, fewer expeditions have successfully reached the North Pole compared to those who have successfully climbed to the summit of Mount Everest.

After a few days of orientation and sightseeing in Moscow that included visiting a number of famed art museums and attending a few cultural programs, we took off from Moscow in a Russian IL-76 plane for Katanga, a small city in Siberia.

It was during the winter season, and we were in the heart of the proverbial frozen tundra. It looked like the entire city was covered with a thick layer of snow. Only a few feet of the mast above the snow told us about the ship buried beneath it! We were holed up for almost a week in a modest snow-covered hotel that would make a Motel 6 in the USA the symbol of ultimate luxury. We were waiting for the weather at the Base Camp Barneo, an eight-hour flight from Katanga, to clear up. We would stroll around the city in our Arctic gear with three-inch-thick insulation to get us accustomed to the severe cold weather we were expecting to experience at the North Pole. We also visited a museum that housed many of the relics of the woolly mammoth that roamed this area over fifty thousand years ago.

During those days, we would venture out of our hotel and visit a few restaurants and small shops that kept the lifeline alive in that snowbound Siberian city. We would venture out only for lunch and dinner in one of only two or three restaurants that served mostly reindeer meat as the main entrée that pushed our taste buds to the limit in their tolerance of repetitive food.

There was no conventional runway at the base camp, rather the Russian transport plane had to land on the frozen ice flat on top of the

Arctic Ocean. The strong current under the ice flat continuously created cracks and ridges at our intended landing site that made it dangerous for the plane to land. We were told many previous landing attempts over the years had ended in disaster. Barneo is a drifting ice base at the North Pole that moves two to four miles a day due to the current of the Arctic Ocean under it. The first North Pole drifting ice base was established around 1930 and manned by a few brave Russian souls. They stayed on the ice base for over two years before they were rescued.

During our stay in Katanga, Siberia, the expedition team members went out to practice cross-country skiing on a nearby frozen lake each day. They were planning to traverse the last one degree (89- to 90-degree latitude), a distance of 111 km, between Base Camp Barneo and the true geographical North Pole on skis. They were to be fitted with Arctic gear and garments rated at minus 80 degrees, before they skied about 10 to 15 miles a day with a sleigh that was harnessed to the waist. The sleigh would carry about 100 pounds of provisions needed during each of the five overnight camping breaks on the way to the Pole.

Finally, we got encouraging information from satellite pictures that allowed us to take advantage of the weather break to land at the base camp. A few American dollars changed hands to secure the clearance from the Russian air traffic control in Siberia. Our Russian team members joked that "everything was possible in Russia with money, particularly if the bills carried the picture of George Washington in green."

Some of the most hilarious moments during the North Pole expedition came from our Middle Eastern team member. When he first showed up in Moscow, he had a long and bushy black beard and could not be talked into taking any alcohol. Then, when we were holed up in our hotel in Siberia prior to going to the North Pole, we finally talked him into taking a sip of vodka. Apparently, he liked it very much as it was evident from a very loud Tarzan-like yell he belted out. Every day his consumption went up to match his increasing liking for the newfound drink he had been missing all these years. Ultimately, he would start getting totally drunk. Then one evening when we had gathered in the lobby to play endless boring games (name that tune, name that movie, name that person, and so on), he showed up completely drunk, and completely clean-shaven. He started to scream with various epithets about the rigid culture that existed in the strict conservative society of his country. One of our Russian friends, Sergei, cracked that the USA needed to follow a different tact in their foreign policy in the Middle East. He suggested that the USA should air-drop caseloads of vodka all over the Middle East, particularly on its university campuses, to change the mood and attitude of the people of the region.

Finally, we took off from Katanga on April 14, 2002, and landed at an abandoned Russian Air Force base on Sredneiy Island for refueling. The Russians had used this base for their intercontinental ballistic missile (ICBM) coordinations and also as a strategic bomber base for flights over the North Pole during the height of the Cold War. After refueling, an AN-24 cargo plane took the team to the base camp, located about 111 km from the geographical North Pole.

We set up our tents at the base camp for the overnight stay. One of the most daring acts was the dash to the toilet (a polite name for a tent surrounding a hole in the ground). The challenge was to dash there from our tent and take no more than a few seconds to get the job done to avoid any injury to the bare skin from the frigid weather—the temperature hovered around sixty to seventy degrees below zero with wind chill and was coupled with strong wind gusts.

From there, most of the team members would trek to the North Pole by skiing for about five days over the moving ice floes and pressure ridges, fighting the cold temperatures and wind as high as twenty to thirty miles per hour. The plan was to cover a distance of twenty to twenty-five kilometers every day and then set up tent for an overnight stay. Very detailed planning and execution were needed to make these tents livable in that harsh and inhospitable weather. The day-night definition must also be qualified in the North Pole with around-the-clock daylight. A few of the expeditioners who opted not to undertake the rigorous and challenging skiing adventures were taken by Mi-8 helicopters to the North Pole.

After we successfully reached the North Pole, we celebrated with the traditional Russian dance in a circle while making toasts with vodka (what else?). The memories of proudly planting the Stars and Stripes on the North Pole and the breathtaking view of the snow-capped North Pole were exhilarating.

We did not trek back to the base camp by skiing; the Russian Mi-8 helicopters flew all the team members back to Base Camp Barneo. However, for the sake of posterity, most of the expeditioners jumped from 6,500 feet from the helicopter to the North Pole with a parachute. Finally, all of them got back in the helicopter to fly back to base camp and then to Moscow.

At the base camp of North Pole (left) and planting
Stars and Stripes at the North Pole (right).

My assisted swim across the English Channel between England and France is a source of many fond life-long memories. I arrived in England on August 23, 2002, and started training to acclimatize to the cold and choppy water of the North Sea along the coast in Folkeston, a small town in Kent.

When the day of reckoning came and I attempted the swim, the temperature of the water in the channel was approximately fifty-eight degrees Fahrenheit. The captain of my guide boat was a very well-known personality in the English Channel Crossing Association. He did all the coordination and paperwork, including coordination with the English and French Coast Guard. The English Channel is one of the busiest shipping lanes in the world, so the boat captain had to carefully maneuver the boat to guide me in a safe manner to minimize the wakes and strong ripples generated by the passing oil tankers and other ships. During my swimming endeavor in the Channel, I had to stop and hold on to the boat several times to wait for the big tankers that my boat captain tracked meticulously to pass by.

Some of my most hilarious memories during my English Channel swimming event occurred at the very start. I was about to start from knee-deep water on the English coast, but the boat captain shouted at me to get out of the water and start on the beach. After all, those few feet in the water would give the perception of compromising the actual distance across the Channel. I wondered how a few feet could be so significant considering the fact that I was about to start swimming over twenty-two miles! After all, the rules needed to be strictly enforced.

Swimming the English Channel (left) and getting ready to start (right).

When I stopped to receive a drink from the boat, the boat captain would throw a bottle in the water tied to a rope. When I grabbed the rope, the boat captain ensured there was sufficient slack in the rope while I was treading water and drinking from the bottle. If the rope was tight, it could aid me by dragging me along, and this would violate the strict rules of the channel swim. Other rules included the prohibition of wet suits. Only a scant nylon swimming trunk, head cover, and goggles to protect the eyes were allowed. The use of grease on the body was allowed as protection from the challenging conditions of the North Sea water.

With temperatures in the fifties, heavy currents, choppy water, and the passing oil tankers and ships, swimming the English Channel is still considered one of the most grueling athletic events and is normally attempted by world-class swimmers, including

Olympic medalists and national champions. Bengali swimmers like Brojen Das, Mihir Sen, Bula Chowdhury, Ararti Saha, and a very few other Indian swimmers have swum the English Channel and are well-known in India. Brojen Das was received by Queen Elizabeth II at Buckingham Palace. Mihir Sen received one of the highest civilian awards, Padma Bhusan, from the president of India. My attempt was not driven by any need to receive high honors, publicity or record. As a matter of fact, I have kept a very low profile for all my extracurricular adventures, including my assisted channel swimming.

When I went to England to swim the English Channel, I did not give myself even a 20 percent chance of success as I did not have impressive swimming credentials. I just counted on my positive thinking. I decided not to spend the money to even register with the English Channel Swimming Association; however, the neutral observer on board recorded my swim with a video camera. I received a certificate from the English Channel Crossing Association that credited me with a successful "Assisted Solo Crossing" of the English Channel between the English and French coasts. The pictures and the video captured the moments and became part of my personal treasures for safekeeping in my memory bank, nothing more.

My direct exposure with Russia first came in the mid-1990s when the Cold War was about to end and the mighty Soviet Empire was in the process of disintegration. Originally, my involvement in Russia started as part of a joint collaboration with a Russian rocket engine company in my capacity as the chief engineer of an aerospace company in the USA.

Our engineers and their Russian counterparts worked collaboratively to adapt Russian rocket engines from their 1960s lunar program so they could be used commercially in the USA. This required many complicated design changes. Many of the engineers in my organization started to travel to Russia while the Russian engineers came to our facilities. A number of engineers in my organization came back with beautiful Russian wives, giving true meaning to *From Russia with Love.* Subsequently, I also started going to Russia. However, my main focus was to get into their astronaut (cosmonaut in Russian) program and get the most out of my time in Russia.

Eventually I got the opportunity to go to Star City in 2002, the Western name for the Yuri Gagarin Cosmonaut Training Center (YGCC) located in Youzny, a city approximately an hour's drive from Moscow. The YGCC in Youzny is in a heavily guarded and walled city that houses the cosmonaut training facilities and the residential flats for the space scientists, cosmonauts, support personnel, and their families. In addition, several American-style homes were built inside the compound to house American and European Space Agency (ESA) astronauts who undertook joint training with Russian cosmonauts before their launch to the International Space Station (ISS).

A life-size statue of Yuri Gagarin (the first human to go into space in 1961) holding a single red rose greets visitors immediately inside the entrance. I have been told that the rose was to show Gagarin's eternal love for his wife who lived in a flat behind the statue for many years after he died following his crash in a Mig 15 in 1968. Even to this date, he remains one of the most revered figures in Russian society. They have preserved his office in Star City in exactly the same way he left it before taking that fatal Mig 15 flight from a nearby air force base. He was being groomed to be the Neil Armstrong of Russia and the first man on the moon, but the Soviet Union lost the moon race. However, even to this date, every cosmonaut who gets certified after completing their training is required to go to his office and take a vow to uphold the honor of the motherland in the best tradition and ideals Gagarin set for his fellow Russians. I had the great honor and privilege to visit Gagarin's office to pay my homage.

The cosmonautic training experience involved either simulators or actual replicas of past and present spacecraft and space stations including the earth-orbiting International Space Station (ISS). Eventually, I spent time in the modules of the Soyuz spacecraft that the Russians used to transport both American and Russian astronauts and cosmonauts to the ISS, their previous Mir Space Station, centrifuge (the largest in the world), the Russian module of the ISS, Orlan Space Suit, vestibular chair, and natural buoyancy pool where astronauts train to work on the underwater replica of the Russian module of the ISS, in addition to other simulators. I also got to do some hands-on experience on their space shuttle, Buran, in the simulator.

The Russians successfully flew their space shuttle once before placing it on display in Gorky Park.

Training in Orlan Space Suit (left)
and inside the Mir Space Station module (right).

| Being monitored at the Control Room while in Centrifuge | At the Control of Soyuz Spacecraft |

After the training at the YGCC in Star City, I came to their mission control center, which is located in Moscow. This is a very impressive center which houses all the controllers who provide the command and controls for all their spacecraft, including communication with the American astronauts and the Russian cosmonauts currently working in the ISS. The NASA Mission Control in Houston and the Russian Mission Control in Moscow share the command and control tasks, taking turns around the clock. The walls of the

Russian Mission Control Center are decorated with pictures of all the cosmonauts who went to space, starting with Yuri Gagarin. My Russian hosts proudly pointed out the picture of Wing Commander Rakesh Sharma from India who went to space and spent a few days at their Salyut-7 Space Station in 1984.

In addition to my helpful and friendly Russian trainers, I was privileged to meet many other individuals who extended their friendship and hospitality. Although I learned to speak Russian eventually, at the beginning I was provided with a bright and beautiful Russian interpreter, Anna Tsikaya, to help me communicate with the Russian trainers. Anna was the head of the interpreter group at YGCC who helped the American and European Space Agency astronauts when they trained with Russian cosmonauts before their launch for space duty in the ISS. Eventually, I met Anna's husband, Ruslan, who was a former colonel in the Russian Air Force. Subsequently, he became a pilot for the Russian Space Agency and transported the astronauts and cosmonauts between Moscow and Baikonur in Kazakhstan, the launch site for most of the Russian space missions. Ruslan was a very tall and handsome man. Even though he had great difficulty with his English, he tried very hard to communicate. Both Anna and Ruslan became my good friends.

Anna invited me to their flat and entertained me with some authentic and sumptuous Russian and Ukrainian dishes. Anna's mother and her best friend Tatiana also joined us.

At the Red Square with Tatiana (left) and at Anna and Ruslan's place for dinner with Ruslan, Anna's mother, their son, Artjom, and Tatiana. Anna, not seen in the picture, was busy cooking (right).

Tatiana, a tall and beautiful young lady (molodoya dieyvushka), eventually became a very close friend of mine. Eventually, we were in a serious relationship and planning to get married. This was the time I was divorced from my first wife. During my subsequent trips, I stayed with Tatiana. She visited me twice in Los Angeles and Sacramento. After two years of intercontinental romance, the relationship ended due to some overriding reasons related to my job. Ruslan was originally from Ukraine while Anna was Russian, the only daughter of a colonel in the Russian Air Force and a mother who was a professor at their air force academy. After dinner and a few shots of vodka, Ruslan and his son played the guitar and sang many Russian tunes. It was a very memorable evening, and I cherish the fond memories of their genuine friendship and hospitality.

Another remarkable and interesting man was Anatoly Mikhiv. He was the local head of Moscow Operations of Aerojet Propulsion Company in Sacramento. I knew Anatoly from my days at Aerojet as the chief engineer. Anatoly provided all the logistical support during my cosmonaut training and drove me in his Mercedes between Moscow and YGCC in Youzny. A heavyset, barrel-chested man, he was one of the most interesting and jovial persons I've ever met. I've never met anyone who could consume so much liquid food as he did (yes, you guessed it right, vodka!). He was also a wheeler and dealer who could talk anybody into doing anything.

One day, after a grueling training session at the YGCC, I asked Anatoly if it was possible to go to the world-famous Bolshoi Theater, which was normally always sold out. It was difficult to get tickets particularly on the day of the performance unless somebody was willing to pay an outrageously exorbitant amount to the scalper. Anatoly told me not to worry with his usual mischievous laugh. He said, "Dawaii, dawaii!" ("Let's do it!"). We went to the Bolshoi Theater about an hour before the show. He bought two of the cheapest tickets from the scalpers with some hard bargaining with just a few rubles above the face value! When we went inside the theater and got seated, we found out that the seats were at the very back of the theater and needed powerful binoculars to get any kind of acceptable view of the stage! When Anatoly detected the disappointment on my sad face, he told me to relax and asked me to give him a couple of hundred rubles. Minutes later, he was back with another burly Russian with a flashlight in hand who signaled me to get up. They guided me through the theater, and just before the start of the show, we were seated in the second row in some of the most coveted seats! My wheeler-dealer friend had worked the Russian system and come through for me. It was one of the most awesome shows I have ever seen! I also realized that bribery is alive and well in all parts of the world and is not an Indian monopoly.

There are many fond memories from my thrilling flight experience to over 85,000 feet in a Mig 25, one of the two fastest planes ever built in history. The only Mach 3 (three times the speed of sound) plane in the USA to this date is the SR-71, a high-altitude reconnaissance plane. It has been openly known for many years that the Russians built the Foxbat (Mig 25) as a defense against the SR-71. Anatoly drove me to Zhukovsky Air Force Base bright and early on the day of my flight so that I could do all the paperwork, and go through a rigorous checklist, medical tests, and a preflight briefing with a Russian test pilot, Popov, and other support crew at the air force base. They took a copy of my American Federal Aviation Agency's (FAA) pilot license. I had been certified and licensed to fly in the USA since 1977. The flight plan was to pull over five Gs and climb up to the edge of space and do a number of exciting maneuvers such as complete 360-degree barrel rolls. By the time the plane reached 85,000 feet with the Mach meter reading 2.2, I saw the stars in the sky above and the curvature of the earth over the horizon. It was one of the most thrilling experiences I have ever experienced.

The successful landing was followed by toasting with vodka with a chorus of "dawaii, dawaii" from my Russian coordinators who arranged the flight. I was then escorted to the office where Popov gave me the certificate commemorating the successful Mig 25 flight. The flight certificate recorded all the flight data (including altitude, speed, g-load among others attained during the flight) achieved during this flight. I fondly remember how two of the Russian lady workers at the air force base labored so hard for a considerable time to locate a G-suit, oxygen mask, and helmet that would fit me.

At the controls at 85,000 feet (left) and waiting
for the crew to fuel the Foxbat (right).

At the control of Mig-25   Landing after flying to 85,000 ft

I suppose the anatomical contour of my body and head was drastically different from those big Russian pilots whose flight gear the ladies had to sort through.

While I have many fond memories from other adventures such as my assisted swim across the English Channel or climbing to the base camp of Mount Everest, the memories from my numerous trips and time in Russia are very close to my heart. I have never claimed or bragged about my richness in a material sense, but I am very proud of my rich bank balance in the memory bank. I met many friendly and wonderful people in Russia. I visited some of the most magnificent art museums in the world in Moscow and Saint Petersburg. I was privileged to enjoy some of the most elegant ballet and opera performances at the world-famous Bolshoi Theater. I was invited to the Kremlin Palace Theater to see a show where some of the top bands of Russia and a legendary singer from Italy performed.

Anatoly and Tatiana took me to many authentic Russian and ethnic restaurants (Georgian, Kyrgyzstani, Uzbek, Azerbaijani, Swedish, and Japanese restaurants among others). Anatoly arranged a lovely dinner for me at a Georgian restaurant in Moscow and made sure that we got to sit at the same table where President Clinton was once entertained during his state visit! He tried to arrange the same menu and the Georgian wine that were served to President Clinton!

The hostess is in ethnic dress (left). At a Kyrgyzstani restaurant in Moscow with Anna, Ruslan, and Tatiana (right).

I took many leisurely walks along the beautiful Moscow River overlooking the Kremlin. Red Square is imposing. I got to visit Lenin's body in the mausoleum in the Red Square. The changing of the guard at the eternal flame in the courtyard of the Kremlin was fascinating.

Russia is the largest country in the world, covers 11 time zones, and 6,592,735 square miles of territory, and has enormous natural resources. It has been under dictatorship or autocratic rule for hundreds of years under the czars, followed by rigid Communist rule after the Russian Revolution in 1917. It is natural that they struggle with their ongoing experimentation with democracy, which has resulted in many social upheavals. The empire that was going to unite the proletariats of the world with equitable distribution of wealth among its masses has now created a vast gulf of differences between its haves and have-nots. The nuevo-rich billionaires from Russia have bought sports franchises like the NBA's New Jersey Nets (now Brooklyn Nets) or the English Premier League team Arsenal while I have also encountered many young Russian mothers holding babies and asking for help while strolling between my hotel and the nearby Kremlin.

I know the Russian people are very talented with a long heritage of art, science, and culture spanning hundreds of years. Once their transformation to a democratic society is complete, they are destined to achieve greatness once again among the community of prosperous nations.

Anatoly and Nadia were very hospitable hosts. They invited me to their dacha (their expensive home in the exurbs) and entertained me with many authentic Russian meals. Nadia always prepared my favorite borsch soup, a very common and popular Russian soup made from beets. I still fondly remember their playful young daughter, Masha,

Anatoly getting ready for the next toast
with Nadia looking on (left) and dinner
with Tatiana's mother at her flat. (right)

who was then a beautiful six-year-old girl, trying to size up all the guests to their home by asking many innocent questions. We called her pachemoochka (meaning "he or she who always asks questions"). Many years then passed by until when I received a heartwarming e-mail request from Anatoly with a picture of Masha who had blossomed into a very beautiful (ochen kracivoya) eighteen-year-old girl. She had graduated from school in Moscow and was looking at enrolling at UCLA for her undergraduate studies. Masha had been born in the USA during one of Anatoly's business trips. Anatoly knew I taught space courses at UCLA as an adjunct professor and was soliciting help and information from me about UCLA. Needless to say, I tried my best to be helpful to this loving father and my friend (moi drook).

CHAPTER 17

My Journey across Many Borders and Cultural Divides

It has been an eventful journey as I wandered through many uncharted courses across many geographical boundaries and cultural divides. I grew up in a Brahmin Hindu family in a predominantly Muslim country and endured deep-rooted persecution. My family was forced to flee from their ancestral home in Pakistan to India as destitute refugees and had to rebuild their lives from scratch. Each troubled spot around the world I have investigated is almost like a mirror image of my own childhood experiences on the Indian subcontinent. As a matter of fact, the harrowing tales of persecution of minority communities all over the world throughout history have a common theme built solely on the intolerance of one segment of mankind toward another with differing religious faiths or political views.

I have traveled long and far since the days many years ago when my family hid in different villages to escape the brutal Pakistan Army and its cohorts. But we did survive, although there have been many dramatic moments during those unsettling and turbulent years that seemed to engulf me, even to this date. Each time it seemed like my life had stalled without any hope of ever moving forward again, but somehow it did move on. Keeping the faith and being determined to overcome and override the harsh events in my family's way have helped me march along and have a reasonably fulfilling and eventful life.

During those turbulent years in my early childhood, I never realized that someday I would go on to serve the National Academy of Science of the United States or establish myself as a widely recognized space scientist and play a key role in many major and high-profile defense and space programs. I never imagined that someday I would find myself in America, the land of opportunity where the sky is the limit for anybody willing to invest their time and energy in an effort to achieve great heights. I never imagined either that someday I would swim the English Channel, visit the North Pole, trek to the base camp of Mount Everest, do cosmonaut(astronaut) training in Russia, be licensed as a pilot, fly one of the fastest airplanes in history, or teach as a professor at some of the greatest universities such as the UCLA. Eventually, the largest university (on a single campus) in the U.S.A, the Ohio State University recognized me with the "Outstanding Alumni for Professional Achievement Award" and The California State Assembly recognized me for "pioneering work in the field of space and rocket science". Only in America, the sky is indeed the limit.

The dramatic experiences I had as a child made an indelible impact on my outlook and attitude toward life. They forced me to seek answers all through my life to help me understand why mankind can be so ruthless and brutal in inflicting unspeakable levels of miseries and atrocities on fellow human beings. I cannot say that my search provided me with any definitive answers, but I continue to seek a greater understanding of the root causes of these human sufferings.

During my search for the elusive answers, I have looked at contemporary events all around the world. I have painfully followed the events in the troubled regions of the world, particularly in the Middle East where millions of people have lost their lives or become refugees. They suffered through no fault of their own except their religious or political identities differed from terrorist groups like ISIS, Boko Haram, Al Shahab, or Laska-e-Taiba who believe it's "our way or no way." These fringe outfits do not represent their mainstream religions, yet have managed to cause great havoc and destruction all over the world. The intolerance toward other faiths or ways of life continues to taint and harm mankind.

The main reason I chose to articulate my life story was not to delve into any detailed discussion on religion. I simply felt a strong need to look into the core beliefs of all major religions to understand why there have been so many conflicts waged and atrocities committed in the name of religion. I discovered the core beliefs of all religions were not contradictory to each other; in fact, they are all based on the same essence of righteousness and the belief in the supremacy of one god.

I have sadly wondered if mankind would have been better served if the tenets common in all religions, even though defined by different formats and day-to-day rituals, were adhered to and practiced. I have become convinced there are only superficial differences in our day-to-day practices of spirituality, and the core tenets described in the holy scriptures of any religion have often been misinterpreted by self-serving religious zealots in their effort to impose their way of life on others. In their attempt to establish their faith as the sole moral and spiritual standard bearer for all mankind, they have resorted to brutal measures all through history. Mankind has suffered and continues to suffer as a consequence with many troubled regions engulfed in sectarian and religious strife. Our planet would be far more livable if we all learned to live and let live.

I was born and brought up in an Eastern culture but spent most of my adult life in a Western culture. It was a fascinating and an eye-opening experience for me to explore the stark differences in the two cultures. This was simply a comparison, however, and did not mean I found one culture was better or worse than the other. Both cultures have endured the test of time for thousands of years. It would be simply wonderful if we all learned to adopt and practice the best norms of both cultures rather than frowning at them. Also, there has been a tendency on the part of the younger generations in many Eastern countries to blindly embrace Western culture in lieu of their own rich cultures that have stood the test of time. This is unnecessary and counterproductive.

I have been forever in awe and wonder about America and the magnanimity of the American people who opened their arms and hearts to welcome and accept millions of immigrants from all over the world. Despite the blemishes and imperfections one can find in American society and its government policies, I believe the United States of America is by far the greatest and most benevolent nation on earth. I doubt if there is any other nation in history that can match the greatness of "America, the beautiful" with its majestic natural beauty and the magnanimity of its people. I would proudly echo what President Ronald Reagan once emphasized. America is a shining city upon a hill whose beacon light guides freedom-loving people everywhere. The USA is a country built by immigrants. Millions of people who have bounced around in many troubled spots all around the world in hopelessness and despair found a welcoming home in America. I am fortunate and privileged to count myself as one of them.

REFERENCES

The following links to various websites refer to the articles and documents that provided the information or substantiated some of the historical facts discussed in this book. In some cases, facts from these sources were included verbatim to maintain their authenticity. The websites were accessed from time to time from 2016 to 2017 during the course of writing this book. Most recently, the links were accessed on January 2, 2018, to check if there was any update to the original content included in the book.

- The Muslim Period in Indian History
  http://www.gatewayforindia.com/history/muslim_history. htm
- Daniel Pipes-Middle East Forum: Submitted by Proud Hindu (India), May 11, 2006, at 07:44
  http://www.danielpipes.org/comments/45331
- Siege of Chittorgarh (from Wikipedia, the free encyclopedia)
  http://en.wikipedia.org/wiki/Siege_of_Chittorgarh
- History of Hinduism (from Wikipedia, the free encyclopedia)
  http://en.wikipedia.org/wiki/History_of_Hinduism
- Core belief of Hinduism (part of Hinduism For Dummies Cheat Sheet by Amrutur V. Srinivasan)
  http://www.dummies.com/how-to/content/hinduism-for-dummies-cheat-sheet.html
- India and Southern Asia Chronology (HARAPPAN CIVILIZATION Ca. 3000-1500 BC)
  http://www.thenagain.info/webchron/india/harappa.html
- Mongol empire (from Wikipedia, the free encyclopedia)

http://en.wikipedia.org/wiki/Mongol_Empire
- Bengali Muslims (from Wikipedia, the free encyclopedia)
  http://en.wikipedia.org/wiki/Bengali_Muslims
- How Islam spread in India
  http://lostislamichistory.com/how-islam-spread-in-india/
- Islam in India (from Wikipedia, the free encyclopedia)
  http://en.wikipedia.org/wiki/Islam_in_India
- The Muslim period in Indian history
  http://www.gatewayforindia.com/history/muslim_history.htm
- Core beliefs of Islam
  https://www.islamreligion.com/articles/10256/core-values-of-islam/
- The origin of the Quran
  http://www.whyislam.org/submission/the-holy-quran/the-origin-of-the-quran/
- Facts about Islam
  http://www.30factsaboutislam.com/
- Hinduism
  http://www.religionfacts.com/hinduism/overview.htm
- Christianity
  http://www.religionfacts.com/christianity/index.htm
- Ten Commandments
  https://www.google.com/search?q=ten+commandments&rlz=1C1SQJL_enUS770US770&oq=ten+commandments&aqs=chrome..69i57j0l5.6149j0j8&sourceid=chrome&ie=UTF-8
- Catholic Bible 101—The Ten Commandments
  http://www.catholicbible101.com/thetencommandments.htm
- History of Buddhism (from Wikipedia, the free encyclopedia)
  http://en.wikipedia.org/wiki/History_of_Buddhism
- Buddhism Basic Belief—How did Buddhism begin?
  http://www.uri.org/kids/world_budd_basi.htm#How did Buddhism begin
- Jainism (from Wikipedia, the free encyclopedia)

http://en.wikipedia.org/wiki/Jainism#Origins
- Sikhism (from Wikipedia, the free encyclopedia)
http://en.wikipedia.org/wiki/Sikhism#The_Sikh_concept_of_God
- The Ten Principle Beliefs of the Sikh Religion (from Wikipedia, the free encyclopedia)
http://sikhism.about.com/od/sikhism101/tp/Top_Ten_Sikh_Beliefs.htm
- Bhai Mardana (from Wikipedia, the free encyclopedia)
http://en.wikipedia.org/wiki/Bhai_Mardana 4857
- European Colonization of the Americas (from Wikipedia, the free encyclopedia)
https://en.wikipedia.org/wiki/European_colonization_of_the_Americas
- "Burakumin (from Wikipedia)"
https://en.wikipedia.org/wiki/Burakumin

 Dr. Shyama Chakroborty has traversed a long, winding, and arduous path since his childhood in a small town on the Indian subcontinent. His Hindu family endured tortuous persecution in predominantly Muslim East Pakistan before immigrating to India as destitute refugees. He came to the USA in his early twenties in 1974 with only $9.57 in his pocket. He went on to obtain a master's degree in mechanical engineering from the Ohio State University, a doctorate in engineering from Cleveland State University, and an MBA from the University of California, Davis.

He is a nationally recognized rocket and space scientist and played a vital role in the development and deployment of numerous major defense as well as space systems for space exploration. He served on various committees of the National Academy of Sciences, the venerable scientific body that advised the President and the Congress of the U.S.A on scientific matters of national significance. He was an adjunct professor of astronautical and aerospace engineering at the University of California, Los Angeles (UCLA). He received the Most Outstanding Alumni for Professional Achievement Award of the Ohio State University in 2013. His pioneering work in rocket and space science was recognized by the California State Assembly in 2016.

Dr. Chakroborty is not just a desk jockey. His extraordinary adventures included an assisted swim across the English Channel, trekking to the North Pole, cosmonaut training, and the legendary Foxbat Mig 25 flying in Russia, among other exploits. Dr. Chakroborty has been fondly addressed as the renaissance man by his coworkers and was introduced as the most interesting man in the world for his versatile talent when he received the outstanding alumni award from the Ohio State University.